Gun Digest's Buyer's Guide to

CONCEALED CARRY HANDGUNS

Jerry Ahern

Published by

Gun Digest® Books, an imprint of F+W Media, Inc.
Krause Publications • 700 East State Street • Iola, WI 54990-0001
715-445-2214 • 888-457-2873
www.krausebooks.com

To order books or other products call toll-free 1-800-258-0929
or visit us online at www.krausebooks.com, www.gundigeststore.com
or www.Shop.Collect.com

Library of Congress Control Number: 2010924668

ISBN-13: 978-1-4402-1383-0
ISBN-10: 1-4402-1383-6

Cover Design by Tom Nelsen
Designed by Paul Birling
Edited by Dan Shideler
Photos by Sharon Ahern unless otherwise noted

Printed in United States of America

DEDICATION

This book is respectfully dedicated to the memories of Mae West and Cary Grant. Miss West, as you'll recall, delivered a since immortal line to Mr. Grant in the 1933 Paramount Picture *She Done Him Wrong:* "Is that a pistol in your pocket, or are you just glad to see me?" The line is one of the most famous double entendres in history and something all concealed weapons carriers should consider.

CONTENTS

ACKNOWLEDGEMENTS

A book such as this would not have been possible without a great deal of generous help. Obviously, those manufacturers who assisted us deserve credit not only for generously making product available, but for doing such a fine job with the respective items they manufacture, items which help to keep us safe and free.

I want to thank my son-in-law, Danny Akers, and his friend and mine now, too, Bradley Fielding. They did a great job. Thanks to Dan Shideler, my editor, for his patience and his support for this book, not to mention his friendship.

Nothing with the name "Ahern" on it would ever get done without Sharon, my wife, my buddy, my photographer and co-conspirator in all that I do.

Jerry Ahern
Jefferson, Georgia
June 1, 2010.

PART 1

THE TOOLS OF CONCEALED CARRY

CHAPTER 1

INTRODUCTION

When concealing a handgun wasn't that important, larger weapons like this Cimarron Arms copy of an 1851 could be employed.

(Cimarron Photo)

For some reason I will never understand, during the latter decades of the 19th century in America, the open carry of weapons declined. Perhaps some people thought they were too sophisticated to be armed, or that being armed somehow wasn't fashionable or some such silliness. Maybe the "upper crust" was becoming afraid of the rest of us and just did something stupid. In some instances, in the post-Civil War period, prohibitions against weapons arose as a tool to deny freed slaves access to arms. And some likely good-hearted but woefully misguided souls probably thought they were doing something to curb crime or make a social statement against violence. Whatever the reason, by the closing years of the 19th century and opening years of the 20th century, being armed at all on the street – even if not openly – was illegal in many locales,

New York's "Sullivan Law" of 1911 being the most egregious example of such restrictions.

Those of us who are sensible, and do not labor under a religious or moral obligation against self-defense, go armed. If we are fortunate enough to live in one of the ever-growing number of "shall issue" states, and have a clean background with the law, etc., we can apply for and receive a concealed carry permit, after the appropriate background checking has been done and, in some areas, a course of instruction taken. Those good people who do not live in "free states," but must be armed, either find the means by which to circumvent draconian anti-firearms laws by getting some sort of legal pass – a badge as a volunteer or reserve deputy, etc. – or just carry discreetly anyway and hope not to get caught. Remember the old aphorism? "It's better to be judged by twelve than carried by six."

We carry weapons in order to protect ourselves, our loved ones and other innocents from violence. It's as simple as that. That is why people have taken up the practice of going armed since the first caveman picked up a rock or the jawbone of an ass. That is

For greater concealability, the Baby Dragoon, sans rammer, was a fine choice. (Cimarron Photo)

Once the most advanced military handgun on the planet, the Walther P-38, this a police turn-in gun imported by Century International Arms, has a five inch barrel. That can be cut for supposed added concealability.

Bond Arms Derringers can be converted from one centerfire caliber to another merely by swapping barrel sets. The trigger guard is also easily removed for a more traditional appearance.

why peasants, serfs and the disenfranchised in general in subsequent eras were denied the use of arms. Those who couldn't defend themselves or their loved ones or just stand up for what was right were far easier to control, subjugate and exploit.

Since weapons are usually no longer carried openly, although there is a growing movement

A derringer is a palm sized handgun, typically, designed to be carried hidden in a pocket, up a sleeve or in a woman's purse. Unlike what we see in the movies, any handgun is going to weigh too much to be held up by a garter on a pretty woman's leg.

Cobra offers derringers of different sizes, depending on choice of caliber.

A derringer sits well enough in the hand, but accurate shooting is a challenge at anything past contact distance for a great many shooters.

in that regard, we have learned to conceal our weapons, and more and more effectively. In the old west, in towns where being openly armed was no longer *de rigueur,* unless one possessed a firearm specifically made for concealed carry – like a derringer – one might employ a "town carry," wherein a full-sized Colt Single Action Army was stuffed holsterless into the wearers's trouser waistband, the loading gate left open to guard against the revolver's slipping and sliding down into the trouser leg.

Small, concealable handguns had been available for quite some time. The single shot pistol from Henry Deringer with which actor John Wilkes Booth murdered President Abraham Lincoln is perhaps the most well-known example. Deringer's pistols were already widely circulated and the word "derringer,"

Many would argue that a full-size .45 automatic – this one is a Detonics USA (Pendergrass) Model 9-11-01 – is the ultimate personal defense handgun. They do conceal well, if you know how.

A full-size .45 is a pleasant handgun to shoot and a well-made model can be extraordinarily accurate.

spelled with an extra "r" in the middle, became as generic in use as "fridge," the shortened form of the trade name "Frigidaire," became synonymous with any refrigerator, regardless of the brand. The most famous derringer ever was the Remington over/under, produced from 1866 until 1935. Using self-contained cartridges, small and concealable, it chambered a comparatively anemic .41 caliber rimfire round and could discharge if dropped. Some of these guns are likely still carried in men's hip pockets and women's handbags.

When men commonly wore vests or waistcoats, a Remington derringer might well be hidden in the vest pocket. As automatic pistols smaller than Borchardts and Mausers started to appear – notably some of the fine designs of John Moses Browning and weapons inspired by his work – it became possible to carry more than two shots in one's vest pocket.

The "vest pocket pistol" is a class by itself, but it's often lumped together with "pocket pistols"

generally. Let's take two well-known examples: the Browning Baby Model .25 ACP, generally considered one of the smallest .25 autos – if not the smallest – ever made, is a vest pocket-sized pistol. The Walther PP or PPK is a pocket pistol.

To paraphrase Gertrude Stein, "A pocket is a pocket is a pocket." But the distinction is worth noting. Today, the most commonly encountered ultra-small pistols aren't pistols at all, but revolvers from North American Arms. The original .22 Short and .22 LR and .22 Magnum Mini-revolvers – especially those with the one and one-eighth-inch barrel – are true vest pocket size. The more recent .22 Magnum NAA Pug, although possessed of a slightly more bulbous grip, is actually an ideal vest pocket pistol.

In a free market economy, manufacturers develop or attempt to develop product based on

The North American Arms .22 Magnum Pug makes a fine ultimately tiny backup or backup to a backup. The Long Rifle Mini-Revolvers like this would sometimes be hidden inside a package of cigarettes.

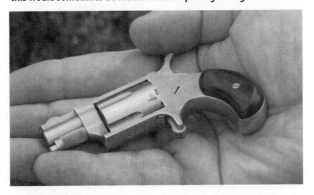

Regardless of what anyone says to the contrary, small handguns for close range personal defense may have to be shot from waist level. The Seecamp, of course, has no sights at all.

The NAA LR Mini-Revolver, in the palm of a hand, has been set up to be worn in a belt buckle, on a chain around the neck or is fitted with a folding grip that holsters the gun at the waist.

what is perceived as present or future consumer demand. Smith & Wesson's first self-contained cartridge revolver, the Model 1, was a seven-shot .22 Short rimfire introduced in 1857 and continued into the 1880s. It was the first revolver to utilize a self-contained cartridge and was the ultimate in modern defensive weaponry. A tip-up revolver, it looked a little like a North American Arms Mini-revolver with a hinge on the top of the frame forward of the cylinder. And, of course, it was bigger than the North American Arms guns.

By the post Civil War period, despite a serious economic downturn, there was still a demand for firearms, this fueled by westward expansion. As cities grew, and as being openly armed was less and less practiced, it was only logical to combine the technological improvements in cartridges – "central fire" over rimfire – and mechanical advances such as stronger break-open constructions, solid frames and double action mechanisms into weapons of a size to be handily carried in an outerwear or suit coat pocket or a woman's purse. Just as in the days of bronze and iron edged weapons, when steel was sought-after as a technological marvel, in the age of firearms it has always been firepower, interpreted either as cartridge effectiveness, or sheer number of rounds between reloadings, or both. When firepower was coupled with reduced size and weight, there was true practical and commercial potential. A five- or six-shot .32 was easily at least as good as a seven-shot .22 Short. And, if the slightly larger size were not a problem, five or six .32s easily beat out two .41 rimfire rounds in a Remington Derringer. The

To conceal a full-size single action, long barrel and all, many would use a "town carry," wherein the loading gate is left open, serving to keep the gun from slipping down.

An original Browning Model 1910/22, with original grips and magazines, the 1910/22 variant intentionally made larger than the more familiar Model 1910 from which it is derived. This was an extraordinarily popular .32 ACP.

Precision Small Arms exports the US-made Browning Baby Model for Fabrique National of Belgium. Marked differently, the guns are sold in the USA as well. There are various options, including finish, engraving, grips and even metallurgy. It is one of the most popular .25 automatics ever made. (Precision Small Arms Photo)

Derringer hung on, of course; John Dillinger was arrested in Tucson, Arizona, in 1934 with one of the Remington Derringers in his sock. In 2009, that Derringer went at auction for $95,000. If memory serves, that's a bigger haul than Dillinger ever made from one of his famous bank robberies. And I wouldn't be at all surprised if an officer involved in that 1934 arrest had a Remington Derringer as a backup weapon stuffed in his hip pocket.

The .25 automatics that Browning designed for Colt and for Fabrique National of Belgium revolutionized personal defense. Not only were these guns small, they were capable of firing a half- dozen shots without reloading and as rapidly as one could pull the trigger; and when reloading was needed, assuming the presence of a spare magazine, firing could be quickly and easily continued. The very flatness of these pistols was essentially a match for the Remington Derringer, as was overall length and, to a lesser degree, height. If operated properly, these pistols were actually safer to carry and, assuming someone bothered to make a ballistic comparison, the .25 ACP under most circumstances more than held its own against the .41 rimfire in every practical regard.

In comparatively little time, Browning had developed pistols in the more powerful and still well-regarded .32 ACP. Within a period of two years – 1903 to 1905 – this led to the same pistol being offered in the even more powerful .380 ACP. The modern age of concealed carry handguns was upon us. Handguns surviving in close to original mechanical and structural condition from this epoch are as serviceable today as they were throughout the 20th century, when the 1903 and 1905 Colts were carried by Prohibition Era plainclothesmen, issued as General Officers Pistols to men like George Patton, worn covertly by the agents who served in World War II's Office of Strategic Services and kept in a pocket, purse or nightstand to safeguard private citizens.

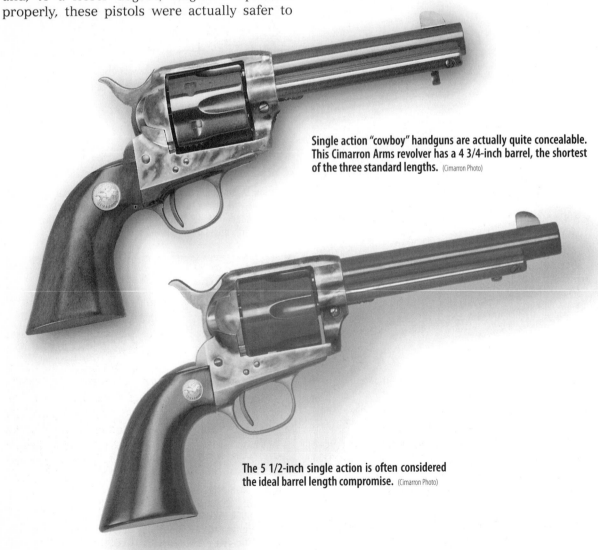

Single action "cowboy" handguns are actually quite concealable. This Cimarron Arms revolver has a 4 3/4-inch barrel, the shortest of the three standard lengths. (Cimarron Photo)

The 5 1/2-inch single action is often considered the ideal barrel length compromise. (Cimarron Photo)

CHAPTER 2

SIZE REALLY DOES MATTER

The Wells Fargo Model was made for concealability. (Cimarron Photo)

Over thirty years ago, we were out testing some guns with our old friend Hal. Hal was a big guy. I'm not exaggerating when I say that Hal carried a four-inch N-Frame S&W in an ankle holster in perfect comfort. That's how big Hal was. One of the guns we were field testing was a .22 Short Mini-revolver. Sharon was afraid that Hal was going to shoot himself in the tip of the finger, his hands so large, the gun so small and the barrel so short. In those days, sometimes I'd carry a Mini-revolver just dropped into a jacket pocket. I had this corduroy sportcoat – wide lapels and everything, as was the fashion in the 1970s – and I lost the little revolver in one of my pockets and actually had to pat myself down in order to find it.

Guns can be too small for concealed carry use, and guns can also be too large to hide.

Generally speaking, you should be able to get at least one to one and one-half fingers on the butt of the gun for a secure hold. If you cannot grasp the gun easily as it is drawn, you are increasing your chances of a fumble when the gun is needed. With almost any handgun you might conceivably carry concealed, two fingers is enough for a terrific hold, the little finger curled under. If you specifically have a gun for concealed carry, you must understand some basic parameters.

With a little modification, such as larger or extended grips, your concealed carry handgun may be capable of pinpoint target accuracy. So

From top left clockwise, Seecamp .32, Beretta 950BS .25, NAA Guardian .380 and NAA Guardian .32, all excellent concealment pistols, the perfect size.

what? That's nice and all, but you don't need to be able to shoot a one-hole group at twenty-five yards. If you can, fine; but, if that means making the weapon less concealable, you may be hitting the bullseye but you're missing the point. That's why we don't put handgun scopes on hideout weapons.

Walther – very sensibly, I might add – would supply their PP series pistols with two magazines, one of which had the finger rest extension, the other without. Sensible people who carried concealed used the finger rest extension magazine as a spare or when plinking or target shooting, using the magazine without the finger rest extension when the gun was hidden on body. Consider the logic. Let's say

that the use of a finger rest extension lengthens the gripping surface by more or less a half an inch. If you buy a handgun with a grip that is a half-inch or so longer, you might very well have one round greater capacity in the magazine. So, if you're going to lengthen the grip and possibly reduce concealability, you may as well get that extra round for your trouble. The idea with a concealable handgun is that it should be concealable.

Some years back, when I was running the Detonics USA operation in Pendergrass, Georgia, we occasionally made up a small number of pistols with the short CombatMaster grip frame and a full-length slide and five-inch barrel. They were called "StreetMasters." The guns were never very popular, but they were extremely practical. The weapon had a quite concealable grip with a barrel length that allowed full ballistic efficiency. It just looked odd. Years earlier, Colt offered a pistol that was set up just the opposite way. The pistol came with an Officer's Model slide and barrel and a full-length grip frame. No offense to the folks at Colt, but, barring someone with a valid need which I cannot begin to imagine, no person with even a basic understanding of concealment issues would ever have bought such a gun for concealed carry. All that gun afforded the concealed carry consumer was greater capacity at the cost of concealability. With a full-size 1911 grip, a full-size 1911 slide and barrel is just as concealable on body.

Within reason, length of a handgun matters little to nothing as far as concealment is concerned, depending on application and carry method. When I do live demonstrations of concealment positions at waist level, I use a six-inch N-Frame, if one's available. The revolver is easy for folks in the back row to see and, if you do it right, a six-inch N-Frame can be concealed perfectly well, although a gun of that length is far from ideal for the task. Grip length, on the other hand, is extremely important. Too long a grip and the handgun will be harder to hide, poking out under the covering garment. Too long a grip as relates to too little length and the gun butt will "fall away" from the body when worn at waist level. This further complicates hiding the gun.

There is physical size and then there's caliber size. If the only handgun you have available or the only handgun circumstances will allow you to hide is a North American Arms .22 LR Mini-revolver, then that's the gun to carry and, hopefully, you'll hit what you are aiming at, should you need to. North American Arms Mini-revolvers are outstandingly well-made. It's just that .22 Long Rifle isn't the ideal defensive round. It's not even remotely close to ideal. That said, Israeli sky marshals and executive protection teams used to carry Walther and Beretta .22

From top left, Detonics USA (Pendergrass) Model 9-11-01 .45 ACP with Crimson Trace LaserGrips, Detonics USA (Pendergrass) CombatMaster .45 in Detonics Black finish, Grandfather Oak Kydex inside waistband holster and SureFire L4 Digital LumaMax.

Clockwise from left, NAA Guardian .380 with Crimson Trace Laser grips, Seecamp .32 on a pocket holster, NAA Guardian .32, NAA Pug .22 Magnum and, smallest of the bunch, a standard Long Rifle Mini-Revolver.

LRs and I doubt any of us would have cared to tell them that using a .22 was stupid.

Assuming a man or woman has the requisite shooting skills and the resolve to risk taking a life if called upon, the better suited the caliber to defensive use, the better the potential results. An old friend I haven't seen in several years carried a Beretta Minx – the tip-up barrel .22 Short semi-auto – in his hip pocket. He was/is a quite gun-knowledgeable guy and I could never quite see why he did that. I mean, as the choices in tiniest semi-automatics went in the late 1970s and earlier, one of the tip-up barrel Berettas was just about as good as you could get. But, that same gun was available in .25 ACP. .25, as anyone will tell you, is not some powerhouse round. My old friend Lynn "Trapper" Alexiou – gunsmith, spring manufacturer, refinisher, writer and video producer – told the story about once seeing a mouse cross the floor of

Left profile of the excellent little Glock 27 .40.

his spring factory. The only thing available was a .25 automatic. He shot the mouse with a square hit, but it escaped. The story is probably apocryphal, but even though the .25 ACP isn't a very good choice for self-defense, as a centerfire round, it's a vastly better choice than any .22 round, if that .22 is going to be fired from a semi-automatic.

For starters, .22 Short and Long and Long Rifle are all rimfires, meaning that the primer compound is painted on the rim. What if a spot – the spot where your pistol's firing pin is going to strike – doesn't have the primer compound? You can't look at a rimfire cartridge and tell for sure. Oops! Quite unlikely, certainly, but extremely likely is the possibility that the more fragile rimfire cartridges can be damaged when you load them into the magazine or will be damaged when they feed. The bullet can separate from the case. What shooter hasn't had that happen at least once when handling a .22 rimfire cartridge? And, lead bullets with no jacket can more easily catch on anything than jacketed bullets can.

There are .25 ACP hollowpoints and special purpose rounds, but since cartridge size – bullet size and weight and powder charge – really does matter, certain rounds just really are better suited to defensive use than others.

These days, unless budgetary or sentimental concerns over-ride one's better judgment, semi-automatic defensive handguns in .22 rimfire or .25 ACP can be bypassed completely for the same size handgun in a much better caliber choice.

Shooting the Glock 27 was a pleasant experience.

That said, I have no idea how many hundreds of thousands or more .25 ACP semi-automatics are in service throughout the world and will be for decades to come. The ammunition is as robust as any centerfire and the .25 ACP generates so little pressure, if the gun is well-made to begin with, it'll essentially never wear out. Anyway, such guns are rarely shot.

Three of the best .25s – only one is still manufactured, to the best of my knowledge, and that in limited quantities – are the Baby Browning, the Beretta 950BS "Jetfire" and the super-inexpensive Phoenix Arms Raven. Yes, the Raven. The guns worked and the people who made them knew the guns inside and out and, when I was a salesman three decades back for a firearms distributor, regular dealer price was $29.95. Yes, under thirty bucks! Every once in a while, we'd have them on special!

The old 950BS Beretta, mistakenly attributed as the .25 Beretta "007" carried in the James

Bond novels prior to *Dr. No* (Bond's gun was a much earlier model, generally considered to be the Model 418 based on the descriptions in Ian Fleming's books), had an eight-round magazine when most .25s had a six-round magazine. Additionally, the weapon featured a tip-up barrel for easy loading and unloading. Field stripping was ridiculously simple, unless you foolishly removed the grips. The magazine release was push button style, hence faster and more familiar to most shooters. The tip-up barrel feature was a special plus for women with poor finger strength. Later models of the basic Jetfire incorporated a thumb safety. The gun could be carried cocked and locked, if one chose. The Berettas I had and, years and years ago, sometimes carried, were always kept at half-cock. I got into the habit with my first Jetfire, one that had no manual safety. That's the only pistol I would ever carry at half-cock, the half-cock notches on single action Beretta pistols supposedly quite strong. A one-armed American Indian who worked in a shoe repair shop made me an inside waistband holster for the little gun and, quite literally, it was one of the best holsters I ever had and was marvelously concealable. That man was as fine a holster-maker as I've ever encountered.

The Baby Browning has the cachet of being wonderful because it is a Browning, and that's true in most regards. The basic gun – whether current limited production under the name PSA/Precision Small Arms (for US sale, guns for sale outside the USA were marked "FN") or the long-gone stainless steel Bauer or the originals that were made in Belgium – consists of few parts. A six-round magazine, base of the

Smith & Wesson's M&P 9C Compact is sized for concealability.

At left, a Beretta "Minx" in .22 Short, at right a well-used Beretta "Jetfire" in .25 ACP, a much better choice for an autoloader.

butt magazine release, with a sliding thumb safety, the pistol is striker fired. It is certainly among the smallest handguns to be had, both in length, height and thickness. Various cosmetic grades have been offered over the decades the pistol has been around and, for a number of years, there was a version offered with an alloy frame. I used to carry a Bauer .25 quite a lot, until I talked myself into selling it. The problem I had with this basic Browning design was the ease with which that sliding thumb safety would slide. And, I saw no sense in carrying a super-tiny .25 auto chamber empty.

In addition to PSA, Beretta, Phoenix Arms and Taurus still offer .25s, the PSA and Phoenix guns single actions. Double action, the Beretta Model 21 Bobcat and Taurus PT 25 are clearly the spiritual inheritors to the Beretta 950 BS's crown (which I award posthumously) as the most practical .25 automatic. I like double action handguns, especially when talking about safe carry of pocket pistols. That said, I would still stick by my top three choices – the 950 BS, the Baby Browning and the Raven. I was born in 1946, so, at my age, I've got a right to be set in my ways with some things. Would I carry a .25 these days? Only if I had to and, for some reason, couldn't use my Seecamp .32, my Guardian .380 or my North American Arms Pug .22 Magnum.

As much as I discourage the use of semi-automatic pistols in .22 LR or .22 Short for defense, because of inherent problems one can have with .22s in semi-autos, I have nothing but praise for the North American Arms .22 Magnums and, if I really can't hide anything larger, the basic one and one-eighth-inch barrel .22 LR. Calling it like it is, a .22 Long Rifle out of one of NAA's reliable and well-made Mini-revolvers, if you rotate ammunition regularly (shoot it off), is way, way better than nothing and should be used, if it must, at or near contact distance against a soft target. It may seem crude, but there's no such thing as not "hitting below the belt" when you are fighting for your life. I view a small, limited sight radius .22 LR as an "eye, ear, nose and throat" gun. I've heard of a practice some police officers use. They carry a .22 Short Mini-revolver that is loaded with .22 Long Rifle cartridges with a portion of the LR cartridges' bullets sawn off, this to have the smallest handgun possible for stashing in a pack of cigarettes or some other hidden on-body location, yet have more "power" than the .22 Short. That seems to me like a great deal of trouble for nothing. The Long Rifle Mini-revolver from NAA is four inches long, while the .22 Short version is three and five-eighths inches long!

When you get to .22 Magnum, though, you're into something more substantial. Many years ago, Freedom Arms, which also made Mini-revolvers, had a Boot Pistol model with a three-inch barrel. Smith & Wesson, at that time, was making a three-inch barrel version of their

The 21A Beretta Bobcat features the convenient and familiar tip up barrel.

The 21A feels almost as familiar to Ahern's hand as the old 950 BS, now discontinued.

justifiably well-respected Kit Gun in .22 Magnum. I was testing both for different articles. Sharon and I had some ductseal – very fashionable in those days for testing bullet performance – and we fired both guns into the ductseal, which is like clay. Regardless of the gun, with ordinary hollow point .22 Magnum rounds, the bullets expanded to roughly .38 caliber and penetrated over two inches. Should we ever be attacked by a claymation figure like Gumby, I'll grab a .22 Magnum unhesitatingly! But, against more commonly encountered enemies, even with one or one and one-eighth or one and five-eighth barrels, the .22 Magnum is better than the .22 LR and is what I would consider the absolute minimum personal defense cartridge.

The NAA Pug is probably the best choice in this caliber, for combining handling qualities and performance. If you pass on handling qualities, the one and five-eighths standard .22 Magnum Mini-revolver will give you a little more barrel through which muzzle velocity can develop. Both are extraordinarily well-made little handguns.

Currently I do not own a .25, because I have no reason to and I am not a gun collector. I may pick one up again, someday, but it would largely just sit at home. I own a Long Rifle Mini and a .22 Magnum Pug. They're available should I need them and I know they are reliable, while the classic small frame semi-autos which began appearing around the beginning of the 20th century are victims of the less-than-stellar cartridges they employ.

CHAPTER 3

MEDIUM FRAME SEMI-AUTOS ON THE RISE

This nickel plated Bersa Thunder .380 is a perfect example of a medium frame semi-automatic in a classic medium frame caliber.

The semi-automatic pistol, which emerged as a type in the very late 19th century, was, of course, the harbinger of the future. No longer do the uniformed police who patrol our streets and by-ways or the troopers in our Armed Forces who stand against America's enemies carry a revolver. It's semi-auto, the wave of the present and the wave of the future, at least until death ray guns come along – which, on a personal note, I really hope don't come along for a long, long time. Even Brinks messengers are carrying semi-autos these days. When I was a young guy in Chicago and Brinks guards carried their guns in one hand

and money bags in the other, I got to see some amazing old revolvers. When I was a kid, I remember seeing a black Chicago motorcycle cop who wore a pearl handled revolver on each hip, the holsters suspended from over-long drop shanks, the gun butts at the level of his hands. I remember a white foot patrolman who carried his stag-gripped revolver in a reverse draw, just like the real Wild Bill Hickok and Guy Madison's portrayal on TV. Those colorful days started fading when the early autoloading pistols proved themselves quite a bit more than a collector's oddity.

The early semi-autos were large handguns,

This blue Bersa Thunder .380 might be considered by some to be the poor man's Walther PPK/S, but there is nothing poor in quality or performance. All the Bersa pistols examined and fired in association with this project worked like champs.

The medium frame is ideal in the hand, large enough to grasp properly and easily, yet not so large as to be harder to conceal. This is a Bersa Thunder .380 in nickel.

The Bersa Thunder Plus .380 is a larger capacity pistol with double column magazine.

of course; our 1911 and 1911A1 and the German Pistole '08 Luger were almost trim little guns by comparison to pistols the size of the C-96 Mauser Broomhandle (which is still a quite formidable weapon, if you can find one with a bore left). What really got people into carrying semi-automatics rather than the familiar revolver were the still smaller autos. We've just touched on the .25s, of course, but they were the super hideout guns. For ordinary citizens who kept a handgun around just in case they needed to carry it, and for cops and military officers and, admittedly, even for some of the gangsters, what was to become known as the medium frame automatic was just the thing.

Medium frame autos really caught on. Even the legendary frontiersman and showman Buffalo Bill Cody endorsed a medium frame auto! Flatter and more concealable than a revolver with a six-shot cylinder, the medium frame was/is a natural to drop into a pocket or use with a holster. In 1929, a medium frame auto was to become the first commercially successful double action semi-automatic pistol in the world. That gun, of course, was the Walther PP, initially produced in .32 ACP (7.65mm Browning), then in .380 ACP (9mm

The Rohrbaugh .380 is small as guns in that caliber generally go.

The Rohrbaugh .380 exists because of worries that the identical gun in 9X19mm would produce unmanageable recoil. The .380 is a nice little gun and the 9X19mm's recoil is not horrible.

The SIG-Sauer P238 is a single action .380, small in size, slender and quite pleasant to work with.

Kurz). For a number of years, PPs were offered in .22 LR. Shortly after the success of the PP, a slightly smaller version, the PPK, was produced, aimed at undercover police use. There have been many variations within the PP series, such as some PPK production with aluminum alloy frames, some in .25 ACP (6.35mm Browning). Walther PP series pistols have been and still are wildly popular. PPs and PPKs have served not only as civilian and law enforcement concealed weapons, but as openly worn service pistols for police agencies and, during World War II, the German military. The original PP in .32 was the most popular of the guns.

Today, Walther PPs are not manufactured under license in the USA by Smith & Wesson, as are PPK and PPK/S models; as this is written, Walther Germany's website shows German manufactured .32 ACP PP Models still available in blue, but I have been unable to ascertain if anyone is importing them into the USA. The PP in .32 was the most popular model in Europe in the entire PP series, the slightly shorter PPK the most well known variant because of the association with James Bond.

Old and modern, this Walther PP in .32 ACP wears Crimson Trace LaserGrips.

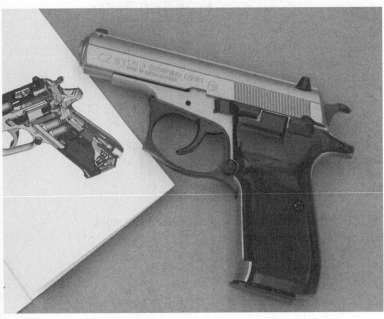

Left profile of the CZ83 with a page from its owner's manual.

The PPK/S came about after the Gun Control Act of 1968 went into effect and banned importation of numerous handguns based on size and other arbitrary factors, the PPK one of these. The PPK/S was a way around the ban, a hybrid with a PP frame and a PPK barrel and slide, the combination making the PPK/S a pistol that could be imported.

As proof that the PP series guns are still considered modern pistols, I'll call attention to the fact that Crimson Trace LaserGrips are manufactured for the Walther PPK/S. I have a set on my Century International Arms imported police turn-in Walther PP .32. Remember, the grip frame of the PP is the same as the grip frame of the PPK/S.

Other famous names in the firearms business, of course, produced at one time or still produce medium frame autos. Remington had one (the Model 51), as did Savage (the most well-known being the Model 1907). Fabrique National of Belgium and Colt both offered John M. Browning-designed medium frames in .32 and .380, the FN pistols being sold under the Browning marque in the United States. The FN Model 1910, otherwise known as the Browning .380, was banned from importation by GCA 68; a target stocked, target sighted, slightly longer version was imported for a short while

At left, a Beretta 70S .380, at right the 1934 Model, a .32. The Model 1935 was a .380 and the 70S is a much modernized version, long since discontinued.

The 1934 Beretta is generally considered a classic of its type. It was the World War II Italian service pistol. It's also the Beretta used on screen when "James Bond" has to swap to the Walther PPK per the orders of "M." An actual Beretta .25, regardless of model, would have looked rather ridiculously small. The 1934 is a .32, just like the PPK Bond is given.

after that. The original was a truly fine looking and practical personal defense weapon. The post-GCA 68 model was not. The Colt 1903 (otherwise known as the Model M) was the issue General Officers pistol during World War II and was among the weapons of America's Office of Strategic Services, the famed OSS, which was the forerunner of the Central Intelligence Agency. At a gun show, recently, Sharon and I spotted an after-market nickel plated version of the little Colt and Sharon was amazed at its slimness.

Colt manufactured other medium frame autos, most recently the Colt Mustang and the Colt Pony, the former a single action, the latter a double action. In size and general appearance, the SIG 238, a single action .380, bears a startling resemblance to the Mustang. The Mustang and Pony were among the casualties when Colt's leadership backed away from most civilian handgun model production during the period of uncertainty before The Protection Of Lawful Commerce In Arms Act was passed in the Senate by better than a two to one margin in 2005, during the Administration of President George W. Bush. Some gun makers, like Colt's, cut back production in order to minimize the potential for punitive litigation brought on by anti-firearms administrations in certain of the cities. Others, like Smith & Wesson, when it was owned by British lawnmower makers before its current pro-gun ownership, had signed a pact with the Clinton Administration, incurring the wrath of firearms rights proponents everywhere. The vote in the House was almost two to one. Six days after the vote in the House, President Bush signed the Bill into law. Other good and promising handguns fell by the wayside, the Autauga .32 among them.

Beretta offers the tip-up barrel Tomcat in .32 ACP and the Model 80 Cheetah series in .380 ACP. Over the years, Beretta has offered numerous medium frames, like the large capacity Model 84 which, for a time, was sold as the Browning BDA .380. One of the most famous and well respected medium frame autos of the 1930s was the 1934 Beretta, this .32 ACP single action being followed in 1935 by a .380 chambering. The pistols have a distinctive look and are quite attractive. Following World War II, Beretta offered a cosmetically altered, more modern looking version of the same basic pistol, sold as the Model 70S, if memory serves. As far as I know, the 70S was offered in .380 and .22 LR, primarily sold in .380 in the United States.

When Smith & Wesson introduced the first stainless steel handgun in 1965 – the Model 60, a two-inch .38 Special J-Frame revolver – the semi-automatic pistol field was slow to catch up. Most people will say that the original Detonics company was the first firm to offer a stainless steel semi-automatic which didn't gall (gouge itself) unless or even if exotic lubrication regimens were followed. However much I'm a fan of Detonics .45s, I believe the Bauer .25, a stainless steel copy of the FN Baby Browning, actually holds that title, although comparing durability concerns between a .45 and a .25 is rather silly.

During the Viet Nam War, considering the jungle environment, a great many persons were interested in rust-resistant personal ordnance. Exotic chrome plating finishes, some truly excellent like the still available work of Mahovsky's Metalife (www.mahovskysmetalife.com), began to flourish and stainless steel revolvers were nearly as dear as diamond encrusted gold ingots.

But it was not just how the gun held up, but what the gun could do that would literally cause a revolution: a man named Lee Jurras started a business called "Super-Vel Cartridge Company" in Shelbyville, Indiana. Talk about a shot heard 'round the world!

The double action Beretta Cheetah .380 is the latest in Beretta's long and distinguished line of true medium frame autos.

Solo shot of the Beretta 70S. This gun originally had bad grips and only one magazine of dubious quality. Searching the Internet found a domestic source for older Beretta parts and the gun, which belongs to a friend, was restored to original usefulness.

CHAPTER 4

DOWNSIZING MEDIUM FRAME CALIBER AUTOS

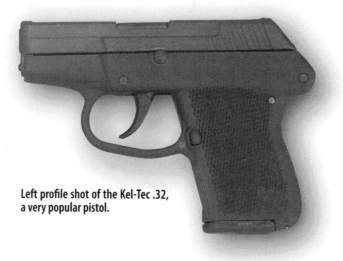

Left profile shot of the Kel-Tec .32, a very popular pistol.

The problem, of course, with smaller handguns had always been that they threw a less effective bullet at the target. Lee Jurras sought to rectify that with the creation of the first high speed jacketed hollow point handgun ammunition. Although Super-Vel Cartridge Company of Shelbyville, Indiana, made a lot of ammunition between 1963 and 1974, their rounds for smaller personal defense handguns achieved the greatest notoriety. I still have part of a box of original Super-Vel .380 hollowpoints, then the ultimate in medium frame semi-automatic ammunition. Lee Jurras sent it to me when I was Associate Editor of *GUNS Magazine,* between 1973 and 1975. It came out of the glove compartment of his Pantera. The Super-Vel cartridges worked so well that he was taking substantial business away from the larger cartridge manufacturers. They learned from him and the abundance of superb cartridges from Remington, Winchester, Federal, Black Hills, Corbon and others might not be available today were it not for his efforts. Lee Jurras is a name that every handgunner should revere.

Because of Lee Jurras, guns like the J-Frame Smith & Wessons and the Walther PPK models were elevated to much more serious ordnance than ever before. As I write this, one of my two usual pocket automatics is in my pocket. Today,

The Kel-Tec .32 and guns like it are palm sized and can be hidden almost anywhere.

it's the Crimson Trace LaserGripped North American Arms Guardian .380, loaded with Remington 88-grain JHPs. At other times, it's my faithful Seecamp .32, loaded with Winchester Silvertip hollow points. Neither cartridge might exist, and, had they not, neither gun would likely exist, either, were it not for Lee Jurras.

Bersa offers the various Thunder Models in .380 ACP, these traditionally-sized medium frame autos. The Walther pistols made in this country by Smith & Wesson, the current Berettas and the two models from SIG-Sauer are also popular traditionally sized medium frame autos. SIG's Model 238, as mentioned earlier, is a pocket-sized single action. The 238 is five and one half inches long, just under four inches high and weighs a tad over fifteen ounces, without magazine. The barrel length is almost two and three quarter inches. Alloy framed, the slide is stainless steel. It is a single action, with this particular gun meaning it will be carried cocked and locked or chamber

The LCP is Ruger's entry into the small, light medium frame pistol market.

empty. Let's assume cocked and locked. And, with that being the case, those persons doing so would have to carry the gun in a holster if they wished to be prudent.

Ahern's trusty Seecamp .32, in his pocket as this caption is written.

SIG's double action medium frame is the 232. It is just over six and a half inches long, just under five inches high and features a barrel that is a little over three and one-half inches. If you get the pistol with an alloy frame, empty weight without magazine is eighteen and one-half ounces. If you go to the all stainless steel model (with stainless steel frame), you are adding another five and one tenth ounces to the empty weight. Magazine capacity is six rounds. The 232, and the earlier 230, as double actions, offer greater versatility in how they can be carried, in my opinion, but are heavier and larger than the relatively diminutive single action Model 238. There are no easy choices when it comes to selecting a concealable handgun, whether for backup or primary personal defense.

While discussing smaller SIG-Sauer pistols, it's interesting to note that the SIG 239, with a capacity of eight plus one in 9mm and seven plus one in .40 S&W or .357 SIG, is 6.6 inches long, just like the 232. The 239 is 5.1 inches high,

making it four-tenths of an inch taller than the SIG 232. The barrel of the SIG 239 is 3.6 inches, identical in length to the 232. The weight factor is substantial. The 239 comes in at 29.5 ounces with alloy frame and the 232 is 18.5 ounces with alloy frame. So, for eleven extra ounces – and I know extra handgun weight bothers a lot of people – you get a pistol available in three of what are usually considered the top four semi-automatic pistol cartridges in the world today. And you get added capacity. If you go with the .40, you can swap barrels, enabling .357 SIG versatility. Data like this makes the intelligent selection of a handgun even more complicated. It is comforting, at least, to know that any handgun you would pick from the SIG-Sauer lineup would be an excellent choice. The most gun knowledgeable man I know, someone who has his choice of a wide range of superb handguns, is quite happy carrying his SIG 239 in .357 SIG.

So, since the SIG 239 is the same size

The Autauga .32 was a promising little handgun, discontinued during the period when certain city administrations were trying to drag the gun companies into court. No action was brought against the company, but the ownership decided to close it anyway.

essentially as a medium frame, but in a caliber normally associated with compact or full-size large frame automatics, what is it?

These days, the old size classifications have become very blurred because of a guy named Larry Seecamp and his late father, and a small manufacturing company on the other side of the country which specialized in explosives. Larry and his Dad did the impossible. They took a .25 automatic sized handgun – which was actually being sold as a .25 and was essentially identical in size to the .25 auto Colt had been selling – and packed .32 ACP into it. Some years later, with these guns successfully performing in the field, Larry chambered the exact same size handgun for .380 ACP. The .380s work and work well.

Meanwhile, those explosives guys, led by explosives expert, engineer and security consultant Sid Woodcock, took the dream of a man who only wanted a small .45 automatic for himself and did the impossible as well. The original Detonics in Washington state offered

the first factory produced (albeit there was a great deal of hand-fitting) 1911 .45 automatic that was about the same size as a traditional medium frame automatic like the Walther PP. Custom gunsmiths had been making seriously cut down 1911s for some years, the result often referred to as "chopped and channeled." There was a waiting list months or years long to send one's full-size or Commander-size 1911 in to some of the top gunsmiths for this treatment, then months more until the gun was returned. Cost was high and didn't even include the original cost of the gun.

After Seecamp began to enjoy great success with his downsized .32 and the larger gun companies saw that the Detonics guns usually worked quite well, other manufacturers of semi-automatic firearms, who, for years, had been seeing their full-sized automatics being cut down by professional gun whittlers, took notice. Smith & Wesson started offering smaller sized versions of the firm's popular 9X19mm

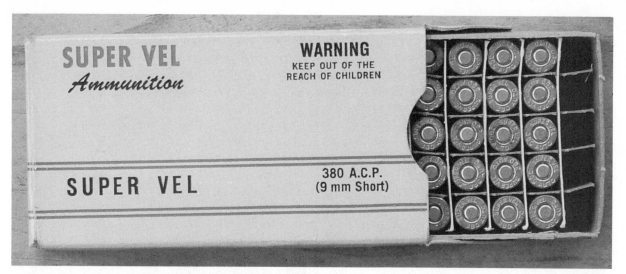

Lee Jurras gave Ahern this box of Super-Vel .380 hollowpoints, taken from the glove compartment of his Pantera. That was in the mid-1970s.

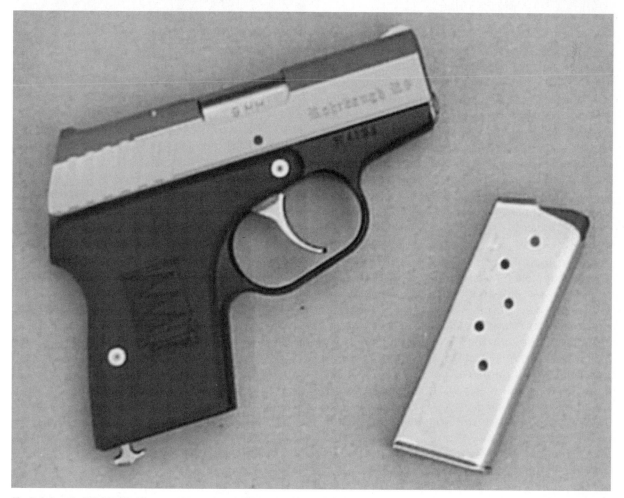

The Rohrbaugh .380, identical in every aspect except caliber to the R9 9X19mm.

semi-autos, inspired it would seem by the ASP and Devel pistols. Colt eventually came out with the Officer's Model .45.

So, now, we have the cartridges that traditionally went into full-size autos being chambered in handguns the size of traditional medium frames. The cartridges that were once chambered in traditional medium frames are now being chambered in guns the size of a small frame.

NAA Guardian .32 NAA, a hot little pistol in a proprietary caliber.

The Guardian in .32 NAA and the Guardian .380 below it, the .380 wearing Crimson Trace LaserGrips.

And the materials are often different. Years ago, firearms had steel frames, except for those comparative few with frames made from aluminum alloy. Spurred on by the success of Glock's pioneering work with polymer frames, companies like Kel-Tec CNC and, more recently Sturm-Ruger, have introduced polymer framed .25 auto-sized pocket pistols. Kel-Tec's first effort with such a pistol was a .32 ACP. The Kel-Tec people were well-versed in working with polymer frames, of course, based on an earlier and larger model. The little Kel-Tec .32 has been extremely well-received. The next project was a .380, this enjoying good success as well. Ruger closed out the first decade of the 21st century with its very first small semi-automatic, the polymer framed .380 caliber LCP, which weighs in at 9.4 ounces empty. The Beretta 950 BS Jetfire .25 weighs 10 ounces empty. See what I mean about the distinctions being blurred?

And then we have the Rohrbaugh, which is also the size of a small frame semi-auto at just 5.2 inches long, 3.7 inches high and weighing only 13.5 ounces empty. There is a .380 ACP version that handles very nicely. But the model getting all the interest is the R9. It's a 9X19mm. That's 9mm Parabellum, the same cartridge chambered in the full-size handguns on the hips of the majority of cops in the United States, the official handgun caliber of the United States military. My Walther PP .32 is 6.5 inches long, 4.25 inches high and has an empty weight of 23 ounces, Crimson Trace LaserGrips included.

While some were, with varying degrees of success, working with already existing cartridges, the people of North American Arms, the Mini-revolver makers, were coming up with new cartridges. Based on work by stopping power expert Ed Sanow, Cor-Bon's Peter Pi and the design staff of North American Arms, the first of the two cartridges is the .32 NAA, a bottleneck .380 case with a .32 caliber bullet. The second round is the .25 NAA. The .25 NAA was inspired by the .25/.32 cartridge, developed by my old friend and world class firearms expert J.B. Wood. It is a fast round, the nominal .25 caliber projectile sitting rocket-like atop a .32 ACP bottlenecked case.

The Tomcat .32 Beretta features the firm's popular tip-up barrel design, far easier than racking a slide to load or unload – and, safer, too.

Bottlenecked cases are noted for ease and reliability of feeding. .357 SIG is a recent and very prominent example of this successful mating of down-sized bullet to bottlenecked case, in that case a .357 bullet on a bottlenecked .40 S&W case. The NAA cartridges incorporate these same concepts. I've recently been shooting a North American Arms Guardian – the .380 ACP frame size – in .32 NAA and have found the results to be quite interesting.

What used to be referred to as "medium frame autos" these days come in a variety of sizes, of course, and can be found in a relatively wide range of prices. The lowest priced .380 auto to be had, as best as research indicates, is from Hi-Point. Pricing starts a little over a hundred dollars and, depending on model, can be about double that. Such low pricing should not be off-putting. Hi-Point has developed a reputation over the years for good, solid value. Cobra Enterprises has bargain priced .32s and .380s along with a wide range of other guns. The FS .32 and .380 models go for well less than two hundred dollars, the CA .32 and .380 models

being even less expensive. The Accu-Tek AT-380II is still quite a bargain, although around a hundred dollars more in price. At about the same pricing level, you'll find the Firestorm .32 and .380.

Smith & Wesson, as this is written, catalogs no .380, but was scheduled to release the new, state-of-the-art, integral laser Bodyguard .380 in May of 2010. It looks very typical of S&W semi-auto profiles, is to be DAO and will have a 6+1 capacity. No word on price. Taurus, well-known for combining excellence of manufacture and performance with attractive pricing, comes in very near to four hundred dollars with the choice of .32 or .380 in the Millenium Pro. The CZ 83 .32 and CZ 83 .380 are several notches higher on the pricing ladder, the CZ reputation for quality respected worldwide.

The Glock Model 25 .380 is the physically smallest of the Glocks, but no miniature. Glock's reputation for quality and durability is unquestioned. The firm makes truly superior handguns. The KAHR P series .380 is another

The magazine release for Beretta's more modern tiny automatics, like this Tomcat .32, is convenient and easy to operate.

of the more expensive .380 pistols; but unless you've taken a KAHR for a "road test," you might not appreciate what superb shooting machines the typical KAHR products are. Precious little larger than the .380 is the Kahr MK 9 or MK .40. These are superb guns, especially the models which have been slicked up at the factory. The Ruger LCP .380 is a fine compromise between pricing and size, a palm-sized handgun at a suggested retail price of just a tad over three hundred dollars.

We return to what many consider the benchmarks for the traditional medium frame auto calibers, the Walther and the Seecamp. Walther PPK and PPK/S Models, produced in the USA under the aegis of Smith & Wesson, although a little altered – the tangs have been slightly lengthened – are still Walthers, the premier traditionally-sized medium frames

for decades and decades. Larry Seecamp's .32 and .380 Models are, of course, what started the size revolution. Talking to Larry recently, I'm not breaking any confidence by telling you – obviously – he's working on some new ideas that may, one day, become reality. In the meantime, both the higher priced (just under eight hundred dollars) Seecamp .380 and the quite reasonably priced .32, lower priced than either Walther model, are considered the "Rolex" of unobtrusive, personal protection handguns. One idea I must dispel, however, and one I must confirm: in tests I conducted, bracketing two Seecamp .32s around one Seecamp .380, I could barely tell any difference in perceived recoil. As to differences between the Walther PPK and PPK/S, the solid steel backstrap of the PPK/S delivers less perceived recoil to the hand than the wrap-around plastic grips of the PPK.

CHAPTER 5

HANDGUNS FOR WOMEN AND CLOSE RANGE SHOOTING FOR ALL

More so than a man, a woman will wisely go out of her way to avoid physical confrontation. And, possibly more so than a man, if trouble starts for a woman, it may well be at extremely close range.

Women often get to corner the market on raw deals and short ends of the stick. Women also frequently get to benefit from the judgment – or lack thereof – of husbands, boyfriends and fathers when it comes to what handgun they may wind up with in their purses or glove compartments or nightstands. If said interested male is gun-knowledgeable, a woman who might not be into guns can, indeed, truly profit from such recommendations. However, if the guy doesn't know a great deal about the subject or appreciate women's special concerns for safety, the woman in question may be better off doing what a girl friend of my wife's used to do in Chicago some forty years ago. The woman's father was in the construction business. He gave

The control on this variation of Crimson Trace LaserGrips is on the side, not the front strap.

her a brick to carry in her purse, which she did faithfully, ready, if needed, to swing the purse at an attacker's head or a more obvious target, quite a bit further south. A gun would have been better, of course, but that was in Chicago, where only the cops and the crooks get to be armed on the street. In those more genteel days, when women often wore gloves, carrying change in the palm of the glove was an instant blackjack or sap.

When our daughter, Samantha, turned 21, we gave her an ideal birthday present for someone about whom we care a great deal. I'd gone to my great friend Steve Fishman, proprietor of Sydney's Department Store and Uniform of Augusta, Georgia, a terrific gunshop, and purchased a very gently used Smith & Wesson Model 640 .38 Special. Sam had been shooting since age seven and once cleaned a table of bowling pins with two shots from a full-sized .45 automatic when she was 12. Eventually, Sam wound up with a nice pair of Crimson Trace LaserGrips on that 640.

So let's talk frankly about women and handguns. If a woman is a uniformed cop,

or a cop in an environment where she is in plain clothes but openly displays her badge, concealment is not a problem – until she's off duty. If a woman is a plainclothes cop, she must conceal her weapon just as a man would, but differently, because – big shock here, guys – women are constructed differently!

Sharon and I knew a fine female law enforcement professional who worked with the U.S. Marshal Service. She wore a blazer to cover her strongside carried weapon. She was a lovely and stylish woman, and it worked great for her. But most women will not alter their clothing style in order to carry a concealed weapon, despite specialized clothing that is available for women, designed to hide gun and holster combinations. I'm sure a lot of this specialized clothing is sold, but most women, like it or not, will carry in a purse. Sure, a purse can get snatched, the gun is slow to access and all that. But if you want a woman you care about – whatever the relationship – to have a handgun there if she needs it, you have to be realistic and realize what she'll do and what she won't do.

The Taurus 809B in 9X19mm features an ambidextrous thumb safety and exposed hammer, two features many people like.

The Taurus 809B is a versatile and easily mastered handgun ideal for experienced or novice shooters alike.

Get her to carry that .45 she's so great with on the range and it'll be at home in a drawer if she ever needs it because the gun is too heavy for her to carry comfortably in her purse. Men should do this experiment. Ask the lady in your life if you can borrow a shoulder bag. Assure her that you're not planning a lifestyle change. Take all the stuff you normally carry in your pockets, along with other items she might need – women do that for guys – and stick it all in

that purse. Then, take that 1911-A1 and a couple of spare magazines and put them in the bag as well. Now, hang this from your shoulder and walk around with it all day. You'll get the idea.

But, the subject here is the guns and not how or how not to carry them. So, what guns are best for women to carry concealed?

I have been asked this question in a variety of ways for decades and I'll tell you some of my stock answers and what my wife, Sharon, carries. How do I know what a woman will or will not carry? As this is written, Sharon and I have been married for over 41 years. That kind of gives me a clue. I have a beautiful daughter and a beautiful daughter-in-law and I've done a great deal of research for this book, other books and decades' worth of columns, articles and lectures on concealed carry gear and techniques.

What I normally recommend as my generic answer concerning what a woman should carry in a purse is a .38 Special J-Frame Smith & Wesson revolver (or, a similar revolver that is set up the same way). Specifically, I'm talking

Tracy is armed with a Glock 22 fitted with Crimson Trace LaserGrips unit and a Surefire 300 WeaponLight.

about the Smith & Wesson Model 640 .38 Special with two-inch barrel (only manufactured for five years and no longer offered new). The original 640 .38 was and is the best handgun of its type ever devised. Almost identical is the Taurus 850 SS2. If blued works for you or your loved one, the Taurus 850 B2 is a good choice. In the lighter weight revolvers, the original S&W Airweight Model 642 with two-inch barrel, the nearly identical Cobra Shadow .38 Special or the Ruger LCR, or the as yet to be released new S&W Bodyguard .38 would work, but not with +P ammunition. They are lighter weight, hence easier to carry in a purse, yet producing more perceived recoil when fired. This is an important concern. I'm prejudiced about this weight issue, I know, but I recommend all-steel construction whenever possible for women (and men, too). The fully enclosed or shielded hammers of these guns make them perfect for quickest access from inside a cluttered handbag or an outerwear pocket. If you can't find any

of these enclosed hammer models – if you're a woman reading this or a man assisting a woman in personal defense handgun selection – take an exposed hammer version of the Smith & Wesson or Taurus revolvers or go to one of the Charter Arms or Rossi revolvers. If you acquire an original S&W Bodyguard or a similar revolver with shielded but not enclosed hammer, there is always the possibility of a coin or some other object getting lodged between the two sides of the shield and preventing proper hammer function. If you really must, get a Smith & Wesson or Taurus in .357 Magnum, still avoiding the exotic metals as much as possible, and never fire anything more than .38 Special +Ps in the revolver. If you can only find one of the exotic metals revolvers –scandium, titanium, etc. – I'd stick with standard velocity .38 Special hollowpoints and nothing hotter than that. Generally, the lighter the weapon, the heavier the perceived recoil and the lighter recoil-producing ammo required.

If a woman has adequate hand/finger strength and can reliably and easily work the slide of a semi-automatic pistol, try a medium frame caliber auto, as discussed in the previous chapters. But try an auto of any description – medium frame caliber or whatever – only if hand/finger strength is not an issue. For a great many women, it is. If an automatic is the best choice, and hand and finger strength is marginal, what comes instantly to mind is a gun such as the Beretta 3032 Tomcat, with its tip-up barrel. The Tomcat can chamber a round inserted directly into its chamber – its slide doesn't have to be cycled to chamber that all-important first round. For years, before there were small frame automatics in medium frame calibers, Sharon carried a Beretta 950 BS Jetfire .25 in her purse. It was a good little gun, despite the caliber, and served her well. The tip-up barrel feature and the minimal finger strength required to work the slide, if she had to, made a great combination. Sharon is as strong as the average woman, certainly, but her grasping finger strength has never been that great.

When Sharon wasn't carrying that Beretta Jetfire, she carried an original Smith & Wesson Model 60 .38 Special two-incher. We put Goncalo Alves combat stocks on the revolver, giving her more gripping surface. The grips did nothing negative as far as concealment, because the revolver was either in her purse or a coat pocket. These days, Sharon's J-Frame is a Smith & Wesson Model 640 .38 Special with Crimson Trace LaserGrips, the revolver loaded with 158-grain lead semi-wadcutter hollowpoint +Ps, just like Samantha's. When this handgun is too large for the occasion, Sharon carries a North American Arms Guardian .32, loaded with Winchester Silvertips, just like I carry in my Seecamp .32.

More so than a man, a woman will wisely go out of her way to avoid physical confrontation. And, possibly more so than a man, if trouble starts for a woman, it may well be at extremely close range.

Although this is not a book about shooting, and I certainly don't consider myself a shooting instructor, it is appropriate to digress with this chapter. The handguns normally selected for concealed carry often have smaller sights, shorter sight radii and grips which may be harder to hold as securely as one might wish. Because of these factors, and especially for newer shooters or totally inexperienced tyros, it is important when shooting concealed weapons that these shooters are enabled to experience

some degree of success at the outset. This is quite practical, too. Most shooting altercations take place at 21 feet or less, a mere seven yards. When one considers how such a statistic is derived, one realizes that a great many shooting situations must occur at well under 21 feet. My point is that for accurate confrontational shooting training and in order to rapidly instill confidence in beginning shooters – as a great many women and a great many men are – targets should be engaged initially at contact range or close to that, when safety considerations allow.

Obviously, when shooting at extreme close range, one must be significantly more conscientious about the potential for ricochets. And one must understand the gun in question well enough to realize its close range limitations when shooting something solid like an attacker rather than something as flimsy as the typical target. Some handguns, for example, can be pushed out of battery and, consequently, will not fire when the muzzle is pressed against a hard surface – like a human sternum or ribcage. 1911 style pistols are famous for this. During World War II, some Allied personnel were taught that certain handguns which might be used by enemy forces could be disabled for an

Demonstrating close-range technique: Ahern prepares to shove an attacker back from his personal space as he readies his gun, an old-style Smith & Wesson Model 640 with Crimson Trace LaserGrips.

At virtual contact range, careful to keep his other hand out of the way, Ahern's laser is in the center ring of the target.

As Ahern takes a pace back, the muzzle rises. His support hand comes onto the gun.

Another step back, the gun coming up but still not at eye level.

The weapon is nearly to eye level, Ahern still another step away from his target.

Both hands on the gun and looking across the sights, Ahern isn't yet in a good position for this type of aimed fire.

At last, Ahern is in a Weaver Stance, the gun on target. At any stage, Ahern could have delivered a center of mass shot. The laser helps, of course, but so does the confidence one can build from starting out so close.

instant by actually pressing against the muzzle of the weapon, when one was faced with a pistol shoved into one's back. In theory, this works. I've seen it done with a 1911, for example, but I really have no interest in finding out if it works in the field and wouldn't recommend anyone else try it.

For the closest range shooting, you need to make enough room between yourself and an adversary that you can access your handgun. Push, shove, punch, gouge, scratch, knee or whatever to get yourself that fraction of a second to step back and put that foot or so or yard or so of distance between you and an adversary in order to draw your gun. Stab the gun toward your attacker's center of mass as you fire, unless you are very close. Then, keep the gun near your hip or pelvis and fire. These techniques can be practiced on a variety of target media, from simple silhouettes to things like Usama Bin Laden targets (Great fun to shoot at and patriotically uplifting, too!) to the full torso mannequin style, so long as the target itself and how the target is mounted or held up is safe for such close range firing and all other factors regarding basic shooting safety are adhered to.

This type of shooting gives instant gratification to a novice. Just always be doubly careful that the shooter's other hand and all body parts are well clear of the target area. In other words, she shoves with her open palm or knees the target, draws and fires. Make certain that hand or that knee is out of the way. Also, in this reactive style of shooting, make certain the novice has enough trigger control experience so she will not prematurely discharge the weapon. Practice these techniques with an empty weapon before a loaded weapon is used.

In order to accomplish this, you must first set up targets at a more conventional distance, but not a great distance. Again mindful for ricochets and other safety considerations, set up a target about six feet distant. After teaching the fundamental safety and handling techniques every shooter must know and engaging in some dry firing techniques, get the new shooter to comfortably do some target shooting on a silhouette, just aiming for center of mass.

Before doing anything that involves aiming, dry firing or shooting, make certain that the gun is being grasped properly. With an empty gun and correct muzzle discipline, pick up the handgun and position it so that the lateral center of the grip is in contact with the center of the web of the shooting hand, the web being the

A good concealed carry gun for a man or woman, especially a beginner, this Beretta 3032 in .32 ACP is easy to shoot and operate.

area between the thumb and the trigger finger. The hand should be as high up on the pistol as the top of the grip section. With a Colt, a Cimarron or similar single action cowboy style revolver, you obviously don't position your hand so the web is immediately behind the hammer. I'm talking about modern revolvers and semi-automatics.

Once the learner has assumed this grip, again abiding by all safety considerations, whoever is instructing should determine whether or not the hand is going to get in trouble if the handgun is a semi-automatic and the web of the hand is fleshy. This is not a great concern with revolvers, because they do not have slides moving out of and back into battery, shot after shot. If the fleshy part of the web is rolling over the grip tang, the retracting slide will cut the skin. You will have to encourage the shooter to either alter the hand's position or, if practical, get a different handgun. Otherwise, your learner will develop a fear of that slide coming back and biting. Thankfully, women's hands will rarely be large enough or fleshy enough to experience such problems.

Once the grip with the master hand has been considered, you must teach what to do with the support hand. I remember watching that great old television series *The Man From U.N.C.L.E.* and seeing Robert Vaughn's support hand go under the magazine base plate of the heavily modified P-38s used in the series. In real life – some guns more than others – cupping the palm under the butt of the gun can exert

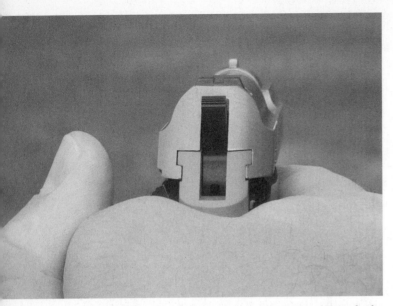

The little Beretta .32's sights aren't large, but they're adequate for the type of shooting required from a small personal protection handgun.

upward pressure on the magazine that can be sufficient to cause a pistol to jam. Not a good thing. When the support hand comes into play, it should be wrapped around the master hand and the pistol grip, roughly so that the middle knuckle of the off-hand first finger is just under the trigger guard and at the lateral mid-point relevant to the grip. This gives a good, solid, secure and comfortable hold that can easily be assumed and reliably helps to control the weapon in recoil.

Once your student is over the idea of the loudness of the report, even with hearing protection, and what perceived recoil there will be, work to tighten groups a little, but remember that you are not teaching bullseye shooting.

Again with an empty gun, have the student practice drawing the gun from wherever it will most commonly be carried. If a purse is where that gun will be in the real world, then don't waste the learner's time teaching her how to get the gun into action from a belt holster. You must emphasize trigger control again and again.

There is great controversy between advocates of aimed fire across the sights and body indexed point shooting. It's a silly thing to argue over. If someone is about to do you harm and you have determined in that micro-second of realization that you must act with potentially deadly force and your adversary is only a few feet away, only someone who had trained in no other technique would take the time to bring the gun up to eye level in a two-hand hold before firing. If your potential murderer might be three feet

or six feet away from you, you must master the technique for body indexed shooting, so that, if this scenario is suddenly your reality, you can shoot as soon as you've cleared your carry system and can stab the muzzle at the target.

To facilitate body index shooting and speed up the process and increase the confidence level, add a laser that can be handily mounted within the gun or, my preference, in the form of Crimson Trace LaserGrips. I talk about Crimson Trace products because I use them on virtually every handgun I have for which LaserGrips are made. The prudent thing is to have the learner work with the laser both on and off, so that a battery suddenly going out – unlikely if the shooter monitors battery service life as he or she should – doesn't prevent the learner from taking appropriate action with the weapon.

The greater the distance to your target, the higher the pistol or revolver can rise after the draw. At contact or near contact distance, get your weapon out and, unless the threat no longer exists, shoot. If someone is twenty or thirty feet away, you'll probably have time to use the sights and, hopefully, move to cover at the same time. Start with the close range and extreme close range shooting and a novice will be getting maximum benefit in the minimum time and can go on from there to further develop needed skills.

As a general rule, when a sudden life-threatening situation arises, promptness of response is at least as important as mode of response. That said, it is only common sense that, if an adversary is extremely close, it would be madness to waste precious time by bringing the firearm up to eye level, acquiring some sort of sight picture and pressing the trigger. Likewise, if an adversary is some distance away – arbitrarily, let's say 20 feet – it would be silly not to use one's sights if time permits. Indeed, at virtual point blank range, extending one's arms in an isosceles or Weaver stance may well be an invitation to have one's weapon knocked aside or worse.

The logical remedy to this predicament is body index shooting, as mentioned. Here's how it is done. Body index shooting from the "hip" or abdomen level at extreme close range is the very specialized and potentially quite useful technique for firing with one hand and bent arm with the weapon as an extension of the shooting hand, while at the same time held extremely close to the body.

Think of the old black and white movies for a moment. The good guy – whether cop, detective,

The Beretta Storm 9mm is ultra modern and very compact, a good choice for the beginner or experienced persons.

amateur sleuth, frontier marshal or cowboy – would get the drop on the bad guy. He wouldn't extend his arm from his body, but rather hold the gun close in at approximate waist level. Of course, in many of those old films, unlike real life, at the precise moment the good guy gets the drop on the bad guy, the good guy also decides to practice his oratorical skills while expounding upon some important plot point or another. But, the positioning of the gun in relation to the gun-holder's body is, essentially, quite valid at close range. Most of us have seen some of the old Warner Brothers films starring Humphrey Bogart or Jimmy Cagney. When they had the "drop" on an adversary, it was actually good, close range technique they were demonstrating.

With this hip shooting technique, the good guy can hold a firearm quite inconspicuously and fire quite effectively at close range. My old pal Sid Woodcock taught me the appropriate technique. After that, it was a matter of practice. On the days when I'm carrying a pistol with Crimson Trace LaserGrips – like my North American Arms Guardian .380 – I practice the technique against a safe backstop, closing my eyes, drawing the gun and actuating the laser, then opening my eyes to see where the laser is pointing. The results are reassuring.

When drawing the weapon, whether from a pocket or some type of holster, try to keep your shoulders level. This may sound simple and obvious. It is neither. When one reaches for a gun, covering garments must be lifted or brushed aside, the body will be moving in such a fashion that the gun arm is either pistoning upward or sweeping from the opposite side of the body, depending on carry technique. The body must recover its equilibrium from such motions in order that the shoulders will become level. A common technique used at close range by handgun armed assassins is to point the gun

The Beretta Storm features an ambidextrous safety.

"shoulders" would be at more or less the same height as one's own. If you are a shorter statured man or woman, someone below average height, once you get the hang of the technique, it might be incumbent upon you to raise the height at which the firearm is held, perhaps from the approximate level of the pelvis or waist to a slightly higher position, this merely by extending the arm an inch or two further forward. This is important to remember because the weapon must be held at a height equivalent to the mid-body point of the target, if one wishes to go for center of mass hits. If instead of hitting, say, at the level of an attacker's sternum, you hit in the abdomen, you might have different results. You are not trying to kill someone, remember; instead, you are defending your life or the life of an innocent by reacting to a threat and the whole idea is to put the attacker down so the attack will cease.

The reasoning behind keeping your shoulders level as you draw and prepare to fire is so that you may enhance hand-eye co-ordination for accuracy. To repeatedly assume the correct hold and stance for an instant response in situation after situation, whether in training or real world use, the body itself becomes the reference to the target, the aiming device, as it were. I have been practicing this since Sid Woodcock first taught me the principles behind the technique and it has proved to be remarkably simple.

As the gun is pointed at the target in practice, you should try to develop the habit of viewing your handgun from above while at the same time watching the target dead on. The slide top strap of an automatic, for example, will be in the lowest boundary of your vision. When using a semi-auto pistol rather than a revolver, you must be especially careful to guard against hot brass hitting your eyes. Safety glasses are very important during practice because of the position at which the gun is held. Make certain that these glasses fit rather closely. I've had the experience of a piece of hot pistol brass dropping between my shooting glasses and my face and burning my cheek. I wouldn't have wanted that brass coming in at a slightly different angle and striking my eye.

In order to speed up the learning process and enhance hit capabilities by instantly correcting one's hold, a laser sighting device can be extremely useful, as noted. Let me emphasize that I am not recommending that the laser takes the place of practice. The laser will merely speed up proficiency by showing you every time where the hits would be if you are dry firing or

and simultaneously step forward and stomp the foot, this to settle the skeletal support in the moment the trigger is pulled.

It is paramount that the drawn weapon's barrel or slide/barrel assembly is kept parallel to the ground. Remember that the body is the sighting system and, if the weapon is not parallel to the ground, shots will either print high or low. At near contact distance, it matters little, but at even a few feet away, resultant error from failure to keep the firearm parallel to the ground will be magnified and the consequence will be a missed shot or shots or even injury or death to an innocent.

Never forget that, with this type of shooting, the target is the opponent's center of mass. Don't go for anything fancy. You want to hit that center of mass and keep multiple shots grouped no more than three or four inches apart. During practice sessions, of course, one is naturally "aiming" for center of mass hits on a silhouette target, one which would be positioned for an average height person so that the silhouette's showing you before triggering a shot that you need to adjust the point of impact.

Albeit that a number of high quality laser systems are available on the market, I favor the Crimson Trace LaserGrips or a laser which is incorporated within a guide rod, in both cases because of the ease of carry and use, but also because they do not alter the natural balance point of a weapon with which the operator may already have developed some considerable familiarity.

Balance of the weapon must be considered as extremely important. Weight and size of a weapon can seriously affect how you hold it. When we're talking body index shooting at extreme close range and you are using different handguns, you may well find that the muzzle will be high or low, depending on the balance point of the weapon and the weapon's weight. For me, at least, a lighter weight handgun will have a tendency for the muzzle to rise, while a heavier handgun's muzzle may have been dead on. The lesson to learn from this is that, perhaps, for consistency with this type of shooting, one should either stick to similarly balanced and weighted weapons or practice so much with each weapon you might use in this context that your body develops the ability to naturally compensate.

Safety must be paramount. Remember that an empty gun practiced with in front of a mirror will hang differently in the hand than a loaded gun will at the pistol range. The weight is unavoidably different. If you are using a semi-auto, as most shooters do these days, it might be a good idea to buy an old, "beat up" magazine, pull the follower and magazine spring and insert some lead fishing weights of an equivalent weight to the number of cartridges the full magazine would hold, plus the one in the chamber. Use epoxy poured into the magazine to keep the weights from shifting around or rattling. If using a revolver, get some empty brass and persuade your friendly neighborhood bullet caster or black powder shooter who makes his own projectiles to add an appropriate amount of weight to those empties.

It's a good idea not to forget that some handguns naturally point high or low for some of us. The method by which you can determine what your own weapon or weapons will do is actually pretty simple. Start out with the eyes closed and just point the weapon straight ahead (obviously observing all prudent safety precautions). Open your eyes and observe where your weapon is pointed. This simple

Balance point, weight and grip angle, when they are just right for your hand, can make a big difference in the quality of your shooting, whether body index shooting or aimed fire across the sights.

exercise will assist you in determining whether the handgun's muzzle naturally points up or down. If you have a handgun that points way off when you do this, you might want to think about whether or not this particular model is a wise choice for you defensively. If you have the opportunity when you are shopping for a handgun to safely perform this little test (without creeping people out), it could save you a lot of money. Balance point, weight and grip angle, when they are just right for your hand, can make a big difference in the quality of your shooting, whether body index shooting or aimed fire across the sights.

Start with the target at nearly point blank range, perhaps only a yard or so away. Be careful lest the weapon is held so close to the body that your clothing will interfere with your pistol's slide operation. As the weapon is walked on target at the range, acquisition of the target with the first shot or shots will become easier and easier.

Getting used to a derringer like this one from Bond Arms, presents a whole set of technique related issues. Danny Akers is at The Firing Lane in Bogart, Georgia.

Mastering close range and distance shooting alone will not be enough. Other elements of close range shooting, to include movement and the like, should be studied and practiced. Remember that in a perceived dangerous situation, your adrenalin will be pumping, your vision will be somewhat distorted and your body may actually tremble because of the adrenalin rush and other aspects of typical human fight or flight response.

The worst mistake a person can make in helping an inexperienced man or woman to acquire a firearm is not teaching that man or woman how to use that firearm, or seeing to it that someone teaches how the weapon is properly and safely used. When your child turns 16, you don't just give the kid the keys to the family car without instruction. One must have confidence both in one's weapon and one's ability to use it as intended in order for the weapon to be worth its weight. A firearm, the mechanics of which an inexperienced man or woman barely understands, will be useless in an emergency, except, perhaps, as something that is thrown at an attacker or used to club him.

Women can be tenacious, deadly fighters when their children or families are threatened, but women are generally raised to be gentle and compliant, nurturing and non-aggressive. A lot of that is changing, of course, with women so frequently engaging in contact sports like basketball and even ice hockey and more and more women getting into physical fitness regimens which may include kick boxing or some other martial art.

Part of helping a woman or a man to be sufficiently competent with a handgun that it will be carried concealed, won't be left at home and will be drawn and brought into action if necessary is assisting the new concealed weapons carrier in the understanding of why deadly force needs to be one of many options and exactly what the use of deadly force implies. If you are a man or woman who is confident you would never use deadly force, you are probably not someone who would be reading this book. So it's simply a matter of priorities, isn't it? Whose life is more important to you? Is the life of a robber or rapist or sadistic thrill-killer of greater importance to you than your own? No one wants anyone's loved ones to have to grieve; but, given the either/or choice, would you rather your attacker's loved ones grieve his passing or your loved ones grieve yours?

SNUB-NOSED REVOLVERS

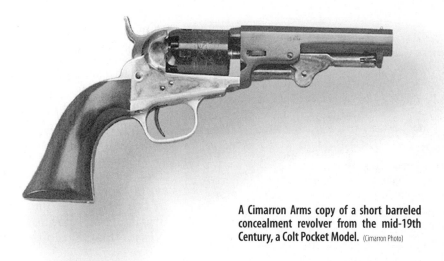

A Cimarron Arms copy of a short barreled concealment revolver from the mid-19th Century, a Colt Pocket Model. (Cimarron Photo)

Although any knowledgeable firearms person will tell you that a semi-automatic pistol is typically a far simpler mechanism than a double action revolver, that same well-informed person will likely freely admit that the double action revolver is easier to operate, whether we're talking about actually shooting or merely loading and unloading of the weapon.

The complications associated with a revolver's mechanism are coincident with the multiple mechanical functions needed for the gun to work, and the fact that, by the very nature of how these mechanical functions are accomplished, there are all sorts of entryways into a revolver for dirt and debris, far more so than for the typical semi-automatic.

Back in my days with *GUNS Magazine,* one of our regular contributors was Colonel Charles Askins. Askins was not just a knowledgeable gun person, but a terrific writer, too. And, he was a truly fine shot. Before World War II, as Askins related in one of his articles, he saw no problems with relying on a double action revolver in the field. But, slogging through Europe in all sorts of rotten weather conditions brought home to him just how comparatively delicate a revolver really was.

But simplicity of operation – firing, loading

Left profile of the Cobra Shadow, a lightweight close copy of the S&W Model 640.

At top, Sharon Ahern's old-style Model 640 .38 Special, below that Jerry Ahern's old-style 640, both with different styles of Crimson Trace LaserGrips. The holster is for pocket carry.

Ahern holds the Cobra Shadow in his right hand, a Model 60 Smith & Wesson in his left. Note subtle differences, like the front of the crane.

and unloading – keeps the small revolvers popular. And, unless the gun is subjected to the harshest of field conditions, as Colonel Askins had to endure with his revolver, the good quality revolver will do just fine. Like semi-automatic pistols, revolvers can be ammunition sensitive, but not to the same degree. The principal ammunition related issue for the double action revolver is primer seating depth. If the primers on the cartridges you place in the cylinder of your revolver are raised, the cylinder might very well not turn. So, yes, you can get a jam with a revolver, but it's unlikely in the extreme with factory loaded ammunition.

Historically, in the United States, the snub-nosed market belonged to Colt and Smith & Wesson. In the mid-20th century, along came Ruger and Charter Arms and the Rossi revolvers from Brazil. Ruger never had a true snub nosed, small frame revolver until the LCR debuted well along in the first decade of the 21st century. In the 1970s, the Taurus revolvers, also from Brazil, began to be noticed in the USA. Smith & Wesson-like and lower-priced, they caught on and grew.

The category of snub-nosed revolvers is usually defined by a nominal two-inch barrel, but many of these same revolvers can be had, at times, at least, with nominal three-inch barrels.

Charter Arms had its ups and downs, but seems, in modern times, to have hit its stride. Built on innovation from the very beginning, Charter has continued this tradition with such things as its mirror image left-hand revolver. Rossi revolvers are now manufactured by Taurus, but as a distinctly different line. Under its own name, Taurus offers a wonderfully full line of snubby revolvers. Smith & Wesson, of course, continues its tradition of world-class revolvers. With Cobra and Ruger offering snubbies, the choices for the consumer run the gamut of pricing and features.

The innovative Ruger LCR is a modularly built .38 Special revolver.

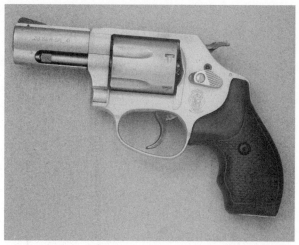

The Smith & Wesson Model 637, like so many concealment handguns, is extremely light weight.

When firing guns like the S&W Model 637 with hotter ammunition, expect serious recoil; you'll get it.

During the Clinton administration years, before legal protection for gun manufacturers was passed by Congress and signed into law by George W. Bush, as noted elsewhere, a number of anti-Second Amendment city administrations went after gun makers with law suits and threats of law suits. The philosophy seemed to be that the cigarette makers had proven to be fair game in the court system, so, why not gun makers? The idea, of course, was to gouge as much money as possible, then force the gun makers out of the civilian arms business. Colt, at that same time, abandoned most of its handgun line, snub-nosed revolvers among the casualties.

A list of the two largest makers of snub-nosed handguns would still include Smith & Wesson, of course, but the principal competitor to Smith & Wesson's offerings is Taurus USA, and that is a situation that is likely to remain.

The Colt Detective Special, as well as the Agent and Cobra, will still be found from time to time as used guns. Of robust design, one of these revolvers in good condition would likely provide a lifetime of service with the proper ammunition choices. And that can be said for all of the snub-nosed revolvers I have ever tried. Treat them properly and they will serve you well.

The Colt revolvers were derived from the Colt Police Positive, the smaller-framed .38 Special six-shot service revolver in the Colt line in the early years of the 20th century. Original swing-out cylinder revolvers on this frame size were introduced as early as 1889. The Detective Special was a Police Positive with a two-inch barrel. The Smith & Wesson J-Frame of 1950, on the other hand, was an enlarged I-Frame gun, beefed up to take .38 Special.

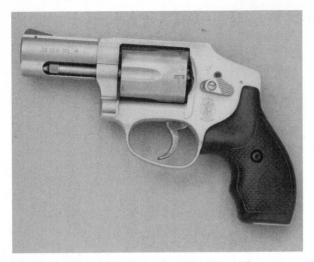

Left profile of the Smith & Wesson Model 642 .38 Special.

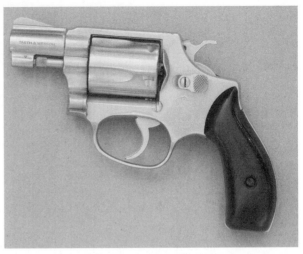

Ahern bought his first all steel J-Frame S&W in 1967. This old-style Model 60 is more recent than that, of course.

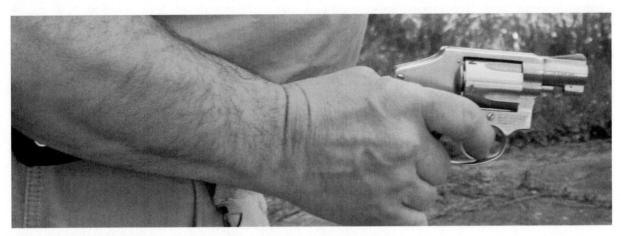

Ahern using body index shooting with a revolver, a skill useful in close range confrontations.

Smith & Wesson produced, of course, snubby K-Frame (smaller medium frame) revolvers, but they weren't small enough. The earliest I-Frame was the .32 Hand Ejector of 1896. The J-Frame five-shooter that so captured the market was the original Chiefs Special Model 36, a true classic that provided the inspiration for all of the five-shot .38 Specials in today's market, regardless of the maker. Other makers' handguns have their own distinctive features and design differences, of course, but that these guns all have marked similarities – frame size, overall length, cylinder capacity and caliber to name the most obvious points – is undeniable.

Because the range of snub-nosed .38 Special revolvers is so broad, the wise shopper will examine as many of these different models as possible, being careful to consider all features.

Weights range from 22-1/2 ounces to jarring featherweights at 13-1/2 ounces. Construction materials can be ordnance steel, stainless steel, magnesium, titanium, aluminum and scandium. Blue and nickel plated finishes are available. You can have gold highlights. You can have multiple colors on the same gun, because of differing metals used. Calibers include .357 Magnum, .38 Special (+P rated), .32 H&R Magnum and .22 Magnum. You can have recoil absorbing grips, fiber optic front sights and lasers.

If you choose a snubby wisely, it can be a tool that will serve you faithfully for life. My first handgun was a snubby revolver and I wouldn't be without one to this day.

CHAPTER 7

WOULD A .38 BY ANY OTHER NAME SHOOT AS STRAIGHT

The S&W M&P Compact is a handy sized 9mm, 9X19mm one of the many variations of a nominal ".38 caliber."

If we date the advent of modern handguns to the successful development of the revolver by the ineffable Colonel Sam Colt in 1836, we could just work our way through the decades going from one ".38" to another. What we call the .38 caliber is really about .357 caliber and can be rounded off to tenths as .36. The .36 caliber was most famously exemplified in the Colt 1851 Navy and its variants, like the concealed carry version which was called the Colt Pocket Navy and developed in 1862, upgraded from .31 caliber, as was the Pocket Police.

Throughout the remaining four decades of the 19th century, part of this period the early cartridge era, the .36 caliber percussion revolvers, whether full-sized six shooters or various smaller ones with five-round cylinders, were carried openly or concealed. Wild Bill Hickok, perhaps the most adept man with a handgun who ever lived, carried a pair of .36 caliber 1851 Navy revolvers. Various other manufacturers offered pocket guns in .38 caliber. The .38-40 became a popular round in Winchester rifles, but also in Colt revolvers,

Hideouts of yesterday and today from Smith & Wesson, the M&P Compact autoloader and an old style Model 60 revolver, all steel.

More shots between reloadings and faster reloading have helped to bring semi-autos to their position of prominence, the gun in Ahern's right hand a Smith & Wesson M&P Compact in 9mm, the revolver a Model 60 of the older, all steel persuasion, and wearing a Barami Hip-Grip, a product Ahern has been using for forty years, as this is written.

The Para USA Para Carry is a nice handling 9mm.

The CZ Rami is a good gun, but it would be easier to conceal if the butt of the weapon were a little shorter, proportionate to length.

enjoying a resurgence, I understand, in modern cowboy action shooting.

Not long after the 20th century dawned, the U.S. Government's new .38 caliber service revolvers were being put to the test during the Siege of Peking (June 20, 1900 – August 15, 1900), when Chinese rebel forces attacked the foreign legations. A year earlier, The United States began fighting against the Philippine Insurrection forces. Marines in the International Relief force which broke the Siege of Peking were drawn from that conflict. The War in the Philippines ended in 1902, but fighting with Muslim and other rebel groups went on until 1913. It was during this conflict against the Moro tribesmen and others that U.S. forces came to the realization that something more

than a .38 Long Colt (less powerful than the standard 158-grain round nose lead .38 Special police load everyone laments) was needed. The .38 Long Colt just didn't have what it took.

While the United States was looking toward a .45 caliber cartridge, the .45 ACP, Europe was looking elsewhere. In 1898, Georg Luger patented his pistol design, influenced by the Hugo Borchardt design of 1893. Luger's toggle action pistol was to combine with the 9mm Parabellum, or 9X19mm, cartridge in 1902. The design and the cartridge together became Imperial Germany's P.08. The 9mm – whether the Parabellum cartridge, the 9mm Kurz (.380 ACP) or the 9mm Browning or the 9mm Makarov – is a nominal .38 caliber, generally firing a .356-caliber bulet.

A Glock 17 Gen 4, the Glock 17 one of the most popular 9mms around.

The Rohrbaugh .380 is compact and pleasant to shoot.

Ruger's SR9C is a typical example of Ruger's excellent quality.

Walther's PPS should be "James Bond's" next handgun.

The 9X19mm is the most popular pistol cartridge in the world. It is the pistol cartridge of the U.S. Armed Forces and the forces of the United Kingdom. It was the primary pistol cartridge of Germany during World War I (fired in the Luger) and World War II (fired in the P-38). It is widely used in submachine guns and has been used in that capacity since World War II. The 9X19mm, with its nominal .38 caliber bullet, reportedly has replaced the .38 Special as the most common chambering for the handguns carried by American law enforcement.

The .38 Special, although much maligned in standard loadings, is still a cartridge very much to be reckoned with when loaded for better performance. It is derived from the .38 Smith & Wesson cartridge, a weaker cartridge which can still be encountered and will not work in .38 Special and .357 Magnum revolvers. The old

.38-44 High Velocity, actually the progenitor of the original Magnum, was never called that because the idea of lengthening the case, if such was considered, was not incorporated into the design. Using a higher pressure loading in the standard length .38 Special, 1930's .38-44 High Velocity was actually the first +P. For the day, certainly, it would have been the equivalent of a +P+ because it matched some early loadings for 1934's .357 Magnum, also a .38, called a "magnum" after the larger-sized champagne bottles, because the case was lengthened by an eighth of an inch in order to prevent .357 Magnum cartridges from being chambered in ordinary .38 Special revolvers or even the .38-44 revolvers of the period.

There was good reason to worry about that occurring – the introduction of an overly powerful cartridge into a handgun designed for

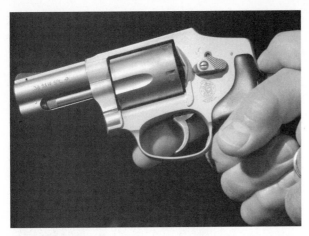

The Smith & Wesson Model 642 of current manufacture, here with a three-inch barrel.

The Smith & Wesson SW9VE proved to be a good shooter.

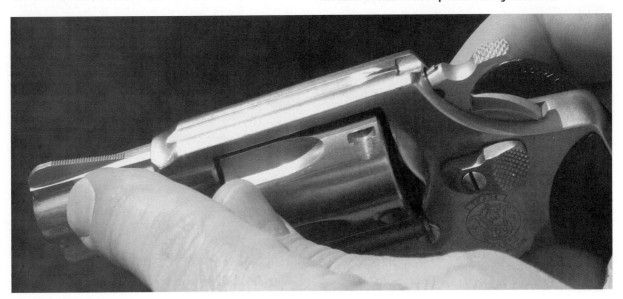

An original Model 60 with serrated ramp front sight.

standard power cartridges – because this was a potentially disastrous occurrence that was not unknown. The classic example pursuant to things .38 caliber is the old .38 Colt Auto and the much more powerful .38 Super. The problem was that .38 Super – essentially a +P version of the .38 Colt – was too hot for safe operation in the older .38 Colt handguns.

These days, there are +P versions of 9X19mm and both +P and +P+ versions of .38 Special and a version of the .40 S&W automatic pistol cartridge necked down into a bottleneck and fitted with a nominal ".38" caliber bullet, which is called the .357 SIG.

When properly loaded, all these ".38s," – the .38 Special, the .38 Super, the 9X19mm, the .357 Magnum and the .357 SIG – are among the very finest defensive pistol cartridges to be had

anywhere at any time. Ballistics authorities are wont to say that the ultimate knockdown power cartridge against a human attacker is a 125-grain .357 Magnum. The trouble is, this is almost exclusively a revolver round. The reason for the existence of the .357 SIG was/is to duplicate that same revolver round's performance out of a semi-automatic pistol. Loaded with a 125-grain JHP bullet, it essentially does just that. As this is written, the Air Marshals, who surreptitiously guard our commercial airliners, use .357 SIG in the SIG-Sauer P250 pistol. I doubt they could have made a finer choice.

It might be possible to cover every possible variation of ".38" within the scope of this book, but I'm not going to do it. I'd rather try shedding light on some of the more interesting examples which can be seen as exemplifying

The Walther P-38 was advanced for its time and is still a fine handgun that's a good shooter.

This much modified Smith & Wesson Model 686 in .357 Magnum wears Crimson Trace LaserGrips.

The Beretta Cheetah is one of the latest in Beretta's long and successful medium frame auto line, a fine .380.

characteristics which are desirable. In previous chapters, I wrote about how men like Larry Seecamp and his late father were able to shrink the concept of traditional medium frame automatics down to the size of small frame autos – a not insignificant feat, to be sure. That said, there are "medium frame autos" to be had these days in calibers normally reserved for full-sized pistols, the smallest of these from Rohrbaugh. The standard R9 is a 9X19mm with 6+1 capacity, weighing 13.5 ounces and having a length of 5.2 inches. The length of a Walther PPK in .32 or .380 is 6.1 inches. Larger slightly is the Taurus PT 709 Slim and, of a similar size but lighter in weight than the Taurus, the Kel-Tec PF-9.

The PT 709 Slim weighs only 19 ounces empty, this with a three-inch barrel, six-inch overall length and a capacity of seven plus one rounds.

If you go for the titanium slide model, the pistol is lighter still. I've tested this gun in a number of ways and found it not only accurate and reliable and extremely pleasant and comfortable to shoot, but, with its handy size, and the way it sits in the hand, the PT 709 Slim is a natural for close range body index shooting from hip or waist level. In an extremely close encounter of the significantly unpleasant kind, a handgun which seems to enhance any proclivity one might have developed for this type of shooting is a definite asset.

Whether you might choose one of the weapons covered in this chapter, or earlier or later in this book, the ultimate weapon, of course, is our humanity. We are physical and we are psychological. If we were discussing philosophy or religion, we'd add spiritual into

The Beretta Storm 9mm sits well in the hand and lends itself to close range body index shooting.

The magazine release and other controls on the Beretta Storm are convenient to use.

the mix. Being true to our nature as mankind developed over the millennia, we have certain biological traits which have helped to safeguard us against animal attack and other dangers. We all know about the fight or flight response, to be sure; but, we must remember other instinctual specifics of human nature. We can sense danger in subtle ways. Yet, to be truly ready to defend ourselves, whether that defense is active (fight) or more passive in nature (flight), we must be fully aware of our surroundings. It is a matter of intelligence, but not the kind that has anything to do with one's I.Q. Rather, the intelligence to which I refer is the gathering of data, collating it in the supercomputer between our ears and reading, understanding and acting upon the results of analysis of the data.

We must be as fully alert to and aware of our surroundings as possible. The late Colonel Jeff Cooper wrote about color-coded conditions of readiness. Condition Red was when the fight was to be joined. Condition Orange was when your awareness of your surroundings was heightened and generally concentrated on something which you were perceiving as a serious potential threat. Condition Yellow is when you're on your toes, on your game, but there's nothing signaling you something even might be about to go down. Condition White is when you are blissfully unconcerned with what is going on around you.

Little children are in Condition White, as they should be, most of the time. This is why they can, occasionally, scare an adult out of his wits as they climb up onto something or run somewhere, totally unaware of what might

be considerable danger. Men generally get more bent out of shape while watching small children. Men do this because we are generally less used to the activity and we tend to look for disastrous occurrences more so than women do. Women take children more in stride. When it comes to what little children are doing, men rapidly fluctuate between Yellow and Orange and sometimes fly into Red. The children know nothing else but Condition White and the typical woman will stay in Condition Yellow and may skip Orange entirely until the child is about to do something that puts her into Condition Red.

For normal day-to-day activities, I recommend never going to Condition White, unless you're the President or someone like that, surrounded by Secret Service bodyguards, or if you're in a bombproof, fireproof, earthquakeproof building thousands of miles from the nearest shoreline or volcano and the building's roof is reinforced against random meteor strikes. Even then, although I might feel somewhat relaxed, I wouldn't still want to go to White. When our hundred pound dog barks and I go to answer the door, I'm wearing a gun which the visitor will never see unless I need to use it. The gun may very well be in my hand; again, the visitor won't see it unless I need to use it. When I'm watching FOX News or whatever at night, if there's not a gun in my pocket, there's a gun on the coffee table right in front of me. There's also a cellular telephone and a small flashlight. Being so equipped is my idea of Yellow. The rest of the time, I'm nearly Condition Orange all the way.

CHAPTER 8

COSMETIC SURGERY FOR HANDGUNS

A Walther P-38, action open, magazine out. There was nothing to do to shorten the grip frame, but some Walther P-38s were customized so the barrel barely protruded past the front of the slide. The practice made the gun better suited to carry inside an outerwear pocket.

Earlier, I mentioned how the quest for those of us who conceal weapons habitually is, within reason, to get the greatest number of the most powerful possible shots out of the most unobtrusive yet most easily manipulated and operated firing platform. Since that is a goal unlikely to be attained, we settle for the best we can get.

But in the 1970s and earlier, there was a trend supported by a small and persistent group of pistoleers who were discontent with factory offerings and wanted something, like a Hong Kong suit, that was tailored to fit. One of the most well-known of these cut-down pistols was the ASP, which, like the Detonics CombatMaster, achieved actual production status. After World War II, the United States Government decided to have trials for a new pistol to replace the 1911A1 as standard. Colt developed the original Commander, which

The P-38 is a very pleasant gun to shoot. Wartime models had steel frames, this post-War police turn-in weapon with an alloy frame.

came to be known in commercial circles as the Lightweight Commander, after Colt offered a steel frame version called the Combat Commander. Smith & Wesson developed a lightweight frame handgun chambered in 9X19mm and very heavily influenced by the Walther P-38, the German service pistol during the recently concluded world war. The double action system, the hammer dropping thumb safety and even the capacity and design of the magazine were very similar.

In an article I edited for *GUNS Magazine* some 35 years ago, as this is written, I recall the late Major George C. Nonte, universally respected for what has been called his "encyclopedic" knowledge of firearms and his prolific volume of work, referring to Smith & Wesson having made some sort of arrangement with Walther of (then West) Germany regarding these similarities. I've never seen or heard any other reference to such a relationship. Be that as it may, the similarities are undeniable. I view this as complimentary to both Smith & Wesson and Walther. The Walther was/is a classic European-looking pistol of the late 19th and early 20th century, with short slide and exposed barrel. It was the first double action battle pistol and years ahead of anything else in design. The Model 39 was unmistakably American-looking, with full length slide encasing the barrel.

Nothing came of the military trials of 1953 and both Colt and Smith & Wesson turned to the civilian markets, where both pistols eventually became quite popular. The Model 39 served as

This Metalife Custom modification to a six-shot Model 686 S&W has everything, including a barrel that has been flatted.

the basis for an entire family of pistols, many of which have survived to this day as the "American Pride" models. And the Model 39 was the first semi-automatic pistol to be officially adopted by an American police agency, the Illinois State Police. This was in 1967. It wouldn't be long until Smith & Wesson developed the Model 59, which was the first of the Wonder Nine pistols – high capacity magazines and double action first shot capability. The 59 was originally produced as prototypes for the U.S. government (as the story goes, for special ops guys in Southeast Asia).

Custom gunsmiths had been working on Colt 1911s and, to a lesser degree, Browning P35 Hi Powers for years, cutting slide/barrel length and reducing grip frame length. FN made a version of the Hi Power with shorter overall length and a shortened grip, but the gun never imported to the USA, at least to my knowledge. Regardless of size, you still had a single action pistol. Jeff Cooper's admonition about double action capability being a solution to a problem he perceived didn't exist notwithstanding, lots of people then and now, even those who truly like the 1911 format, saw and see that, for various

law enforcement duty and military applications, a double action pistol is safer and easier to use. This is certainly true for the novice or casual shooter.

Even the much heralded breakthrough design of the Walther P-38 was not immune from those persons who wanted a smaller handgun that was still a P-38. The "Gestapo barreled" P-38 was a modification wherein the five-inch barrel of the P-38 was cut down to protrude only far enough forward of the front face of the slide to allow positioning a front sight on the barrel. Decades later, Walther would produce a P-38 variant known as the P-38K (for 'Kurz," meaning short) which had a barrel that was shorter still, the front sight being mounted to the bridge of the slide. This pistol came about around the time that other double actions were getting shortened.

The ASP, designed by Paris Theodore of Seventrees, a holster making firm, used Smith & Wesson Model 39s and the upgraded Model 39-2 as the basis for an extensively slicked up, "melted" and length- and height-shortened pistol that had 7+1 capacity, rather than 8+1. Anyone

The 686 can be easily concealed. The round-butt modification to this weapon improves handling qualities.

who tells you that something like that – making a handgun one round shorter for a shorter, hence more concealable grip – makes no difference, likely doesn't carry concealed weapons very well concealed. The grip shortening does make a significant difference in waist level concealability. The ASP achieved moderate production status, perhaps more famous for its "Guttersnipe" sight, which utilized no front sight and directed the eye rather than requiring sight alignment. Paris Theodore went on to other pursuits and Armament System Products of Appleton, Wisconsin, now famous for their expandable police batons, took over. I don't know how many of the guns were produced in Wisconsin.

Firearms designer – some would say "firearms design genius" -- Charlie Kelsey worked on 1911s and other weapons but is best known for The Devel. The Devel was the flagship firearm of Devel Corporation, Kelsey's company. He chopped and channeled Model 39 and Model 59 pistols, following in the ASP tradition, then went on to make them better, more user friendly and reliable.

Meanwhile, Armand Swenson, renowned as one of the finest pistolsmiths ever, was working on advanced ergonomic and performance modifications to 1911s. Although Swenson is not known for chopping and channeling (although he did some), his extended thumb safeties, front strap checkering and myriad other successful refinements transformed a military pistol into a combat and competition pistol in many ways that had not been done before and had not been reliably available to the shooting public. Other gunsmiths were cutting down the 1911s, but nobody was offering a gun that came that way. Except for the Star PD, a sub-Commander-sized .45 about the size of today's Colt Officers Model, there was no production version of a small .45. And the PD was not a 1911, although its controls and operation were quite similar.

Making a 1911 much smaller than Commander-sized was a process not easily understood. A man named Pat Yates wanted a .45 auto that was about the size of a medium frame auto, but he could never get it to work. Along came Sid Woodcock, who was able to get the explosives company with which he was involved – as this is written, Sid is still one of the leading explosives experts in the United States and has served as a consultant and expert witness in many high profile criminal cases – to take up the manufacture of such a gun. Through trial and error and a lot of whittling, this man Sid Woodcock, with his vast amount of firearms experience and an intimacy with handguns few men possess, was able to realize Yates' dream. The result was the Detonics CombatMaster .45. Springs and many other concerns lie behind the success of the design, but the use of a three and one-half-inch barrel is key to the pistol's reliability. The original firm endured many business problems – none having to do with the quality of that original small .45 – before being reorganized and, as this is written, there is a new Detonics company underway. It will be good to see these groundbreaking handguns return.

The Detonics, by the way, was also the first firearms manufacturer to successfully employ stainless steel in the production of a major caliber automatic pistol. I carry one of these little .45s – a Pendergrass, Georgia-built Detonics USA pistol – on a very regular basis. These days, of course, many firms make shortened handguns in .45 ACP, 9x19mm and other calibers and many of these are in stainless steel.

The first stainless steel handgun was Smith & Wesson's Model 60, a revolver of course. And, although there were and are short barreled, smaller gripped revolvers, even in calibers larger than .38 Special, there was quite an industry in modifying revolvers as well. The interest in this practice was for the same reason – more firepower into a smaller and/or more convenient package.

I've had several revolvers of this type and enjoyed them immensely because they were handguns which filled a niche not filled by production revolvers. One of these, which I no longer own and really wish I still did, started out as a four-inch blue Smith & Wesson Model 29 in .44 Magnum. The revolver was done for me by Mahovsky's Metalife and, aside from being given Metalife's outstanding electrostatic chrome binding process finish, Ron Mahovsky action tuned the revolver, added a crane lock at the front of the cylinder and round-butted the revolver down to K-Frame round butt proportions, so that a set of Pachmayr SKC grips – K-Frame Compact size – could be used. Did it hurt to shoot this gun with a butt cut down to such proportions? Not a bit! With Federal 180-grain JHPs in the cylinder, that N-Frame .44 was an extremely pleasant gun to shoot.

Two other cut-down revolvers Ron Mahovsky made up for me are still part of the family, one of these starting out as a four-inch blue, square butt Smith & Wesson Model 13 in .357 Magnum. After Ron worked on it, the revolver was transformed into a Metalife Custom Special. The revolver now has a three-inch barrel, slab sided, my name engraved on one of the barrel flats. The rear sight is a K-Frame adjustable. There's a crane lock. The action job Ron did is buttery smooth. The square butt was turned into a perfect round butt, so perfect I was able to replace the grips which Ron originally put on the revolver – they just didn't appeal as concealed carry grips -- with classic checkered walnut, round butt grip panels. The gun was, of course, Metalifed.

Ron gave a similar treatment to an early Smith & Wesson Model 686. The revolver has a four-inch, slab-sided barrel, my name on one of the barrel flats, gold filled. The 686 has one of Ron's terrific action jobs and a crane lock, of course. And, the revolver was round-butted. For years, I kept Smith & Wesson Goncalo Alves combat stocks on the weapon; but, in recent times, I have removed these and replaced them with Crimson Trace LaserGrips. The 686 Ron Mahovsky did for me is the most perfect revolver I own. Before Ron had even touched it, the four-inch Smith & Wesson, straight from the factory, outshot a six-inch Colt Python that had been action tuned.

In the cases of all three revolvers I've described, there was nothing on the market that incorporated that combination of desired features. The K-Frame round butt grip profile on a four-inch .44 Magnum – it was also Mag-Na-Ported – would have been the kiss of death for commercial sales, because so many people like would have thought the gun would prove torturous to shoot. Mine was not the first Ron made. At the time, one would periodically read stories of very manly guys getting freaked out by the horrific recoil of a four-inch Model 29. And why wouldn't they? Rather than recoil absorbing wrap-around Pachmayrs, they'd either stick to factory wooden grips or the Pachmayrs that were really skinny and provided no cushioning across the revolver's backstrap. And of course these storied shooters likely used either 240-grain loads or hot handloads. No wonder the guns hurt! Mine didn't.

Smith & Wesson, indeed, made the Model 13 .357 Magnum in three-inch round butt trim, but without adjustable sights or Ron's fantastic action work. And as for the L-Frame, in those

A gun like this Taurus 809B is an attempt – a successful one – for a factory gun to be produced with every modification someone could want.

days a 686 came with a square butt grip profile and the only way to have a round butt four-inch L-Frame was to make it yourself or have someone make it for you.

Over the course of time, as the 1970s turned into the 1980s, the various gun companies got on the semi-automatic pistol bandwagon as it concerned smaller, slicker, more easily concealable pistols in serious calibers. We no longer had to blue-sky about really slick semi-automatics, like old friends Willard Christopher or Bruce Butler and I would do when we were all students at Lindblom High School in the early sixties. We no longer had

to conjecture concerning what this maker or that would do – the makers were doing it by the eighties and nineties and are doing more and more of it today.

Revolvers are another issue altogether. In part, at least, I'm way less than thrilled with the directions in which some revolver lines are going, yet there are promising things on the horizon. One of the advantages of being in my sixties as I write this is that I can use age as an excuse for liking a good many double action revolvers the way they used to be, as opposed to the way they are today.

CHAPTER 9

BIG BORES AND BEYOND

The Springfield XD40 certainly qualifies as a big bore concealment pistol.

Because of modern developments in metallurgy in both the guns themselves and their springs, it is possible, as we know, to pack a larger caliber into a smaller package. Yet, sometimes, package size is not that serious an issue for concealed weapon selection – within reason, of course. In the aftermath of the first *Dirty Harry* movie, veritable legions of cops wanted to carry big N-Frame revolvers, the Model 29 .44 Magnum with its (then) six and one-half-inch barrel being the most sought after of the lot. With the right holstering, a weapon of such size can be effectively concealed when coupled with the right clothing. That said, a firearm like that is a little large for most of us, no matter how much we like the big bores. And a .44 Magnum is really quite a bit less than ideal for anti-personnel use.

Once I was out shooting with my old pal Ron Mahovsky of Mahovsky's Metalife. At the time,

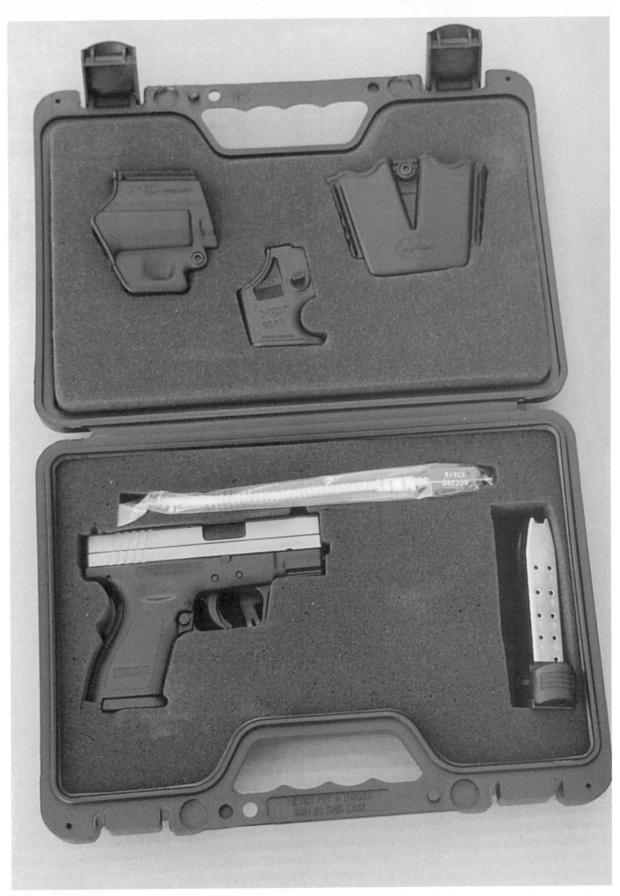

The Springfield XD9 is an interesting weapon. Is 9X19mm a big bore round? Or, is it on the fence?

The Bersa Thunder .45 – a nice shooter – is a definite big bore, some people contending that .45 ACP is the ultimate anti-personnel pistol round. It's not -- .357 Magnum generally gets the title – but .45 ACP is very good.

I owned a really nice six-inch barrel Model 629 .44 that Ron had gunsmithed for me. The gun was a great shooter. My favorite load was the Federal 180-grain JHP. The informal outdoor range at which we were shooting had a rusty old school bus languishing on one side of the property. The bus was already shot full of holes, so Ron and I tried an experiment. Ron fired at the back of the bus with my .44, through the cavity where the right brake light had been. The bullet punched through the brake light cavity and through a number of old seats in the bus and came out the front end of the bus.

At another time, Sharon and I were doing an article dealing with a .44 Magnum Desert Eagle and a nearby county SWAT Team helped us out. The range they used – a terrific set-up – had an automobile as one of the targets. It was a full-sized American sedan, a box of bowling pins on the back seat. Using the same 180-grain Federal .44 Magnum load once again, we had a bullet that penetrated the driver's side rear door, took a chunk out of a bowling pin or two and exited through the passenger side rear door. Penetration like that is a little much for some uses.

As relates to big bores or even smaller calibers in more amply-sized handguns, let's just say, for the sake of argument, that we will go no larger than a four-inch N-Frame Smith & Wesson revolver or a 1911-sized or Beretta 92-sized semi-automatic as potential concealed weapons. The top end, caliber-wise, should exclude hotter, more penetrative .44 Magnum and .41 Magnum rounds. The .45 Long Colt, .45 ACP, .45 Auto Rim, .45 GAP, .357 Magnum, .357 SIG and the various +P and +P+ loads in 9X19mm and .38 Special are the upper end of things. The

Controls on the Bersa Thunder .45 are easy to use.

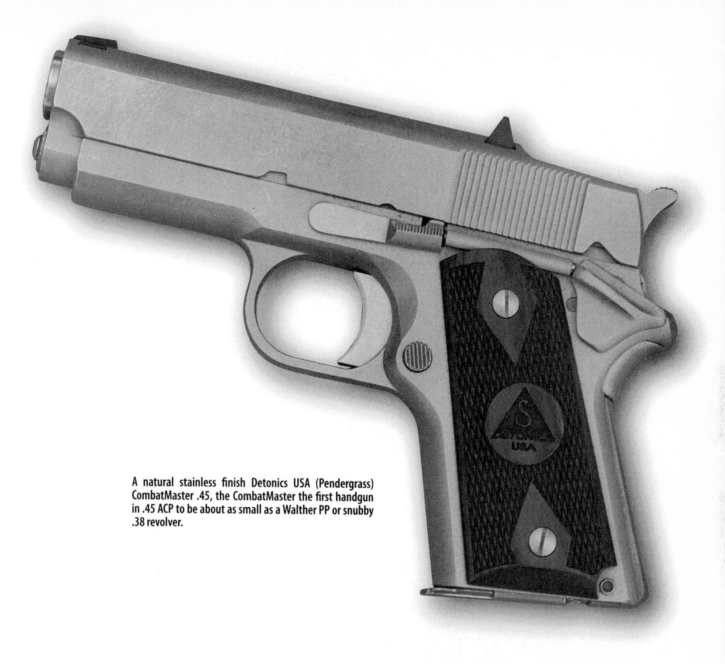

A natural stainless finish Detonics USA (Pendergrass) CombatMaster .45, the CombatMaster the first handgun in .45 ACP to be about as small as a Walther PP or snubby .38 revolver.

widest range of possible loadings exists in .45 ACP, .357 Magnum, .357 SIG, 9X19mm and .38 Special. Depending on the handgun you select, you'll have plenty of choices as you search for the right load.

The problem historically with big bore handguns has been their correspondingly large size. That is no longer the problem as this is written. There are any number of handguns of quite concealable size which are chambered for larger pistol calibers. Revolvers, with a few exceptions, like the Ruger LCR, with its non-metallic frame, or the Taurus Judge, which is both a .45 Long Colt and a .410 shotgun, depending on what one loads, have morphed into exotic metals with built in lockable safety systems.

Just how can you properly conceal something the size of a full-size Government Model .45 semi-auto? I think I shocked people once in one of my "Field Issue" columns in *GUN WORLD Magazine,* and I credit my editor there and decades' old friend Jan Libourel for his courage in printing this observation. I credited not only the late firearms writer and combat shooting expert Jeff Cooper for the popularization of the 1911 as a carry gun in the post-World War II period, but the late mystery writer and sometimes actor Mickey Spillane for doing so through most of his main characters, and "Mike Hammer" in particular. It's how you wear the gun that counts when it comes to concealment and a full size .45 automatic, when worn stuffed into a trouser band, is not a hard handgun to

This Detonics Model 9-11-01 is a full-size .45 that is extremely pleasant to shoot. It's a Detonics USA (Pendergrass) gun.

conceal. When you involve a holster, it's harder, but doable. "Mike Hammer," of course, packed his U.S. Government Model Colt Automatic in a "speed rig" under his left shoulder, his suit coats specially tailored to provide padding under the right shoulder, compensating for the bulge made by the .45 and the "speed rig" – a speed rig presumably something like the old reliable Bianchi X-15 "snapdraw" shoulder rig – under the left side of his coat.

If you think that's a bit extreme – and, in those days, guys wore suits and sports jackets a lot more – you'll love what some people did. I'm not asking you to do something weird, but stretch out your off-gunside arm a little, flex and feel the muscle, etc., coming from your chest into your arm. As stories have it, some guys, who were perennially armed with a good-size "gat" in a shoulder rig, would have that muscle and flesh surgically cut back in order to have the same effect as the tailored sportcoat, without having to shell out the fees to the tailor. Any female readers, or guys who are certain they are alone, may feel free to say, "Ohh, yuck!"

These days, there are much better options for carrying a big caliber handgun. For one thing, a lot of big caliber handguns are available in small packages. For another, holstering options have changed a great deal since the 1950s and 1960s.

Earlier in this book, I mention the three pioneering small size production .45s, namely the Colt Lightweight Commander, the Star PD and the Detonics CombatMaster. The CombatMaster is about the size of the Walther PP, although weighing more. Firing the CombatMaster is not at all unpleasant, its recoil being only slightly more than that of a full-size 1911. When I was running Detonics USA, each pistol was tested before it was pronounced ready to ship. The slightest hint of a problem and the pistol was taken apart, inspected, rebuilt and tested again. What this meant was that for a year or better, when the person who had been doing the testing could no longer do it, Sharon and I would take a batch of pistols to The Firing Lane in Bogart, Georgia, and I'd do the shooting and Sharon would record testing results, etc. Detonics USA was a small handgun company, to be sure, so I might only test fire thirty or so handguns in a single session, some CombatMasters and some of the five-inch barrel, full-size Model 9-11-01. The full-size pistols were obviously more pleasant to shoot, but the CombatMasters were not punishing at all.

Sharon will sometimes shoot my personal Model 9-11-01 and, even though her hands have always been recoil sensitive, she experienced/ experiences no discomfort. Our daughter, Samantha, was firing a full-size .45 by the time she was 12 and experienced no difficulty.

When I first started getting involved with handguns, I remember reading various hairy-chested accounts about the terrific recoil generated when one triggered a shot from a 1911. Obviously, these super heroic guys had to be shooting an alternate universe 1911 which generated a great deal more recoil. While on that subject, it is well to repeat that obvious fact about a .45's knockdown power. As Sir Isaac Newton advised in his Third Law, "For every action there is an equal and opposite reaction." Any firearm which can launch a bullet generating enough power to knock down without fail whatever it hits is obviously too

powerful for a person to hold when that round is triggered, because it would most assuredly knock down the person holding it – or rip the shooter's arm off. Perceived recoil is necessary, allowing us to absorb the shock of launching a projectile down range.

Too much recoil is another matter. The late Jerry Rakusan, Editor of GUNS Magazine before, during and after my stint as Associate Editor (1973 to 1975), years before had worked for Klein's. A great many persons reading this will be too young to remember seeing an ad on the back of a magazine for NRA Excellent Condition Lugers for $49.95 and similar bargains. The slogan was, "Nobody undersells Klein's." Klein's gained international notoriety of the worst kind as the company which unwittingly sold the actual Mannlicher-Carcano carbine associated with the assassination of John F. Kennedy. Before that terrible incident, however, Klein's was a thriving gun business and it was not uncommon for customers to bring in firearms in need of repair. Jerry was working there when a well-dressed older lady came in with her husband's double barreled 10 gauge that was in need of repair. The woman's husband had not informed her concerning the nature of the problem. Jerry took the shotgun to the store's basement range. In an attempt to ascertain what sort of work was needed, Jerry loaded both barrels, put the shotgun to his shoulder and – I bet you can guess what happened! Both barrels discharged at once and knocked Jerry to the floor. Thankfully, nothing was broken – except the shotgun!

Recoil from conventional large caliber concealable firearms is generally not of great concern. Usually, the bigger and heavier the handgun, the gentler the recoil impulse the shooter will experience. Do not, however, succumb to the fallacious argument that recoil in a concealed weapon doesn't matter at all because, when you really need to use the gun in self defense, the recoil won't matter. That may be true, but a gun so punishing to shoot will not be practiced with sufficiently that you'll be able to perform at maximum efficiency with it.

So, if your clothing style and lifestyle will allow you to carry a larger caliber handgun, so much the better. Not all larger caliber handguns are physically larger. The Rohrbaugh R9 is sized somewhere between a Seecamp and a Walther PPK, so it's not very big at all. Most larger caliber handguns are larger than that. My smallest big caliber handgun is a Detonics USA (Pendergrass) CombatMaster, a handgun

Danny Akers was always into guns and shooting, but Ahern is pretty certain he's hooked his son-in-law on .45s, this one Ahern's Model 9-11-01.

that I have carried for several years on a fairly regular basis. In the decades before that gun was built, I'd frequently be found with one or two original Seattle Detonics .45s.

I've used a variety of carry methods. The most well known of these methods was one I shared with our character "John Rourke," in our series *THE SURVIVALIST*. Rourke (constantly) and I (only sometimes) carried twin stainless Detonics CombatMasters in a double Alessi shoulder rig. My old friend Louie Alessi has since passed away, but his company carries on his tradition of quality of manufacture and excellence of design. Unlike John Rourke, my encounters with brigands and invading armies were extraordinarily infrequent (thankfully); so, most of the time, I opted for a single shoulder rig when I wore a shoulder holster. The Alessi shoulder holster style both Rourke and I prefer incorporates a pull-through snap which closes through the trigger guard. Obviously, you would not use this style of closure with something like a Glock. Alessi also offers conventional thumb breaks. The offside piece on the single diagonal shoulder rig was a single mag pouch which carried horizontally and held the magazine in position by means of a magnet within the pouch. Very secure, yet very fast, I found the single rig and the double to be outstanding.

I occasionally carried a Detonics CombatMaster in an ankle holster, also made by Alessi. It was good to have that option, but that sort of carry with a gun weighing over two pounds wasn't something of which I cared to make a habit. Most of the time, in those days, I would carry in an Alessi inside waistband holster, known as "The Hideout." With a perfect FBI cant, this holster was worn and worn.

I've also had great luck with an inside waistband holster from Grandfather Oak, this made of Kydex rather than leather. Extraordinarily light weight, this holster's angle is adjustable for either strongside or crossdraw use.

With the larger guns particularly, the angle at which they are worn on the body very much determines their concealability – or the lack thereof. The FBI cant to which I referred is a term for an angle of carry originally practiced by the FBI back in the days when a six-shot revolver was worn strongside on the right hip, the weapon drawn and fired with one hand while the left hand, balled into a fist, was drawn up over the heart, the idea to slow down a bullet, I'm told. That way, I guess, you could get shot in the hand first and know the excruciating pain associated with that for the split second before the bullet tore a hole in your heart. Left-handed agents probably had to reach over a little more to shield the heart. But the angle of carry was really good and has stayed with us. With a handgun worn openly in the field or in competitive shooting games or merely at the range, a straight drop carry is fine. Persons suffering from carpal tunnel syndrome (which I had always thought referred to persons who were afraid of being caught in a carpool while traveling through a tunnel) have an easier time grasping a handgun worn this way, the draw not requiring bending the wrist. I've seen it argued that this is a faster

presentation method, too. I don't dispute that, but a straight drop conceals very poorly with any handgun of decent size.

With the FBI cant, consider that there is an imaginary line drawn between the toe of the gunbutt and the uppermost portion of the weapon's muzzle. This imaginary line should be parallel to the side seam of the trouser leg, but not coincident with it. The holstered weapon will usually be worn somewhat to the rear of the side seam of the trouser leg.

If you keep this imaginary line in mind, the angle of your handgun will be such that the muzzle is pointing somewhat rearward and the all-important butt of the gun is drawn more in line with your torso. What you are doing is keeping the weapon and holster in line with your body plane as seen from the side. This is the ideal angle for a handgun when worn concealed for a strongside waist level draw.

Earlier, I mentioned a heavily customized, round-butted Smith & Wesson .44 Magnum four-incher that I had some years ago. When I carried that revolver – which I did with some actual frequency – I used a diagonal shoulder holster and the revolver and holster concealed surprisingly well. I honestly don't remember the make of the holster.

When the Beretta 92 in 9x19mm was selected as the new U.S. military pistol, I recruited Samantha for shooting once again. There were some persons actively complaining that the wide body magazines made the pistol too large for our G.I.s to hold onto. I figured that if my then not quite adult daughter – as an adult she's 5' 3-1/2" – could manage the Beretta with her girl-sized hands, the typical U.S. Marine or Army Ranger could handle the grip size. Sam handled the pistol with aplomb.

But concealing the Beretta 92 was often a problem. The handgun is about the length of a 1911, but quite a bit thicker in the butt. I had a special holster made – an inside waistband rig – that worked quite well; but, in order to conceal the weapon properly, the Beretta had to be worn deeper down, the gunbutt front strap essentially contacting the upper edge of my trouser waistband. In the final analysis, this is one time I'll say they did it one hundred per cent right in the movies. When Bruce Willis wore a Beretta in the first three *Diehard* movies, it at least always started out in a DeSantis shoulder holster. A diagonal shoulder holster works well with the Beretta 92 and guns of similar profiles. When Mel Gibson wore a Beretta 92 in the *Lethal Weapon* films, the pistol was worn holsterless inside the trouser waistband. With the safety on, this is the most concealable carry I found to work effectively with the Model 92 Beretta.

One of my all-time favorite handguns is the SIG 229 in .40 S&W. Smaller than the Beretta, but not much, the 229 works quite nicely holsterless inside the waistband, but most of the time when this is the gun I carry, it's in an old Galco Miami Classic shoulder rig. Sometimes, instead of a shoulder rig, I'll use a Ken Null Vam holster. The holster was designed to be worn while driving, but it works quite safely and well when one is standing or moving about. The Vam carries the handgun essentially parallel to the waist. It's not the most concealable holster, but it's still okay in that regard. Where it really shines is in the unmatched access it provides while seated, while still being safe to wear when not seated. And it is the fastest holster I've ever used.

When a heavier caliber revolver is the order of the day for me, although I have some other excellent holsters, my Metalife Custom Smith & Wesson 686 with Crimson Trace LaserGrips rides in a Miami Classic from Galco, the shoulder rig being a very comfortable and concealable carry system for my "six-shooter." If you can live with the comparatively low capacity and the generally slower reloads utilizing Safariland speedloaders or Bianchi Speed Strips, so long as the weapon can be effectively concealed, a good old-fashioned four-inch barrel wheel gun in .357 Magnum loaded with 125-grain JHPs is a very hard handgun to beat for anti-personnel use. With heavier bullets, although what you have in the cylinder will generally have to do, such a revolver is regarded as effective against wild or feral dog attacks (and attempted predation by similar-sized animals).

I can carry my full-size Glock 22 in a Galco Miami Classic with four spare magazines pouched on the offside. If I want to carry my Glock 22 with my Surefire 300 Weapon Light attached, I have a Blackhawk Serpa belt holster that can be worn with conventional belt attachment or on a paddle.

CHAPTER 10

WHAT'S OUT THERE?

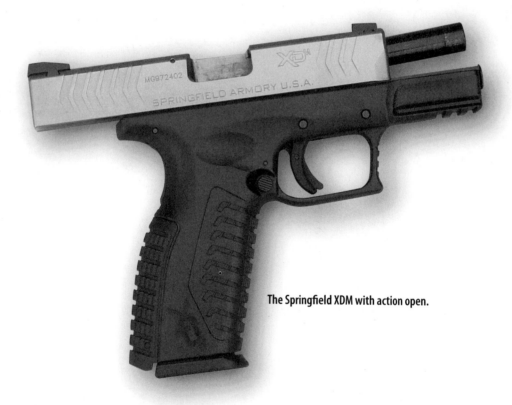

The Springfield XDM with action open.

Companies from Armalite to Wilson Combat all offer handguns which are well suited to personal defense and concealment. Some companies are, of course, historically well known for making some of the highest quality personal handguns to be had and, in several cases, their "track record" goes back well over a century and a half or even longer. **Colt** unfortunately only produces variations of the Government Model .45 and custom shop versions of the Single Action Army these days. Their outstanding revolvers are sorely missed by many, as are other automatic pistols of quite concealable size in smaller calibers, namely the Mustang and Pony. Smith & Wesson maintains its title, as far as I know, of being the largest handgun producer in the world, with the possible exception of entities which may devote their handgun production to high volume military runs.

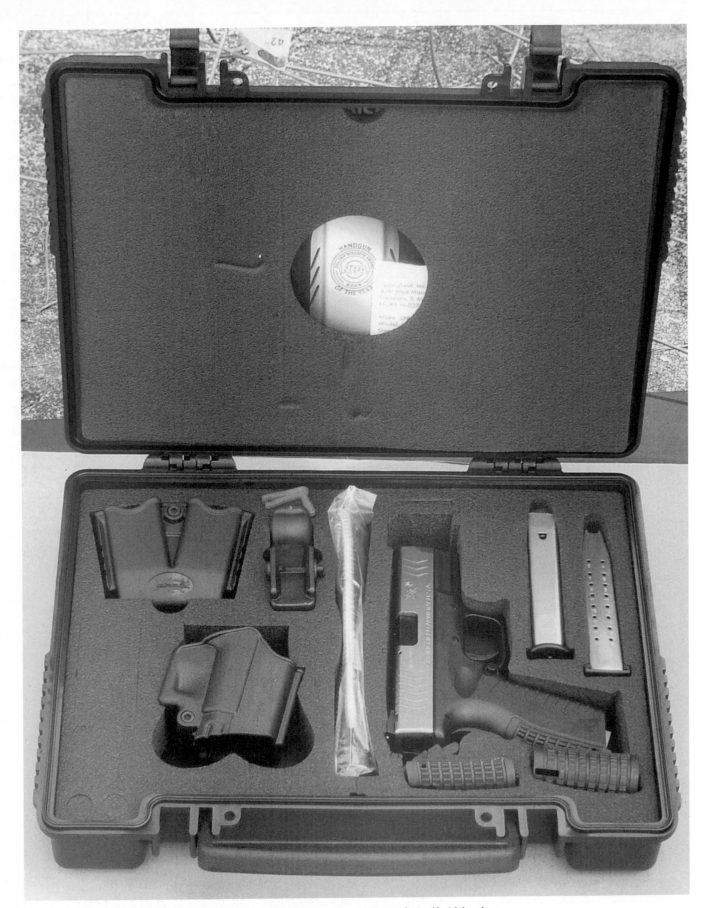

The Springfield XDM kit. Initially a rifle company, Springfield made a solid name for itself with handguns.

Beretta, the world's oldest gun making company and still family held, currently produces what has become the US military pistol, the Beretta 92F, along with a whole host of other handguns. Nothing that has come about because of the wars in the Middle East and complaints about problems with the Beretta 92F in that environment should be considered a condemnation of the gun or the 9mm caliber. Instead, there are complex issues that are environmental – like sand that is as fine as powder – and the use of only hardball full metal jacketed 9mms in the military context. **SIG-Sauer** offers a full range of both single action and double action and double action only pistols in .45 ACP, .40 S&W, .357 SIG and 9X19mm. You can buy a state of the art double action pistol that can be transformed from one size to another or you can acquire a traditional 1911. Aside from Colt and SIG, Smith & Wesson, Taurus, Auto Ordnance and Wilson Combat, just to name a few, offer 1911s as well. Here's a partial list of firms offering larger caliber handguns which are well suited to concealed carry by those who take the time to learn the skills necessary.

I mentioned **Armalite**, which offers a fine 9mm pistol, and **Auto Ordnance**, owned by Kahr Arms. **Les Baer** offers full size and compact pistols in not only .45 but the little considered but still quite excellent .38 Super, which, depending on how it's loaded, is similar in performance to the 9mm or .357 Magnum. We mentioned Beretta, of course, but there is also **Bersa**, of course which has compact .45s, 9s and .40s.

John **Browning**'s second most well-known pistol, which turned 75 years old in 2010, is the Hi-Power. It's sometimes known as the GP, for Grande Puissance (French for "High Power"), or simply P-35, after the year of its introduction. It is available as always in 9mm, but is also offered in .40 S&W. It is well to remember that when Smith & Wesson produced the Model 59, what they were doing – albeit this is an over simplification – was incorporating the P-35s double column magazine into their already existing Model 39. **Charles Daly** offers an enhanced 1911 as well as a 9mm. The eclectic firm of **Cobra** offers its Patriot .45, diminutive derringers and a revolver so close in appearance and function to one of the models from Smith & Wesson that grips will even interchange. I earlier mentioned Colt, of course, and it's well to remember that, in addition to .45 ACP caliber

in their Government Models, they still offer a .38 Super. **CZ**, which became so famous for the CZ 75 despite being behind the Iron Curtain of the then-USSR, offers the CZ 75 9mm and offers also a .45. These well respected Czech pistols have always been world class. **Dan Wesson**, a name usually associated with competition revolvers, offers its own .45. If you want to go to something really big, the Desert Eagle from **Magnum Research** isn't only for old Arnold Schwarzenegger movies. Firing a Desert Eagle .44 Magnum is essentially as easy as firing a steel frame .45 automatic. I would rather, if I were going to use one of these guns for self defense, opt for .357 Magnum instead, this a better anti-personnel round. CZ-like in their appearance, the Baby Eagles are available in 9mm, .40 and .45. The reconstituted **Coonan Arms** is well on its way to offering a unique 1911-style pistol chambered for .357 Magnum, and it should be available by the time you read this.

European American Armory offers both full-size and compact pistols in 9mm, .38 Super, 40 S&W and .45 ACP. Ed Brown has secured a fine reputation for well done 1911 pistols. **Firestorm** offers a .45 as well. And of course, there's **Glock**. For a company which had never manufactured a firearm of any sort and got into a situation where they could have the opportunity to offer a handgun to the Austrian military because their trench shovel was such a success, they've done rather well. To my knowledge, they do not offer full size, medium size or compact .38 Supers. But, if it's any size of 9mm, .40, .45 ACP, .357 SIG or even their own .45 GAP that you need, Glock makes it.

HK, which got started in making world class firearms by manufacturing some of the world's most well known assault rifles and submachine guns, has become equally well-regarded for various pistols in 9mm, .40, .357 SIG and .45 ACP, their pistols ranging from compact size up into guns which are longer than typical and threaded for suppressors, these of course for the military and law enforcement market. **Hi-Point** is noted for its extremely economical pistols and does, in fact, offer handguns in 9mm, .40 and .45. From all accounts I have knowledge of, although these are some of the least expensive handguns you can buy, the company has earned a solid reputation for making a reliable product.

Kahr Arms, mentioned earlier in association with their Auto Ordnance brand, was and is a true leader in the production of pistols the size of medium frame autos which are well built,

.40 caliber is a good size, formidable when pointed at you.

accurate, reliable and good looking. Some years back, I had a Kahr MK9 Elite 98. At the time, this was a top of the line pistol for Kahr Arms and it was remarkably pleasant to shoot, had a great trigger and was as good a handgun as anyone could ask for. Kahr offers pistols in 9mm, .40 and .45 that will answer many people's need for a heavier caliber handgun.

Kel-Tec, which came on the scene with its P-11 9mm and made a huge splash with its little .32 ACP and subsequent .380 pistols, is offering those same excellent 9mm pistols, known for light weight, rugged construction and reliability. Years ago, I had the occasion to be in conversation with a K-9 officer who had stumbled on a violent crime in progress and used his 9mm Kel-Tec to take charge of the situation and save his own life. Needless to say, he was a happy customer. **Kimber** offers a full range of some of the most attractive 1911 style pistols to be had. Whether it's their undercover style pistols or something that is designed for match shooting, these extremely well made handguns in .45, 9mm and .38 Super clearly place Kimber as one of the highest volume 1911 manufacturers and as an industry leader. My own experiences with shooting various Kimbers have been nothing short of excellent.

The **Korth** 9mm, made in Europe, is rarely seen, despite its fine reputation because one Korth will cost you more than ten Kimbers. I have no personal experience with this pistol which starts its pricing at $15,000, but I would imagine it has to be one fantastic shooter. I wonder how many magazines it comes with?

Olympic Arms offers a wide selection of pistols ranging from numerous 1911 variants to pistol versions of the AR-15 rifles and carbines they offer. Olympic has a good reputation. Such a gun – pistol-sized AR – would require some unique techniques for concealability to be achieved.

Para USA offers both single and double action pistols in 9X19mm and .45 ACP, in standard or high capacity variations. A double action Para that I've recently shot performed extremely well and these guns have earned a good reputation. Para started out selling large capacity magazine frames on which you could build your own 1911 and comparatively quickly moved on to produce finished guns and progress to their current offerings. The first time I had my hands on a Para product was when a friend asked if I'd like to try the .45 he'd built. Fisting a .45 with a wider grip frame felt odd, but the gun worked well.

Rock River Arms is a well-respected gun maker and well rounded, offering AR type pistols. Rock River also offers .223 and .308 rifles and offers its AR-15 based pistols in .223 and offers rifles in .40 S&W and 9X19mm. Their PPS – Performance Piston System – concealables are interesting.

Ruger handguns in larger calibers such as 9mm and .45 enjoy a well deserved reputation for being good shooters as well as good values. A number of people whose shooting expertise is unquestionable and whose opinions I trust have said to me, "Try my Ruger!" I have, and they were right. Their Ruger handguns shot just great. When we had our holster business, a perspective customer called and asked us if we could make holsters that would allow him to carry two full-sized Ruger 9mms up his sleeves, just like Antonio Banderas had done in the second "Mariachi" movie. Ruger automatics are quite concealable, but not that concealable!

Sabre Defence makes a pistol very similar in appearance to the CZ-75, in both 9X19mm and .45 ACP. The pistols are made in Switzerland and are available with frames machined from stainless steel, titanium or aluminum. Sabre also makes AR-type rifles sold to the U.S. government as well as .50 caliber machine guns!

To try to catalogue what **SIG-Sauer** offers would be pretty useless since they are always coming up with model improvements and variations. Over the years, I have fired and owned numerous SIG pistols and I still do and I've never handled or had one that I could complain about. Whether in 9mm, .40, .357 SIG or .45 ACP, you can't go wrong with one. I have a brace of SIG 229s with Crimson Trace LaserGrips, both pistols in .40 Smith & Wesson. I also own a .357 SIG barrel to swap into either of the guns and a .22 Long Rifle conversion kit to slip onto either of them. So, I have two handguns with three caliber capability. Not bad.

Much the same can be said about **Smith & Wesson**. My first handgun was a Smith & Wesson revolver, as I mention elsewhere, and I am a great fan of their revolvers generally. Although I've owned Smith & Wesson automatics, it took me a while to warm up to them, in all honesty. That said, Smith & Wesson automatics that I've fired recently – and they are all in heavier calibers – have all impressed me terrifically. Whatever you buy from Smith & Wesson, whether revolver or automatic, it is finely made and immensely serviceable. With the exception of **North American Arms**

The CZ Rami is an example of a firearms line that was largely unavailable to the USA during the Cold War, and because of that largely unknown, except to people really "into" guns.

Mini-Revolvers and my **Cimarron** stainless single action, every revolver I own is a Smith & Wesson, one of them at least a century old and still serviceable. And, speaking of North American Arms, I have a lot of respect not only for their miniguns but for their .25, .32 and .380 Guardian semi-autos as well.

Springfield Armory started in the handgun field by making variations on the 1911 and, to this day, still does that. The firm gained initial notice with the superb M1A rifles, semi-auto only copies of the M-14. But, in addition to their fine 1911 pistols, the Springfield X-D, which is made in Europe, has proven itself to be a versatile pistol in 9X19mm, .40 S&W or .45 ACP, with a wide range of model variations and features. You can have the guns in three different sizes, ported or not and even choose black, Dark Earth, green, or "Bi-Tone" finish.

Taurus offers everything from 1911 style pistols to 92 style pistols to 9mms smaller than a Walther PP to 9mm police duty/battle pistols that are compact full size and include every feature you could possibly want in a semi-automatic pistol. I'm talking about the 809B, a superb 9X19mm. Taurus has become a United States handgun maker to be reckoned with, regardless of revolver or automatic, regardless of caliber, features or finish. Taurus pistols are still quite competitively priced, but they are not a bargain alternative. There is a Taurus within my reach as this is written.

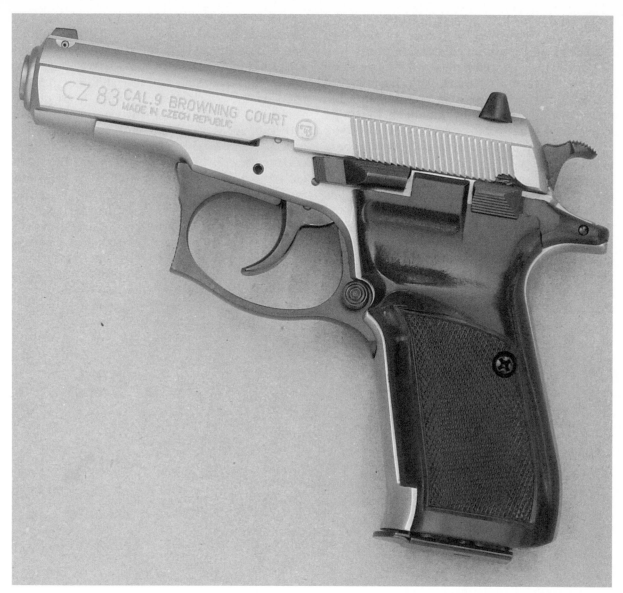

The CZ83 .380 has a definite European look to it, but American shooters have ben admirers of fine European firearms for generations.

U.S. Firearms is making an eclectic mix of reproductions of original Browning/Colt style pistols in both .45 ACP and .38 Super. The 1911 pistols use Armory high polished blue with fire blue accents and are recreations of the historic originals. U.S. Firearms is well-known for their super-accurate reproductions of single action revolvers as produced under the blue dome in Hartford. A look at their 1911s will not disappoint.

Walther has kept pace with the times and, although its original pocket guns are still offered, guns like the P-99 in 9X19mm and .40 S&W and the really excellent PPS in those same calibers are ample proof that you can buy a superb Walther pistol that is as modern as the date on your calendar. It must be remembered that Walther has been innovating and setting design standards for only a little bit more than a century. That tradition continues.

Last, but by no means least, as they say, is **Wilson Combat**. Wilson the man was trained as a jeweler and started working on guns because he liked them and could bring his jewelry making skills into this area of endeavor. Wilson guns, Wilson gun parts and Wilson magazines all have an enviable reputation for consistency and quality. I don't know how many other makers use Wilson parts such as safeties or slide stops, but I do know that when you pick up a gun with another name on it, part of that gun may have started out with a Wilson product.

The point of this exercise has been that it's very easy to know one or two or a half-dozen brand names for heavier caliber handguns; but, you are doing yourself a disservice if you don't find out what else is out there. And I haven't even mentioned the excellent one- and two-shot big bore derringers made by **American Derringer** and **Bond Arms**, among others.

As this is written, spring is in the air here in Georgia. But, when the weather is quite a bit cooler and I know I will be outside and won't be taking off my coat, I often wear my Pacific Canvas And Leather M3 shoulder holster, the popular "tanker rig" for the .45 auto. My Detonics USA 9-11-01 is a perfect fit and, so long as the coat isn't open to show the cross body strap looped from my right shoulder to the holster beside my left ribcage, the rig is quite concealable. You can't beat it for quick donning and doffing, great comfort and easy access to the handgun, whatever you're doing. The first one of these holsters I ever saw when I was just a kid actually had a built-in spare magazine pouch and was said to be a shoulder holster used by the World War II Office of Strategic Services. That particular variant on the M3 – described as an O.S.S. holster – was worn one Saturday morning by the host of a WLS-TV children's program airing in Chicago, the show called "Adventuretime Theater." It was hosted by a man named Charles Homer "Chuck" Bill. The show ran 1940s-ish adventure serials. Can you see a guy M.C.-ing a kids' program these days while wearing a .45 automatic? Coming from Chicago? Talking to "Herman the German Moose," who was mounted on the wall? Some people really have forgotten how to have fun. *"Ding-hoy, little feathermerchants!"*

CHAPTER 11

IDEAL HANDGUN CHOICES

Ahern has found J-Frame S&W revolvers "ideal" for many of his carry needs for over four decades. The gun is Ahern's old-style all-steel Model 640 with Crimson Trace LaserGrips.

I was talking with Karl Rohrbaugh by telephone the other day, Karl being the inventor/designer of the Rohrbaugh R9 and a veteran handgun instructor. He recounted how his students would ask him, "What's the best handgun for self defense?"

Karl would respond, "The one you've got with you."

There's a great deal of wisdom in that response and there's nothing flippant about it.

The answer must be looked at in several ways. First, you've got to have a gun on you. Second, whatever gun it is you're carrying, you should be certain you can operate it efficiently under stress. Third, you should select that handgun – or those handguns – with care, since it or they will be the firearm(s) with which you'll be able to respond to a threat, and not the gun or guns you left locked up in the safe at home.

I am not a gun collector. I have gathered

Ahern likes the SIG 229. In .40 S&W, Ahern has a .357 SIG barrel for it and a .22 LR conversion kit.

many guns over the years and, because of various urges or necessities, divested myself of many guns over the years, as well. A person who collects guns has a theme. For example, one might wish to collect one of every variation of Walther PPK models ever produced. Or, one might wish to collect handguns associated with famous cowboys of the silver screen, such as Roy Rogers and Gene Autry and Tom Mix and William S. Hart. Sharon doesn't collect guns; but she does collect souvenir spoons, has hundreds from all around the world and from as far back as the early 1930s. Sharon says I collect gadgets. She's right. My Dad, Jack Ahern, loved multi-use tools and such and I've taken to that quest as well. Sharon says I collect movies on DVD. I guess I do that, too, come to think of it.

But I don't collect guns. I gather guns. Gathering implies no theme at all. For example, although my abiding firearms interests are

concealable weapons and tactical firearms, I still own and enjoy my 7-1/2-inch Cimarron Arms stainless single action in .45 Long Colt. Even though I've got a terrific Original Dirty Harry shoulder holster for the cowboy revolver, it's not something I consider a concealed weapon in the modern sense – but I can conceal it. The reason I have it is I like it. I don't do cowboy action shooting or quick draw. I just enjoy looking at the gleaming stainless steel revolver and once in a while taking it out and shooting it. It's great fun and the Cimarron Arms revolver is so well made that I'd stack it against an original Colt any day of the week. I use a dueling stance, firing one handed, just like men on the frontier used to do it better than a century ago. I like it, but I didn't collect it.

I have gathered to myself an eclectic mix of concealable handguns for virtually every occasion. The reason those guns and accessories

Ahern likes the Glock 22 for some purposes, this gun equipped with a Crimson Trace LaserGrips unit and a Surefire X300 WeaponLight. This shot was taken in broad daylight.

do not constitute a collection is that acquiring them was purpose driven, not theme driven.

The ideal concealed handgun choice is a very individual thing. I can more easily tell you what is not ideal. If it hurts you so much to shoot the gun, for instance, you won't shoot it enough and you very well won't have the confidence and skill level adequate to the task of defending your life or the life of a loved one or innocent with such a handgun. If the handgun is too big or too heavy, you'll find excuses to leave it at home and also find yourself running the risk of being unarmed when you really, really need to be armed. If the handgun is not a weapon of good quality, your

confidence in the weapon – if you are confident in it – may be misplaced and this may be revealed to you when you need the handgun the most. If the option exists to carry a heavier but still manageable caliber and you really don't want to bother, so carry a gun the caliber of which is marginal for primary defense, that is the time you may find yourself attacked by a drugged-up wildman who feels no pain and is built like the proverbial little brick house.

You should, most professionals would agree, carry the maximally effective handgun circumstances allow. Just what are those circumstances?

Right profile shot of a Detonics USA (Pendergrass) CombatMaster .45. The CombatMaster is one of Ahern's favorite handguns.

Let's dispel some myths first. As I mentioned, Sharon says I collect movies. Whether I actually collect or just gather, I obtain movies that I like to see and hopefully Sharon can tolerate. Movies are a great source of grossly inaccurate information about how to carry firearms. Some movie people – like John Milius or Michael Mann or Tom Selleck – take the gun stuff extraordinarily seriously. Cudos to them. That's terrific and aids in the suspension of disbelief that's part and parcel of an enjoyable film experience, regardless of the genre. But often in films, we see gun-related things that are so unrealistic we either laugh or have to try very hard to ignore what we've seen so we can still hope to enjoy the movie. In the James Bond films starring Pierce Brosnan, wherein Bond first starts carrying the Walther P-99, we have a fine example. Brosnan is a fine actor, of course. But, reality is reality. Now, certainly, Bond could and would have his wardrobe hand tailored. He's not one of these off-the-rack chaps. In order to conceal a firearm that large in a shoulder holster, however, under a closely fitted tuxedo

jacket, the opposite side of the jacket – the right side for a right handed man – would have to be built up and out so that the comparatively large bulge made by the P-99 or any handgun of similar size wouldn't look so out of balance as to be obvious. The thing most people forget about when it comes to movies is that, almost always, the hero only wears his gun under his coat if the scene calls for the gun to be there. That's why, in those other scenes within the film, when the hero is presumably carrying his gun concealed but never has to access it, the cut of his wardrobe is never in question.

There are limitations imposed upon us by both societal convention and sartorial custom. In a work I wrote some years ago dealing with concealed carry techniques, I opined that the ideal covering garments for concealed carry would be the habiliment associated with a traditionally dressed Moslem woman. Under a burka or chaddar, two variations of the all-consuming head to toe veils they are wont to wear in public, a submachine gun, an assault rifle or a combat shotgun could easily be

Loaded with 230-grain Federal Hydra-Shoks, the CombatMaster .45's a formidable little gun and perfectly pleasant to shoot.

concealed. If the woman were tall enough, she might well be able to hide an RPG. There's a comforting thought!

Clothing and what is expected of us greatly determines what kinds of handguns and other weapons we can effectively conceal without special equipment. Let's take one of my favorite pet peeves. It's so hot outside one might think that all the furnace doors of Hell had been left open. And here's this guy wearing a photographer's vest. He's not carrying any cameras or related gear, but he keeps that vest on despite the fact everyone around him is about to succumb to heat prostration. Or how about the guy who keeps his sportcoat on at an outdoor event like a cookout, when the summer sun is beating down mercilessly and every other guy is in his shirtsleeves? These are people trapped by the clothing they're using to cover the hardware they're carrying. Anyone who knows anything about concealed carry will spot them immediately. Don't you find yourself looking a little bit extra hard at everyone who's wearing a fanny pack these days? You should.

There are two approaches to the summer heat problem I have posed as interfering with concealed carry. Either go to a smaller gun for normal carry, one which can be pocket carried, crotch carried or ankle carried (ankle holsters are generally to be avoided when wearing shorts); or, get special equipment. Such special

equipment could be something like the Covert Carrier, normally just for smaller handguns, a specially modified grip plate or grip sleeve with a very discreet clip which is barely visible at the waistband and keeps the totally submerged weapon from falling down through the trouser leg. If you can wear a shirt outside the pants and this lack or formality will not be out of place, conventional inside waistband holsters or the wonderful Barami Hip-Grip can be employed. With this latter solution, you can conceal larger handguns.

If this option – the shirt worn outside the pants – isn't an option for you, then a specialized holster is in order. One fine example is the Galco SkyOps, a holster Galco makes for Air Marshals and sells to the general public. It's an inside waistband holster with a hook-like piece rising up from the muzzle end of the holster, this attaching to the wearer's belt. The shirt can be tucked down over the gun and holster combination, the shirt tail between the holster and the belt attachment piece. Mitch Rosen and others make variations on this basic theme. When you need the gun, you have to pull up the shirt tail and then draw the gun. This would take some considerable practice in order to achieve fluidity and some acceptable degree of speed. Rest easy – I suspect that our Sky Marshals practice quite a bit.

I cannot tell you what gun you should carry, but I can tell you some of the guns that I carry and why. As I think we've established, I'm always armed whenever and wherever it's legal. And I strongly dislike hot weather. That said, a Seecamp .32 or a NAA Guardian .380 with Crimson Trace LaserGrips – one or the other – is always with me. A partial list of some of the larger guns that I favor and actually carry with some degree of regularity includes, but is not limited to, the following:

• Smith & Wesson Model 640 .38 Special with Crimson Trace LaserGrips; "two-inch" barrel; five-round cylinder

• Smith & Wesson Model 60 .38 Special with Barami Hip-Grip; "two-inch" barrel; five-round cylinder

• Detonics USA (Pendergrass) CombatMaster .45 ACP; three and one-half-inch barrel; six plus one with standard magazine; accepts full-length seven-round magazines which hang out

• SIG-Sauer P-229 with Crimson Trace LaserGrips; twelve plus one standard magazine; ten-round magazines held in reserve, left over from magazine capacity limitation silliness

• Detonics Model 9-11-01 .45 ACP with or without Crimson Trace LaserGrips; five-inch barrel; seven plus one with standard magazine

• Smith & Wesson 686 .357 Magnum with Crimson Trace LaserGrips; heavily customized and action tuned by Mahovsky's Metalife; four-inch barrel; six-round cylinder

A trio of ideal handguns which all work well with one another for concealed carry. A full-size .45 and a snubby .38 and a pocket gun make a terrific combination. The .45 is a Detonics USA (Pendergrass) Model 9-11-01. The snubby is Ahern's old-style S&W Model 640. The pocket gun is Ahern's Seecamp .32.

Ahern has found a Seecamp .32 and a front pocket holster an ideal carry for quite a number of years. As this caption is written, the combination is in Ahern's pocket.

The NAA Pug in .22 Magnum is a fine little extreme close range defender and easily hidden.

I keep a 15+1 capacity Glock 22 in .40 S&W with Crimson Trace LaserGrips and Surefire X-300 WeaponLight in reserve. There's a 17+1 Taurus 809 B in 9X19mm immediately to hand. Its Picatinny Rail will also accept the Surefire X-300.

Other guns get trotted out for other reasons, of course, and the guns mentioned above were selected for their defensive purpose based on several factors, not the least of which is their excellence and reliability. The clothing you'll wear, the ambient temperature, the people with whom you will associate and under what circumstances, in what areas do you travel

(crime rates, etc.) – all figure in when selecting the appropriate handgun and how to conceal it. Let's take an example that bears serious consideration. If you were to be attacked, would you anticipate a lone attacker or multiple assailants?

I remember years and years ago watching the late, great Jack Benny's television show. Actor and producer Sheldon Leonard comes up to him on the street, brandishes a handgun and demands, "Your money or your life!" In reality a man of great generosity, Benny's persona was that of the consummate cheapskate. He doesn't answer his would-be robber. After a few beats, Sheldon Leonard demands an answer. Jack Benny replies, "I'm thinking about it!" Encounters on the street aren't usually comedic in nature. And, there won't be any time to carefully think about a response. If the possibility of multiple attackers is a viable one, forget any handgun that isn't equipped with a high capacity magazine.

I've read some opinions from persons whose judgment I respect that magazine capacity should be considered over caliber, i.e., my 15+1 Glock 22 in .40 S&W should be set aside in favor of my 17+1 Taurus 809 B in 9X19mm, despite the fact that .40 S&W is arguably and demonstrably a superior caliber in a number of ways. The assumption here is not so much predicated on encountering a gang of street thugs, although the logic could certainly apply, but rather, in these post-September 11 days, terrorists. Although I don't dispute the logic, because of my style of carrying, I just happen to dismiss the idea of two extra rounds here or there being a factor in my decision making. Hopefully, I won't find myself regretting that sometime in the future. Only time will tell, of course.

When choosing which handgun or handguns you will carry, you must determine, to the best of your ability, the range of circumstances in a potential violent encounter involving you – not the guy in the movies or the guy whose firearms book or article you've just read. Then, after an objective evaluation of those circumstances and your clothing and societal/ social requirements, choose your weapons based on logic and your personal reality.

CHAPTER 12

HOW SHOULD YOU CARRY ONE OF THESE THINGS?

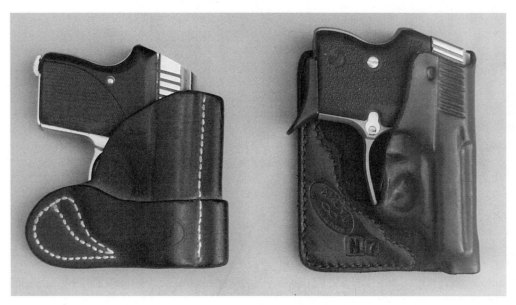

At left, Ahern's Seecamp .32 and its pocket holster, at right Sharon Ahern's NAA Guardian .32 and the holster it rides in when she has it in her purse.

I've written two books dealing with carrying concealed weapons. Although I immensely enjoy writing, it is my source of income. That said, if you want in-depth coverage of how to carry firearms and other concealed weapons, I suggest acquiring my book, *Armed for Personal Defense*, published by Gun Digest Books. However, it bears consideration within the scope of this book to touch upon how and where concealed handguns can be carried.

Handguns can be carried on body in a holster, on body without a holster and with a mechanical aid (Hip-Grip, Covert Carrier), or on body without mechanical aid. Holsters can be carried off body in purses, briefcases, specially constructed notebooks, hollowed-out books, diaper bags and even grocery bags – the brown paper kind. An example I use in *Armed for Personal Defense* involves a stake-out or other anti-crime activity in which someone poses as

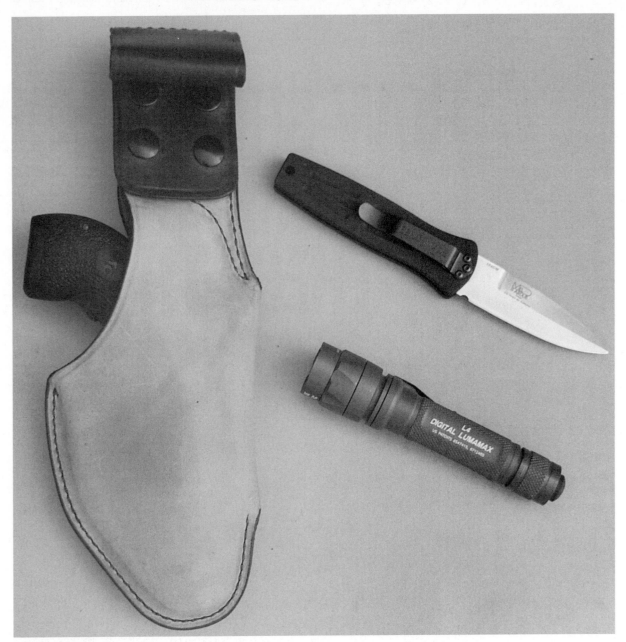

This Ken Null crotch holster carries a S&W Model 640. The knife is a small automatic from Benchmade and the tactical light is from SureFire, the L4 Digital Lumamax.

what used to be called a "wino" but would, these days, be referred to as an "alcohol challenged person, victimized by societal pressures to accept a capitalistic lifestyle." You take a long-barreled handgun – say a Smith & Wesson 586 with a six-inch barrel or a Smith & Wesson 629 with a similar length tube or even my Cimarron Arms stainless single action in .45 Colt with seven and one-half-inch barrel – and place it in a brown bag, of the type in which one might place a liter or so bottle of wine or a fifth of whiskey. Position the weapon with the butt of the weapon downward so you can hold the weapon by the

barrel, as if the barrel were the neck of a bottle. Crumple the bag around the barrel and, every once in a while, pretend to take a pull from the bottle. If you can count on not getting busted by the cops for public drunkenness, this is a terrific way to have a large and powerful handgun immediately to hand.

Sharon and I used to carry guns in the bottom of a diaper bag, back in the days when disposables were a novelty and the really foul stuff was in the bag. Nobody in his or her right mind wants to search a diaper bag packed with stuff like that. Off-body carry merely requires

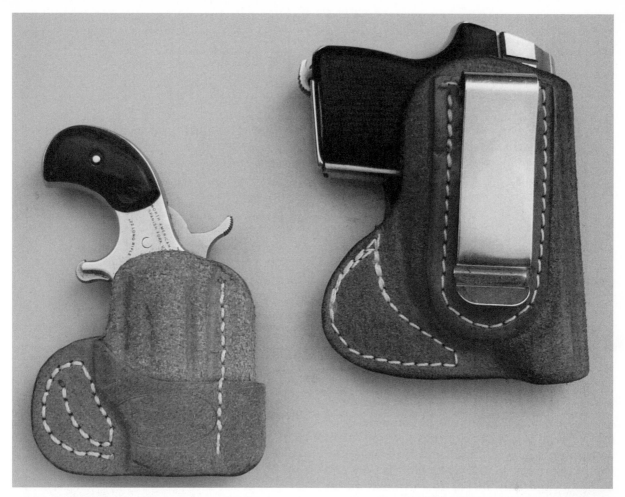

At left, a front pocket holster with a one and one-eighth-inch .22 LR North American Arms Mini-Revolver. At right, a Seecamp .32 in an inside waistband clip holster.

A Seecamp .32 with Covert Carrier clip to use in lieu of a holster.

creativity, but must also be evaluated in light of how readily the firearm can be brought into play should it be needed. The other day, a friend remarked that he wished he could somehow persuade his wife to carry a handgun on body instead of in a purse. I told him that, typically, unless a woman is a law enforcement officer or involved in some similar activity, women just won't carry that way, preferring instead to carry off-body in a purse. If it's that or not carrying the gun at all, off-body is better than nothing.

When it comes to on-body in a holster or without a holster, here are the basic positions. Assuming a right-handed individual, strongside carry would be on the right sight of the body, somewhere between the right kidney and the right hip bone, the butt of the gun pointing rearward. Small of the back carry would be between the right kidney and the spine or over the spine – not a good move for physical/medical reasons, in the event of a fall or long periods of being seated. The gun butt can be pointing toward the midline of the body or outward. Deep crossdraw, wherein the gun is worn just aft of the left hip bone, butt forward, and is accessed with the right hand. The handgun can also be accessed with the left hand by utilizing a reverse

Ahern's Guardian .380 with Crimson Trace LaserGrips in a Grandfather Oak Kydex front pocket holster.

Not something to wear every day, of course, Ahern reaches for a Remington 870 12 gauge in a Sam Andrews shoulder rig.

or twist draw. If a right-handed person carried butt forward behind the right hip bone for a right handed draw, this is also a twist draw. Wild Bill Hickok wore his 1851 Navy Colts this way and he did alright until he sat down to play poker and left his back exposed. Crossdraw, wherein the handgun is positioned between the left hip bone and the navel, the butt of the gun pointing toward the body's mid-line. Appendix forward, also affectionately known as the "felony carry," especially absent a holster, wherein the gun is worn over the appendix, between the navel and right hip bone, the butt of the gun pointed away from the mid-line of the body.

That takes care of waist level carries. These can be accomplished with or without a holster or a mechanical aid, inside or outside the waistband. A holster or mechanical aid makes these carries safer and more reliable. One requires a holster for most of the other carry positions. Most noteworthy of these alternate positions are those wherein the weapon is suspended from the off-side shoulder, either straight up and down in a vertical shoulder holster, straight upside-down in an upside-down shoulder holster or horizontally/diagonally in a horizontal/diagonal shoulder holster.

If the correct shoulder holster is chosen and one's covering garments are appropriately sized, shoulder holsters can effectively handle a wide range of handguns, unless you're too

big or too small. Unlike my earlier reference to James Bond's tuxedo, more casual clothes or "unconstructed" jackets, like Don Johnson wore in *Miami Vice,* will cover a correctly worn shoulder rig with a pretty decent-sized handgun. For example, I have an original Galco Miami Classic, just like the kind used in the television series. I use it with a SIG 229.

The gun can be suspended somehow from the waistband and worn holstered down inside the pants in a crotch holster – what a nice name! – wherein the gun is accessed by either pushing up on the holster from the muzzle end by a hand positioned in a side trouser pocket or by unzipping one's fly and reaching inside to grab the gun. This carry is particularly useful for men using a public urinal.

On the other side of the Andrews rig is a Glock 22 and there's also extra ammo for the shotgun. Sam is one of America's finest holster makers.

Ahern draws his old-style Smith & Wesson Model 640 from a Galco Ankle Glove ankle holster.

A two-inch barrel revolver or a semi-automatic of medium-frame size is about as big as you can go with normally cut loose fitting trousers. I have a Ken Null holster of this type for a two-inch barrel, five-shot revolver, a Smith & Wesson Model 640. Probably something the size of the Guardian .380 would be ideal. I would not consider this carry for primary use, but only for the carriage of a second or third gun.

The thigh holster is positioned by putting the holster and gun combination, butt rearward usually, as follows. A right-handed person, usually a woman or traditionally dressed Scotsman, affixes the thigh holster to the inside of the left thigh. One hitches up and reaches under the skirt or kilt to draw the gun. Since merely affixing the holster around the thigh wouldn't be reliably stable, there will be a belt of some kind which encircles the waist, from which the holster is pendant on a slender strap.

Small, potent caliber autoloaders are the best choice for this style of carry. In years gone by, .25 autos were popular for this method of concealing a handgun. I've seen holsters like this designed to carry a snubby .38 Special revolver, but I should think that would be the largest style of handgun to be considered. In lecture situations on concealment, I've gotten feedback from women concerning this carry; and, it seems, some women cannot get to where they feel comfortable with a gun on the thigh worn between the legs. One woman I recall recounted that she holstered the gun on the outer side of the right thigh, wearing full skirts so the gun and holster combination didn't profile. She did a good job of her concealed carry, because I didn't spot the gun at all.

The leg carry positions a holster on the calf, between the knee and the ankle, necessitating raising the trouser leg quite a bit in order to access the gun, which a right handed person would position on the inner side of the left leg, butt rearward. This carry is particularly practical for women wearing ankle length skirts or dresses.

I would recommend nothing larger than a snubby .38 revolver or medium-frame size semiautomatic. But, since women are so often bereft of pockets, I wouldn't consider it at all inappropriate for a woman to carry a small frame autoloader, but in .32 or .380 unless a .25 auto is all she has.

An Andrews belt slide for the Detonics CombatMaster .45.

A Glock 22 in a Blackhawk! Products leather inside waistband holster.

The ankle holster is tragically misunderstood. A right-handed person would normally carry an ankle holstered gun on the right side of the left ankle, the gun positioned butt rearward. If there were some reason why one could not carry in that fashion, the fallback position would be on the left side of the right ankle, butt forward. Movies aside, a right-handed person never, ever wears an ankle holster on the right side of the right leg. Not only would the gun be quite poorly concealed, but it would constantly get banged into things in the normal course of day-to-day activities. The types of handguns I recommend for ankle carry are neither large nor small, but medium-sized. I've carried a handgun as heavy as two pounds six ounces on my ankle at times. I'm talking about a Detonics CombatMaster .45 with six rounds loaded. Before anyone thinks I'm carrying chamber empty, that's not the case. The "loaded chamber indicator," which is the lower rear edge of the magazine follower in a standard six-round CombatMaster magazine, only protrudes when there's a round in the chamber and six rounds in the magazine. I feed the first round from the magazine into the chamber and leave the magazine one light. But I digress. Thirty-eight ounces plus the weight of the holster itself is really pushing it for ankle carry.

Conversely, if you wear a pistol the size of a Seecamp or even a Guardian .380 on your ankle, you'll have more holster than you have gun. That ratio is always a bad idea. What I recommend for ankle holster carry is a two-inch barrel .38 Special revolver or a medium frame autoloader; and, these days, that could mean a 9X19mm like the Taurus PT 709 Slim or something similar. Go any bigger than that when you choose a gun for ankle carry and the gun and holster combination will likely prove to be heavier than you would prefer.

Pocket holsters are the last of the conventional holstering categories. There are front/side pocket holsters and hip/back pocket holsters. Hip pocket holsters are worn with the flat side out, the butt of the gun pointed away from the midline of the body, the gun accessed with what is variously called a twist/reverse/cavalry-style draw. In one's enthusiasm to get the handgun into action, one must always be mindful of prematurely triggering a round and shooting oneself in the gunhand side of the derriere.

Front pocket holsters are the ultimate in concealed carry convenience. Pocket holster carry, for men certainly, is an ideal means by which to be armed with a medium to small frame semi-automatic or even a two-inch barreled revolver. When Sharon and I had

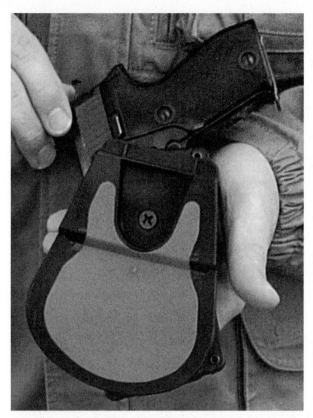

This Fobus Paddle Holster is quite well made and a great way to carry a number of SIG-Sauer models, in this case.

Ahern's used SIG P6 (P225) worked well in this Fobus holster.

When a handgun is accessorized with something that slides onto a Picatinny Rail, like this Glock 22 with SureFire X300 WeaponLight, carry options are more restricted. But, searching, you'll find good holsters which will accommodate this combination.

our holster business, we regularly received requests for front pocket holsters for the Glock 26/27. With heavy material dress pants, this can work. With jeans or other closer fitting or lighter weight fabric pants, smaller guns would be better.

I recommend – based on personal preferences – something certainly not much bigger than the Guardian .380. As indicated elsewhere in this book, my most frequently carried pocket holster handguns are the Guardian .380 and my trusty old Seecamp .32.

A well-made pocket holster will yield the gun reliably, without coming out of the pocket with the handgun. It is a perfectly normal gesture for a man to casually thrust a hand into his front pocket. If you practice the technique, you can even have the handgun fully drawn without anyone being the wiser. If the possibly bad situation goes away, the handgun can be re-holstered without being seen.

Concealed carry techniques, as with any other worthwhile endeavor, must be studied and practiced. The more necessary to truly conceal a handgun, the more polished must be the technique and the more carefully considered must be the choice of firearms. It should be remembered that a provision of many concealed carry permits is that the gun stays concealed and is not flashed. As this is written, more and more people are experimenting with open carry in areas where this has a legal basis. Even if you are in an open carry jurisdiction, good concealed carry technique is a skill set you should cultivate and perfect to the very best of your ability.

CHAPTER 13

WHAT ELSE YOU SHOULD CARRY

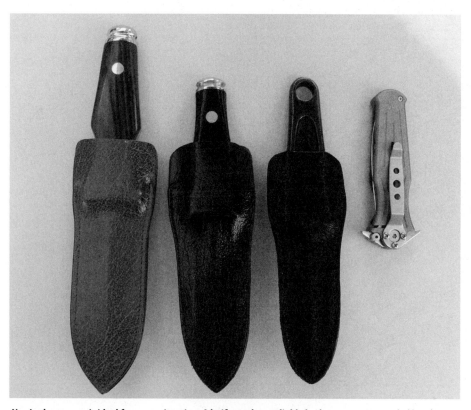

No single weapon is ideal for every situation. A knife can be a reliable backup to your concealed handgun.

Carrying a handgun alone is certainly better than not being armed, but can be severely limiting. There are a lot of things, for example, which you can't do with a handgun. When was the last time you cut open a box with a handgun? My point is, a handgun on its own is not the complete answer. To augment the handgun, one should regularly carry at least two reloads – spare magazines, speedloaders or Bianchi Speed Strips. One should also carry a stout knife that is capable of performing ordinary tasks and equally well-suited to defensive use.

I am addressing, of course, the most basic concept of a "battery." I've read the old line, "Beware of the man with only one gun; he probably knows how to use it." I don't argue with the logic that, indeed, someone with only one gun might well become extraordinarily efficient in its use; but I see the concept as hopelessly simplistic. Certainly, if all you can afford or all the law allows you is one handgun, by all means learn it inside and out. Conversely, it would be hard to imagine one handgun being ideal for all situations.

As much as one might wish it to be so, no one single weapon – be it the most labored-over 1911 or the most innovative of the modern high-tech pistols – is ideal for every situation. Nor can it be said that one weapon will always be enough. Even the best weapon might be subject to failure and, assuming virtual perfection, tactical situations change and require tactical versatility. Indeed, in an ideal world, we could all walk around with our personal assault rifle of choice conveniently slung on body as casually as a man or woman carries a briefcase or a woman carries a purse. But this isn't an ideal world and no single weapon will serve every purpose which comes along in the course of events anyway, even an assault rifle. And going openly armed, unless some sort of police or military uniform accompanies the armed condition, is the stuff of panic in many parts of the USA, especially in our post-9-11 world.

As this is written, there is a groundswell open carry movement in states where open carry is not proscribed by law. I understand that one

If you reside in an area where automatic knives are legal, or if your occupation qualifies you to use automatic knives, automatics can be a true asset. Assisted opening knives can be even faster into action. Movie imagery aside, automatic knives are handy for normal activities because they are easily and safely opened one handed. These are from Benchmade, the larger of the two knives an AFO Model, the smaller designed by Mel Pardue for Benchmade. Both have safety locks on the spine.

state's law may allow open holstered carry of a handgun that is unloaded. I don't wish to rain on anyone's parade, but carrying an unloaded handgun openly is not something I would do. If you really needed to use a handgun, what would you do? Point the gun and shout, "Bang!?" To those who wish to do this, I say by golly, if it's legal, do it. I would not. Decades ago, I was in areas where carrying a handgun was illegal. In the course of my daily activities, I needed to carry a handgun, so I did. I'm not recommending that one ignore a law just because it's silly, of course, but if having a handgun on your person is that important, unless you're the world's fastest handgun loader, I see no value in an empty gun. Yes, you can hit someone with the gun and, especially if it has a steel frame, it'll work for that. But, an expandable baton would cost less, be easier to carry and work better. Just my opinion.

For many reasons, the prudent person who wishes to be armed for self-protection and the protection of innocents and has the financial ability to do so builds a concealed weapons battery.

I like to think that I am a "prudent person," although I'm sure there are plenty of people who would argue that I'm not.

The following suggestions assume that someone lives in an extremely weapons friendly jurisdiction or is a peace officer affiliated with a department which practices an extremely intelligent weapons policy. Certain of the edged weapons and most of the impact weapons included here – not to mention the practice of multiple gun carrying – will be frowned upon in many locales, i.e., "illegal." When that is the case, improvise and stay within the law, however silly the law might seem – unless that's suicidal. The true warrior will find his weapons all about him. My wife's nephew, George, whom I've known since he was going on seven – we think of him like an oldest son, really – was taught by his dad to haul his fist back, grab off his shoe and use the shoe like a blackjack or sap, that is to say if a brick were not available. George was a fantastic bar fighter, but that's another story.

The handguns and other weapons to which I refer here are my individual choices and representative of a type, only. I have always preferred S&W hideout revolvers, for example, using them since 1967. You may prefer a Ruger or Taurus or Charter or an old Colt or a Rossi or a Cobra. The concept is what counts.

Before commencing to build a battery, the term itself must be understood. A "battery," in

the context of a book that is a guide to concealed carry handguns, is a grouping of weapons which complement one another so that where one weapon is inappropriate to a specific task, another will be ideal or close to ideal.

To properly comprehend the basis for this concept, consider the following. You are hunting mule deer, a .243 Winchester caliber rifle in your hands. Suddenly – stay with me on this – an enraged grizzly with blood in his eye charges at you from out of a thicket. Now, suddenly, you are terribly under-gunned. No one weapon will do everything. Add concealment to the equation and the variables increase dramatically.

In the modern world, largely because of the media and other societal factors, weapons are feared by much of humankind. In 2008, Georgia, the state in which Sharon and I live, liberalized its restrictions on where permit holders could carry, to include certain restaurants and public parks. I read an interview with a woman who vowed she would stay out of parks with her children and stop eating out in restaurants because of the change. About a year later, restrictions on carrying in National Parks were lifted across the country. Kind of hope that lady at least has cable! Although irrational, this sort of attitude is fact. Concealability is not only important, but, for most carry situations, it is legally mandated.

Let's start with handguns. To be properly outfitted in your battery of defensive on-body ordnance, you will need some sort of very small handgun which can be concealed with virtually any attire imaginable. Although lots of people have suffered eventually lethal wounds with a .25 automatic, today there are vastly better choices. Of course, if a .25 is all you have and all you can afford, learn to use it well. Otherwise, choose something a little more powerful. My personal choice in a .25 was always the discontinued single action Beretta 950 BS Jetfire. The Baby Browning and the stainless steel Bauer .25 copy were always excellent .25 ACP handguns. The once ubiquitous Raven, despite being one of the least expensive handguns around, worked quite well.

A wide range of truly world-class super-small handguns are currently quite readily available. The Seecamp or Guardian or Kel-Tec .32s, for example, are all fine choices and you might well want to consider carrying one of these or their .380 ACP counterparts on a regular basis, no matter what other weapon or weapons you might be wearing or have to hand. The 60-grain .32 ACP Silvertip from Winchester has a 63% one-shot stop rating, and even the 71-grain .32 ACP solid has a 50% rating, these figures according to Marshall and Sanow. Without sounding too facetious, I hope, if a .32 is all you've got, you may want to consider double taps! The .380 cartridge will give you better performance out the gate, but that doesn't make the .32 ACP something to sneeze at. As mentioned elsewhere in this book, the North American Arms Guardians are also offered in their bottlenecked .32 NAA and .25 NAA chamberings, hotter performing still. Then too, there's the 9X19mm Rohrbaugh R9. However, no gun like any these is the perfect solution. What makes them so worthwhile is their concealability and portability.

I carry a Seecamp .32 or Crimson Trace LaserGripped Guardian .380 at all times, while Sharon carries a Guardian .32 unless she's carrying her J-Frame S&W. The North American Arms Guardians are easier to disassemble than the Seecamp – at least for ten-thumbed yours truly. The Guardian .32 is about the same size as the Seecamp in .32 or .380, while the Guardian .380 is somewhat larger. Any product from Seecamp or North American Arms is something to believe in; both entities stand behind what they make and are universally respected throughout the industry. I was into the Seecamp long before

Five from SureFire, from the top the M3 Combat Light, the E2L Outdoorsman, the L1 Digital Lumamax, the L4 Digital Lumamax and the 6P LED. SureFire's 123 A batteries are boxed beside them.

NAA even thought of the Guardian .32. As far as NAA semi-automatics go, the Guardian .380 deserves an extremely serious look. It has sights, which may or not be of value in a handgun of its size and intended purpose – close range defense – but the importance of Crimson Trace LaserGrips being available as an accessory or as standard equipment cannot be minimized. The Guardian .380 is the smallest handgun for which Crimson Trace offers its wonderful product in standard form and the addition of these grips to a Guardian .380 extends its effective range to target considerably. This proclivity results in the Guardian .380 being a more formidable weapon than either its size or caliber might initially suggest.

The next element of the battery is what has always been called a small frame revolver or what used to be called a medium frame automatic. I say "used to" because guns such as the Kahr MK9 or SIG 239, despite more powerful calibers, are the same size as the .32 ACP and .380 ACP medium frames of a short while ago; many of these are still hanging around. Excellent guns though these older designs are, why carry a .32 when in the same size handgun you can have a 9mm Parabellum or a .40 S&W? Before getting into the medium frame auto concept too heavily, let's consider something less controversial: the snubby .38.

I believe the original Model 640 J-Frame Smith & Wesson .38 (now discontinued) to be the best personal hideout revolver ever made. Period. For several decades, I have used J-Frames with the marvelous Barami Hip-Grip, which obviates the need for a holster, the hook-like shelf on the right grip plate going over the waistband or trouser belt and keeping the gun from sliding through. These days, one can find oneself in a true quandary, however, since the Crimson Trace Lasergrips are so excellent with these guns as well. The Model 640 .38 or original Model 60 with exposed hammer – my personal favorites – are among those handguns no one should be without. Excellent revolvers of similar size are available from Taurus, Charter, Ruger and Cobra, used guns from Colt, as well.

If a snubby revolver is not to your liking, it is – or should be – back to the semi-autos such as the Kahr and SIG models to which I've already referred. These, and the pistols like them from other sources, can be seen as the "new medium frame" autos, as discussed elsewhere in this book.

Whatever "mid-size" handgun or handguns you select for this portion of your battery, whether revolver or semi-auto, you must decide how to approach the carry weight issue.

Once you move into calibers larger than .22, .25, .32 ACP or .380 ACP, perceived recoil can become a serious consideration. Even some .380s can be a bit stout. There are different schools of thought concerning this matter. I have always been of the opinion that having a gun which is too lightweight in a caliber with the potential for generating a stiff recoil jolt will preclude practice. Whatever your decision, weigh the facts (no pun intended). In handguns of this mid-size variety, I have always preferred steel frames so that the weapon is more pleasant to shoot. If I were going to a non-steel frame revolver, I would try to stick with an aluminum alloy frame if I were going to use anything heavier than .38 Special +P and I would avoid .357 Magnum with any lightweight frame.

To round out the handgun portion of a concealed carry battery, one needs a pistol with enhanced magazine capacity. By a weird chain of events, I wound up trading for a .40 S&W SIG 229 some years ago. It was a gently used pistol and it proved to be exceptionally accurate for me. Sometime later, I put Crimson Trace LaserGrips on the pistol. Magazine capacity is twelve rounds, plus one in the chamber (12+1). If thirteen rounds before reloading aren't enough to get me through a bad situation, a fourteenth, fifteenth, sixteenth, seventeenth or even an eighteenth round probably won't help me very much either.

Going beyond the ordinary definition of concealed weapon, if you anticipate truly serious trouble and, for some reason, can't stay home or go the other way, a legal length pistol grip shotgun could be the solution. Almost certainly, an ordinary Concealed Carry Permit will not authorize you to carry a concealed shotgun. If, however, it is legal, then it would be hard to make a better choice than a Remington 870 with a Pachmayr Vindicator Kit installed. This is not a "Witness Protection Shotgun," nor a "Sawed-Off Shotgun," both of which would be NFA (National Firearms Act) weapons, i.e., forbidden for civilian ownership unless you have the appropriate federal tax stamp and the permission of your local law enforcement agency . Barrel length of the original police riot shotgun was 18 inches. It still is. The Pachmayr Kit merely replaces the wooden "trombone" handle and the buttstock, giving the shotgun a pistol grip with no shoulder accommodation. In recent times, I have replaced the Pachmayr fore-end with a Surefire unit incorporating a high intensity tactical light. Under appropriate outerwear, with a proper sling or holster, the shotgun so equipped could be concealed.

In a great many jurisdictions, no matter how gun friendly, impact weapons – that is, something designed to hit someone with – are frowned upon, at the very least, for civilian use. If you can legally carry an impact weapon, one of the expandable batons like those from ASP is ideal. As the baton is flicked open, it makes a very distinct sound which is easily recognized. I favor

this standard style of expandable baton, but I also have an expandable which is reminiscent of a tonfa. A conventional flat sap, for those who are skilled in its use, can be an extremely versatile weapon. An acquaintance of mine, a one-time police officer, literally saved his own life with one. Sap gloves – again, predominantly a piece of police equipment – look and wear like ordinary heavy leather gloves, unless you know how to recognize them, but powdered lead shot is packed into the knuckle and first digit area

Sam Andrews made this outstanding belt holster for Ahern's Detonics USA (Pendergrass) CombatMaster. The matching double magazine pouches are interesting. The one at left is for standard six-round CombatMaster magazines, while the one at right is for full-length magazines, which also work in the CombatMaster.

of the four fingers. Such gloves can be used to deliver a punch or employed with a slapping motion, as one would typically do with a flat sap. My late father-in-law was never into guns, but he kept a spring sap – a type of blackjack – near his front door, just in case.

Impact weapons may be nice to keep as part of a collection, etc., but are generally something to be included in a civilian's concealed carry battery only under the most exceptional conditions. If you are attacked in your home

and need an impact weapon, everything from ordinary hammers to your Lodge cast iron cookware will do very nicely.

Folding knives, on the other hand, should constitute a portion of everyone's concealed carry battery. There are so many excellent knives from which to choose. I invariably seem to carry one or another from Benchmade. Their AXIS Lock, however it is employed – automatic, assisted opening or manual opening – is a delight to work with.

A lockblade folder of some type is your best choice. Avoid a knife that is double edged. If you need to use it for anything other than anti-personnel situations, the knife will prove less than convenient. Also, in a great many states, double edged knives are considered daggers or dirks and cannot legally be carried. Why make trouble for yourself? Remember that a concealed carry permit does not allow you to break weapons-related laws. Unfortunately, most boot knives are double edged. In some areas, automatic opening knives are okay to carry, while in some areas they are illegal. If you want a knife that opens more rapidly than a knife with an ordinary thumb stud, acquire an assisted opening knife. I have an assisted opening knife made by Benchmade which opens more rapidly than one of their best (in my opinion) automatic knives. Both the assisted opening knife and the automatic utilize the same AXIS Locking system. Butterfly/Bali-Song knives are another option. They are quick to get into action, versatile and flashy to operate. They are also illegal in a few places. Check laws in your area. If you do elect to carry a Bali-Song, go to www.amazon.com and hope you can find one of my old pal Jeff Imada's *The Bali Song Manual* so you can learn more than simple opening techniques and realize the full potential of this extremely versatile knife design. Unless you already are a Bali-Song expert, however, DO NOT get a double edged Butterfly knife, since much of what you will learn in terms of openings and closings involves allowing the spine (upper, unsharpened side) of the blade to contact your fingers. With a double edged knife, you'll cut yourself, and likely rather badly.

Just as you'll need maintenance equipment for your firearms, perhaps one of the all-encompassing kits from Otis, you'll need a few things for your knife. Specifically, you'll need some type of ceramic "sticks" for routine sharpening. You'll want a light machine oil for honing the edge, if you are skilled enough to use a stone properly. I've never been good with a stone. My son and my son-in-law, fortunately, are both good men with a stone. But you'll need the oil anyway, to lubricate the pin on which the blade pivots as it opens and closes. Break-Free, which you can certainly use on your guns, works well on knives, too. You'll also need one of those compressed air canisters of the kind used to blow clean computer keyboards and similar equipment. Compressed air may be handy with your firearm, of course, but it's really quite useful with your knife. Folding knives are carried in pockets, by their very nature, and, just like pocket carried handguns, they pick up pocket lint. If you get enough lint around the pin on which the blade rotates, you can actually prevent the knife from fully and safely locking open. The compressed air will take care of that and should be applied before you lubricate.

When I was first getting started going armed, my super hideout was either a Beretta Jetfire .25 or a Bauer .25. My more serious handguns were either an old blued S&W Model 36 on a Hip-Grip or in an inside waistband holster or a Walther PPK/S in some sort of inside waistband holster or, at times, in a wonderful shoulder holster Bianchi used to offer just for PP series pistols, the "Gun-Qwik." It was the fastest shoulder rig there was. My knife was my old Puma, the one the size of a Buck 110.

Some forty years later, after much of a lifetime going armed, it is understandable that I have my own preferences, likes and dislikes, if you will. The important thing is that I've thought through my concealment needs from the likely and the everyday to the extremely unlikely and have equipped myself accordingly. Have I ever found it incumbent upon me to carry a pistol grip shotgun concealed? Never. But do I know how to conceal it, should the need arise? Yes, I do. Much of the time, that little Seecamp .32 or Guardian .380 will be the only firearm I have on body, some of the time not.

By building a concealed carry battery and becoming familiar with all aspects of it, you are giving yourself options which could save your life, the life of a loved one or the life of some other innocent. When you look at it that way, the logic behind a concealed carry battery is inescapable.

To properly equip yourself for the concealed carry condition, ideally you should have at least one of each of the following. You will need a small handgun, one that can be hidden on body with the most minimal amount of clothing, as one might dress on the hottest summer days.

You might move up to the 9x19mm Rohrbaugh R9. The gun is even offered in .380, should 9mm recoil be something which worries you.

When I first discussed this pistol with its inventor, I asked a question I could not help but pose. "Does this gun recoil like the Seattle Detonics Pocket Nine pistols of decades ago?" If the answer had been in the affirmative, I wouldn't have included one in this book. The Detonics Pocket Nine was one of the most unpleasantly recoiling and painful handguns I've ever fired in my life. It was a straight blowback.

If you select a semi-automatic and the weapon comes with only a single magazine, acquire at least two more magazines at your earliest opportunity. This is because magazines become damaged or even lost and a semi-automatic pistol, at best, is a weapon that is usually awkward to load single-shot without a magazine, while some semi-automatics won't work at all because of a magazine safety, a feature I have never liked. If your pistol is an excellent one, but the manufacturer decides to change it or take it from the line, spare magazines may become horribly difficult to find. Get at least two and keep them safe, after you have satisfied yourself through as much test firing as the budget and common sense will allow that these spares work as well in your pistol as the original magazine that came with the weapon. If there are extended magazines available for the gun, certainly avail yourself of one, should you wish to; however, the idea with a gun carried for concealment is that it should be concealable. Keep the extra length magazine, should you purchase one, for special occasions.

If you really come to feel that this handgun is the best of its kind for you, the smart thing to do – especially in these weirdly uncertain times, finances permitting – is to acquire several more spare magazines. Then, consult the literature and go to a trusted gunsmith. Inquire which parts might be the most likely to malfunction, break or wear out. Acquire those parts and put them away for possible future use. This idea applies with any firearm you feel might be of true staying alive value to you. If you can afford it, the best way to make certain you have replacement parts is to acquire a second identical gun that can be cannibalized as needed. Little things like extractors, etc., should be acquired as individual items so the "reserve parts" gun doesn't have to be hit for such simple items. If you are not handy, as they say – I have ten thumbs, myself, as already indicated – find someone who can show you how to detail strip the gun in question and replace and tweak, as needed, the suspect parts.

Next, you need at least three spare magazines (or speedloaders or Bianchi Speed Strips) for your main or primary handgun. You'll probably note that most firearms people advise you to carry two reloads for your primary handgun. I don't disagree with that at all. However, what happens if you lose or damage a magazine (or speedloader or Bianchi Speed Strip)? You need that third unit to be held in reserve for such contingencies. As mentioned concerning the tiny hideout handgun, if you realize this handgun is THE handgun for you, take steps to acquire more magazines and a spare parts gun and miscellaneous spare parts.

Years ago, one could calmly proclaim that only factory original magazines should be considered as spares for semi-automatic pistols. Factory originals are still a great idea, but companies like Pro-Mag offer some very well-made magazines you may very well wish to consider. For certain handguns, the original equipment magazines for which are no longer available, Pro-Mag or some other firm may be your only option. Original equipment magazines can be horrifically expensive if the handgun in question has been discontinued, even assuming that such can be found. And, just because two original equipment magazines are supposedly identical, there is no valid reason to suppose that one magazine will function exactly like another. I know, that should be the case. But it's not. I have a Walther PP .32 with one original magazine, several original magazines not original to this particular handgun and a Walther PPK/S .32 ACP magazine marketed by Smith & Wesson's Walther operation. Several of the magazines work quite well, but only one of these magazines is fully reliable in all regards.

Speedloaders, of course, are cylindrical devices which are pretty revolver specific and carry a full reload for your revolver. They can only be used effectively for a full reload. You must open the revolver's cylinder out of the frame, smartly hit the ejector rod as you invert the revolver so that the empties will fall clear, then re-orient the revolver and apply the speedloader in such a fashion that all five or six or however many cartridges line up essentially perfectly with the charging holes in the cylinder. Then, you must perform some function which releases the cartridges from the speedloader and into the charging holes. Just

personal preference here, but I've always liked the Safariland speedloaders because release of the cartridges is accomplished merely by pressing the center of the speedloader against the revolver's ejector star – it doesn't take any extra motion – and the cartridges release. Safariland speedloaders are essentially foolproof. The only problem with speedloaders is that, pocket carried, they'll pick up lint. They can also pick up a coin that'll jam at the center of the circle described by the cartridges. If you don't notice it until you're reloading in a life and death battle, it could prove to be awkward.

Bianchi Speed Strips are a wonderful and simple invention. A little bit of metal, a little bit of neoprene or whatever, and they work. You take six cartridges and insert them one at a time into the strip, the case head securing inside a pre-sized receptacle. There's a tape on one end, for holding the strip. If you aren't in a huge hurry and you need to replenish only one of two or more charging holes, not a problem. Partially stroke the revolver's ejector rod so that the case heads rise up enough from the cylinder that you can pluck the empties – you can tell by the indented primers, of course – from the cylinder. Then, position one or two cartridges held in the Speed Strip at a time, give a little tug or twist and the cartridges are pried out and slip into the charging holes. Each Speed Strip is set to accommodate as many as six rounds and, to my knowledge, they are only made to accommodate case heads commensurate with .38 caliber cartridges, such as .38 Special and .357 Magnum. Nice and flat, of course, they hide well in a pocket, even the outside breast pocket of a sportcoat. Cylinder-shaped speedloaders are available in other calibers. Remember? Dirty Harry used speedloaders in the movies.

You'll want your primary handgun, your backup handgun, two reloads for your primary handgun and you'll want your knife. Some people go so far as to make certain that their primary and backup handguns will digest the same ammunition, maybe even be capable of functioning with the same spare magazines or other loading devices. Let's say you carry a Glock 22 as your primary firearm. A logical backup, if you can handle the size for concealment, would be the Glock 27, which is, after all, pretty small. Both are .40 S&W caliber and the fifteen-round magazines for the Glock 22 will go into the Glock 27, which could be handy if the Glock 22 were somehow put out of the fight and you had no spare magazines for the Glock 27.

When I was a little boy, one of my favorite programs from those early days of television was *The Range Rider*, which starred Jock Mahoney as the "The Rider" and Dick Jones as his young sidekick, "Dick West." I was always impressed that, on those rare occasions when The Rider and Dick were disarmed, they always had spare guns in their saddle bags. In a more contemporary vein, I've read in the writings of my colleague Massad Ayoob the very sage advice that it is wise to have an identical duplicate to your primary defensive handgun. You don't have to keep it in your saddlebags, but you should keep it, Massad goes on to caution, in the event you need to use your weapon in an altercation. Until properly adjudicated, that weapon will very likely be held as evidence. Assuming you wind up under no prohibition from being armed, is that point in your life really the time you'll want to learn the ins and outs of an unfamiliar weapon, or have to go out and buy a duplicate of the gun temporarily being held pending the outcome of an investigation or trial?

As our character John Rourke in *The Survivalist* novels we wrote was wont to say, "It pays to plan ahead." And it does!

CHAPTER 14

A "LASER" SIGHT

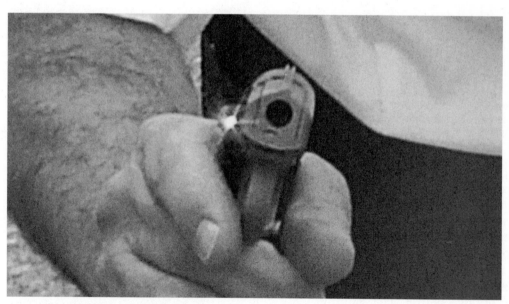

The Guardian .380 from North American Arms is fitted with Crimson Trace LaserGrips, thus becoming a much more formidable firearm at greater range.

Around 1974, Sharon and I, along with our old pal Harry Theodore, did a film project – this was before everybody or really anybody had video cameras – dealing with a weapon that was equipped with a laser. Back then, "Dr. Evil's" air-quotes around the word "laser" would have been pretty apropos. All most of us knew about lasers was that Gert Frobe had tried cutting Sean Connery in half with one in the blockbuster movie *Goldfinger*.

When the movie was made, there was no laser available that could have cut anyone in half. Laser technology was in its infancy. When Sharon and Harry and I made that film, the laser in question was mounted on a weapon about the size of a Thompson submachine gun, which was a good thing because the "Laser-Lok Sight," which cost more than the weapon on which it was mounted, was about the size of an automobile muffler.

From left, clockwise, a SIG-Sauer P229, a Detonics USA (Pendergrass) Model 9-11-01, another 229 and Sharon's old-style Smith & Wesson Model 640. All are excellent guns and all are fitted with Crimson Trace LaserGrips.

Time passed and laser sizes shrank. At last, lasers were appropriately sized to be used with a pistol. The earliest models, some of which didn't mount securely, were attached to the front of the weapon's trigger guard. In recoil, especially if a mounting screw were not perfectly tightened, the laser unit might wiggle and what zero the laser had with the weapon's bore would be lost.

The idea with a laser sight, of course, is to zero the laser with the bore at a specific distance, the laser beam and the point of impact from a bullet fired through the barrel intersecting at distance "x." If the laser mount moved, that intersection point became meaningless. The other problem associated with this style of mounting or installation was that special holstering was required, much as would be the case today should you decide to equip a pistol that features a Picatinny rail with an under-frame tactical light. Attaching something forward of the trigger guard and under the dust cover necessitates a different holster profile.

Next came the laser units which were one with a pistol's recoil spring guide rod. These

When you add a laser to a short sight radius handgun like this old-style S&W 640, you extend accurate reach and add versatility. Given that an assailant has a modest degree of sophistication, said assailant should realize that where that red dot is on his chest is about where the bullet will strike.

lasers, more compact still, did not require special holstering and, if properly made and installed, did not shift out of position under recoil. The one problem was that, typically, one would have to send the pistol off to the people who manufactured the laser so that the unit could be installed. Some people don't like

A Glock 22 in .40, Ahern's old-style S&W Model 640 and a Detonics USA (Pendergrass) Model 9-11-01. All these handguns have Crimson trace LaserGrip units. The ones on Ahern's snubby .38 are the smallest of the Crimson Trace models for the J-Frame Smith & Wessons. If you have not considered a laser, you should consider one.

The SIG 229 is an outstanding pistol on its own. This one, however, is vastly more versatile with its Crimson Trace LaserGrips unit and a spare barrel that allows using .357 SIG ammo as well.

shipping a valuable handgun unless there is no other choice.

Along came Crimson Trace with still another approach, this one neither requiring special holstering nor shipping the firearm back and forth for fitting. The Crimson Trace lasers, pre-zeroed at the factory to fifty feet and easily adjustable by the user, should a different zero be required or desired, were incorporated into the grips, specifically the right grip. Special units for the Glock were developed, since the grips of Glock pistols are part of the frame. Continuous work concentrating on miniaturizing the units has allowed a fully operational laser and power supply to be integrated into grips dimensioned to fit a handgun as small as a North American Arms Guardian .380. The Guardian .380's grip panel surface on either side is approximately two and three quarter inches from top to bottom, 1-3/4 inches front to rear. Lasers have come a long way from being the size of an automobile muffler and costing more than the gun.

The word "laser" is an acronym. It means "Light Amplification by Stimulated Emission of Radiation." Makes you really appreciate acronyms, doesn't it? In many of the practical applications we see for this hitherto magical technology, the light emitted is a coherent frequency visible light that is manipulated by the use of lenses. Other types of lasers can be infrared or x-ray. A verb is sometimes made from the word laser, that verb being the ridiculous-

An assailant's eye view of a 229 with its laser.

sounding "laze." So, when you activate the switch on whatever laser unit may be on your pistol, you are actually "lazing." The most basic idea of how a laser works is that light is inside a reflective casing and energy – with your pistol laser that energy come from the batteries – stimulates the light and causes it to bounce back and forth between two mirrors, one of these mirrors being partially transparent. The ingenious thing, at least to me, is that the light passes through the semitransparent mirror and is focused through a lens and this is what is the

actual laser beam. Most laser light that we are going to see in association with firearms is red, but green lasers are gaining in popularity. The wave length, of course, is what determines the color of the light that we see. Lasers, aside from mounting on pistols and assault rifles, carry communications, read barcodes and help to adjust our eyes so we don't need glasses. Laser light can be in a continuous wave or pulsed. As this is written, the United States military is involved in the testing of a mobile laser cannon which is not a sighting device, but an actual

With an empty revolver, Ahern flashes the laser beam against the palm of his hand. Typically, Crimson Trace LaserGrips are sighted for fifty feet from the factory, meaning that is the distance at which the laser beam and the sights intersect.

This Smith & Wesson Model 686 is an extremely accurate revolver. Adding a laser has added versatility.

I honestly cannot see such technology being allowed to filter out of the military sphere into civilian use – at least not intentionally.

The laser's development, just like the telephone and the incandescent light, was not born without controversy. Albert Einstein proposed the theoretical maniputon of light and microwaves in 1917. It was not until 1960 – three years before *Goldfinger* – that a functional laser was first demonstrated. But, earlier than that, a Columbia University student named Gordon Gould and two gentleman working for Bell Labs, Schawlow and Townes, had done groundbreaking work and thus began a conflict between Gould and Bell Laboratories that resulted in a nearly three decades-long lawsuit pitting Gould vs. Bell Labs. The lawsuit began in 1960 and was settled in federal court, in Gould's favor, in 1987. Next time you turn on your CD player or DVD player or watch *Star Wars,* thank Mr. Gould. If a laser is used as part of a weapons

weapon. As energy output increases and size decreases, it's not hard to envision a day when lasers the size of smallish handguns – ala the "hand phasers" of *Star Trek* – will be a reality.

If concealment and holstering demands don't preclude its use, adding a tactical light to a handgun equipped with a laser affords even more tactical versatility. The Tactical light is a SureFire X300 Weapon Light. The X400 model incorporates its own laser.

The reason there can be a set of LaserGrips on this .32 ACP Walther PP is that Crimson Trace makes a model for the Walther PPK/S. Both pistols have the same grip frame.

system for other than sighting, the object is to stimulate the surface with pulse emissions that will cause the target to break down.

One of the most innovative and broad-based producers of lasers as handgun sighting systems is LaserMax. LaserMax offers laser sighting systems which can be attached to Picatinny Rails, stacked with tactical lighting systems – a terrifically versatile approach, allowing a wide range of end user customization options – or incorporated into guide rods.

Beamshot is well-known for offering a line of red and green lasers that can be adapted to various firearms, when coupled with the appropriate Beamshot mounts. Laser Aiming Systems offers a green laser that is designed to work with Glock pistols with Picatinny rails. Surefire, the weapon light and tactical light people, offer infrared laser units visible only with the aid of night vision equipment, and a

continuous beam laser combined with an LED light, allowing sighting and tactical illumination simultaneously with one unit, designed for use with Picatinny Rails. The light can be operated with the first finger of your support hand, keeping the trigger finger free.

For handguns that need not be concealed, whether used tactically or for ordinary shooting activities, under-frame mounting of laser sighting devices is quite practical. For handguns which will be concealed, those lasers incorporated into guide rods, such as the lasers from LaserMax, or those incorporated into replacement grips or able to be adapted to non-replaceable grips, such as those from Crimson Trace, are the most practical. Laser assisted sighting should never take the place of marksmanship training and practice, but a laser is a definite asset I wouldn't want to be without.

CHAPTER 15

SIGHTS

The fixed sights on this Glock 17 Gen 4 are easy to see, hence enhance accuracy potential, especially in a hurry.

Although some defensive shooting at extremely close ranges does not require sights, and some few handguns are even made without sights – the Seecamp .32 and .380 are prime examples – the sighting system found on a defensive handgun carried for concealment can be quite important and may mean the difference between surviving a gunfight or becoming a casualty.

Look at a black powder Colt like the 1851 Navy and you'll see a prominent front sight, but no rear sight. The rear sight notch is actually built into the hammer. When the weapon is cocked, you sight through the head of the hammer. When you think about it, seeing as the only way to fire a single action revolver is to cock it first, such an arrangement makes quite a lot of sense.

Traditionally, a handgun will have an

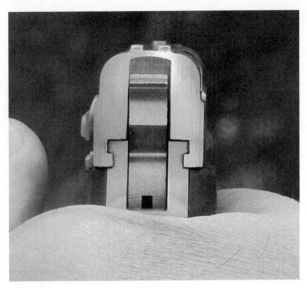

The sights on this nickel plated Bersa .380 were adequate, the gun a good shooter.

Ahern's eyes went into operation in 1946 and seeing the sights on this Ruger LCP, even with glasses, was not easy at all.

elevated front sight and some type of notch at the rear. The Smith & Wesson fixed sight revolvers are a perfect example. The front sight is a serrated ramp; on some later models that ramp is fitted with an orange insert or retrofitted to incorporate the insert. The rear sight was a square notch cut into the frame top strap. With the ramp sight being integral, this was and is an outstandingly robust arrangement for a handgun that may see rugged use. The problems presented by this arrangement are a lack of adjustability without resorting to files and the low profile of the sights to begin with. Of course, low profile sights are less likely to snag on holsters or clothing and also less prone to getting banged around. The ideal situation is to find the happy medium. Among the numerous handguns fired in association with this work, some sighting arrangements were found to be truly excellent, some satisfactory and some few all but detrimental to good marksmanship.

Front and rear sights of the traditional kind are certainly the most commonly encountered, but the variations, some rarely seen, some quite frequently encountered, bear mentioning. As a concealed weapons guy, I've always been more interested in low profile sights on the flatter handguns with the shorter, more easily concealable grips. That said, a handgun I always wanted to own and never did – one specimen passed through my hands once – was the .380 caliber Browning Model of 1910. About six inches long, flat and sleek, this 6+1

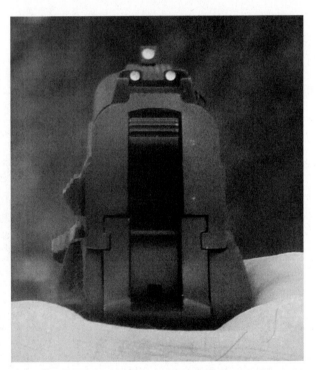

Ahern found sights on the Bersa pistols uniformly good, this model the Thunder .380 Plus, the larger capacity variant.

.380 had a sight arrangement that was milled into the slide, a channel given a treatment rather like stippling. The very front of the channel had a little bump, while the rear of the channel had a little notch. Nothing protruded above the channel. I don't think you could ask for harder to use, smoother to carry sights on a concealable handgun designed to be dropped in a pocket holsterless. I've never seen another sight arrangement like it.

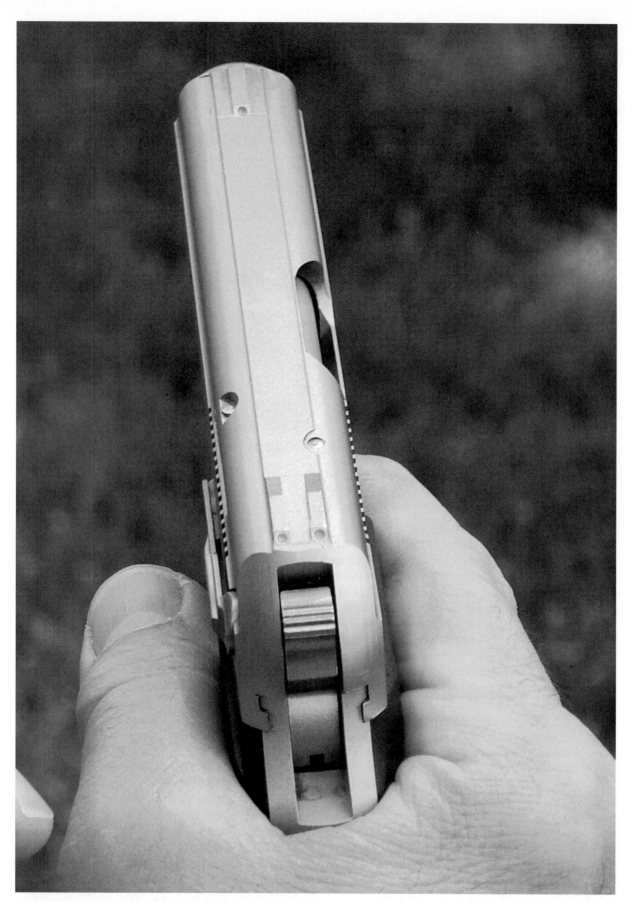

Looking down on the fixed sights of the nickel-plated Bersa Thunder .380.

The Ruger LCR's U-shaped notch rear sight and black front sight were not easy to pick up for Ahern. Ruger offers the LCR with XS Sights, the front sight carrying a Tritium dot for enhanced pick-up qualities. The thirteen point five ounce revolver is offered in .357 Magnum as this is written.

The Ruger SR9C's sights were quite easy to work with.

But the idea of a track for sighting was tried and many people liked it. Called the "Guttersnipe Sight," there was no front sight blade, ramp or bump. The rear sight was an open notch and this was the sole aiming device. The sight was reportedly quite effective at acquiring the types of targets at the range one might work through in a defensive/concealed carry situation.

A more modern and quite unique approach to the idea of quick pick-up sight picture is the Goshen HexSite. What holster designer/maker and all-around gun guy Tim Sheehan addressed with the development of the Goshen HexSite – my great old cop friend, Lew Wilson, first told me about the sight – is the problem of being able to see your sights, see the target and see what's going on around you. You'll want to keep both eyes open, if you can. For older, self-taught shooters like me, especially those who are right-handed but have a right eye that's weaker than the left eye, shooting with both eyes open is challenging at times. The HexSite allows you to do just that – shoot with both eyes open while looking through the rear sight, which allows

you to line up your sights while focusing on the front sight.

The HexSite itself is manufactured using "... advanced composite polymer HexZite-22, shock impact, abrasion and weather resistant." Lew, a guy whose opinions I seriously trust concerning firearms, raved to me about this sight. Sheehan is a very "gunny" guy and has always taken concealed weapons carry extremely seriously. The HexSite could create some holstering issues, depending on what you use. Go to the website – www.goshen-hexsite.com – and you'll be able to see the sight for yourself.

Radioluminescent sights – otherwise called "night sights" – can be extremely useful in a variety of ways. Even if you don't use them for shooting at night, as a gunsmith once pointed out to me, they can be used for finding the handgun in total darkness, should the weapon be beside you as you are sleeping . I have night sights on two handguns, and an odder pairing couldn't be found, I'd wager. The first of these two guns is a Glock 22 .40 S&W, while the second is a North American Arms .22 Magnum Pug.

To Ahern's knowledge, no pistol's sights have ever stirred as much controversy as the rear sight placement on a Detonics CombatMaster. Pat Yates, whose idea the gun was, supposedly liked to thumb cock. When Sid Woodcock designed an actual working gun, he left the feature in. That's one story, at least. Ahern always liked the rear sight being set somewhat forward because he was far-sighted and it gave him a better sight picture.

Both guns came that way. Typically, such sights consist of a small ampule of radioluminescent material, tritium. Trijicon (www.trijicon.com) is the household word for such sights; the sights are ruggedly built and, in most cases, are able to continue functioning for twelve years or longer. Once the tritium gas is exhausted, new ampoules of tritium gas can be placed in the sights and you're back in business. Trijicon claims that marksmanship at night with their high visibility three dot sights is five times better than without their sights. I don't doubt that in the slightest.

My Glock 22 has everything but whitewall tires. It is fitted with Trijicon night sights, has the Glock specific Crimson Trace LaserGrips unit and, much of the time, sports a Surefire X-300 WeaponLight on its Picatinny rails!

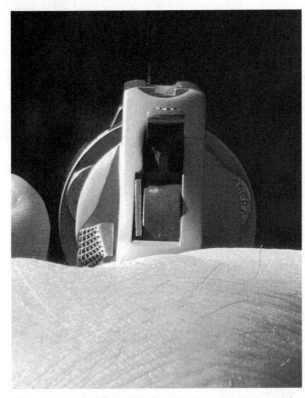

The rear sight notch on a S&W, like this 637, is somehow easier for Ahern to pick up. That might be attributable to using sights like this since 1967.

Top view of the S&W Model 637's sights.

CHAPTER 16

WOULD YOU BUY A USED HANDGUN FROM THIS MAN?

Ahern's Glock 22 was a reconditioned gun when Ahern acquired it. To look at it or shoot it one would never have suspected it wasn't brand new.

As this is written, Sharon and I are planning on stealing away from the office for a few hours on this coming Sunday to go to a gun show. Now, if, by chance, you're an anti-gunner who just happened to stumble across the book and open it to this chapter, let me assure you that we are not planning on buying a LAW Rocket, a machinegun or a nuclear weapon. Gun shows are nice events where generally nice, law-abiding people get together over a common interest in getting good deals on firearms and

accessories. In fact, if you are an anti-gunner, you should probably close this book right now.

Great deals on great handguns can often be found at gun shows or in gun shops by investigating the used guns that might be languishing there. Depending on the gun and excluding any rarity or special collector value – in other words, an ordinary handgun – if you find the used gun of your dreams and it's in pretty decent shape, you can expect to get it for about three quarters of suggested retail

Like most European police uniform duty handguns, this Walther PP .32 show considerable holster wear but was shot precious little. If you don't mind the holster wear, such guns are a true bargain.

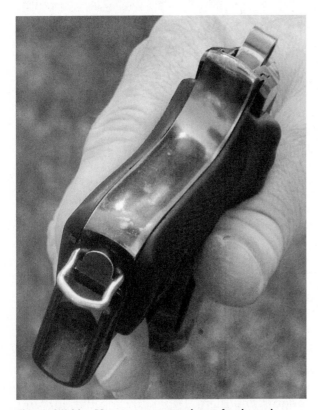

This used Walther PP even sports an attachment for a lanyard.

on that same handgun in brand new out of the box condition. By way of example, let's say you're looking for a handgun that would retail brand new at $600. You find a nice looking used specimen at the local gunshop. Chances are good that your friendly neighborhood gun dealer paid the person from whom he purchased this quality pre-owned handgun $300, which is fifty percent of suggested retail. You'll probably have a good chance of seeing a price tag on that pre-driven handgun that was only used by a little old lady on Sundays that is right around $450. If your dealer traditionally works on narrower margins, he or she may pay less than fifty percent when acquiring the used handgun and/or may lower the price below seventy-five percent of suggested retail. Good for you if you are the buyer of that used handgun.

But, what do you look for when you are considering the purchase of a used handgun? You can't kick the tires. The first thing to do is to look for obvious signs of neglect or abuse or accident. Deep scratches or gouges in the metal surface or the finish can literally mean the gun was banged against a hard surface or dropped. A young man we knew years back who worked in a suburban Chicago gunshop related how he'd broken off the spur on the hammer of his S&W Model 66 2-1/2-incher when his gun came in contact with a toilet. Sharon and I were

This is, apparently, a factory original case for the Colt automatic inside.

Apparently, a cleaning rod came with the cased pistol. The gun itself seems to be in fine shape for what appears to be a Pre-War pistol. Colt .25s – there were several variations – were well-respected little handguns.

burglarized once shortly after we were married, when we both worked out of the house and lived in an apartment. A revolver was stolen, only to be recovered some weeks later during an arrest. The thief had sold the handgun and, when the "customer" was busted, he dropped the revolver to the sidewalk. Another hammer spur bit the dust.

Rust on the exterior of a handgun will sometimes indicate there'll be rust and/or pitting elsewhere, where you can't readily see. Wherever there is rust, no matter how superficial it seems, there will be some pitting. If you find the pitting and no visible rust, look harder. Ask permission of the seller to draw the slide of an automatic pistol rearward or open the cylinder of a revolver. Try to have a bore light of some kind available in order to be able to look inside the barrel for signs of excessive wear, perhaps even the total absence of rifling in a truly older gun. I've had Bolo Mausers with so much of the rifling gone the pistol couldn't print a round on target that wasn't keyholing (the bullet is spinning like a football, thrown by someone who can't throw a football, and hits the target sideways). Use the bore light to look for signs of rust in the barrel as well. If the handgun under scrutiny is a revolver, use the bore light to inspect the charging holes in the cylinder.

If no bore light is available, an ordinary flashlight may help quite a bit. If that's not available, look through the muzzle opening while holding your thumb nail or a business card at the other end in such a manner that your nail will bounce ambient light from an overhead fixture into the barrel. You'll get a pretty good look that way. Again, if a revolver, do the same thing with each charging hole.

If the handgun is a semi-automatic, carefully inspect the magazine to determine that it is original equipment, that the feed lips aren't dented, dinged, beaten up or otherwise showing obvious signs of damage. Check around the base of the pistol butt to see if there's a lot of scratching or finish loss, indicating a lot of rough magazine insertion. Take a pen or pencil and slowly and carefully depress the magazine follower – the elevator on which the cartridges rise to be chambered – and make certain it goes down smoothly and raises up when pressure is released.

Examine the sights for obvious damage and, if they are screw or drift adjustable, make certain, as best you can, that they'll still adjust and aren't a loose fit that will move under recoil.

Hold the semi-automatic handgun up toward the light, looking between the slide and the frame for the telltale sliver of light one can usually see. Make sure that sliver is even throughout its length. Try to jiggle the pistol's slide laterally and see what kind of movement you get. Too much and there may be excessive wear to the frame rails or the slide. Examine the rear of the semi-automatic pistol where the frame and slide interface and look for a relatively smooth match

The Colt .25 even has a diminutive grip safety.

This SIG P6, when sold commercially in the USA known as the 225, was a police turn-in gun , the P6 a popular duty weapon and a fine single column 9X19mm pistol.

– it doesn't have to be bang-on perfect. Make certain, as best you can, that the recoil spring or springs seem to have retained their ability to pop the slide forward smartly. While the slide is open, if you haven't done so already, give what you can see of the interior another look.

Inspect the slide externally, looking most carefully just aft of the ejection port and under and around where a recoil spring guide rod or recoil spring plug emerges. You are looking for telltale cracks which might indicate an improperly heat treated slide or excessive use of over-pressure ammunition – or both. Don't buy a handgun with a cracked slide. Examine what you can see of the portion of the frame in closest contact with the slide for evidence of cracks as well.

If you are buying a revolver, after getting permission to open the cylinder, look immediately at the cylinder bolt, this being located at the lower rear of the frame opening, protruding from the frame as a little bump, longer front to rear than it is wide, but very small. If it looks banged up, you'll probably also find that the notches on the exterior of the cylinder into which this cylinder bolt goes will be worn and damaged looking. Finish loss can be an indicator of ill-treatment. If you find this, it's evidence of someone slapping the cylinder into the closed position or, worse yet, jerking the revolver to the right so the cylinder gets enough momentum to crash into the frame opening. I call this the "Alan Ladd cylinder flick," named

for something which takes place in the classic Bob Hope and Dorothy Lamour comedy mystery, *My Favorite Brunette*. The late, great Mr. Hope, one of our very finest Americans, plays a baby photographer who wants to be a private detective, just like the guy who has the offices on the other side of the hall. That guy is Alan Ladd. Alan Ladd checks his revolver's load. Later, when Bob Hope tries flicking the cylinder of his revolver closed, of course, the cartridges fall out. Whether you get a laugh or not, the cylinder flick is bad for the revolver.

With a revolver, you can convince the firearm that the cylinder is closed and in place by pushing the cylinder release catch in the opposite direction from when you wish to open the cylinder. Then you can cock the weapon and/or pull the trigger. Ask permission of the seller to do this. Many people who consider themselves knowledgeable concerning handguns have an unreasoning fear of dry-snapping a handgun. With a rimfire weapon, this can do damage to the firing pin. With a centerfire, you can pretty much dry snap all you want. But ask and make certain the weapon is pointed in a safe direction. Look for the advancing hand as it moves when the trigger is pulled, the advancing hand found in the rear of the frame opening. Make certain the advancing hand doesn't look damaged and also look at the little nub at the center of the cylinder. The cylinder flick will beat that up as well. The raised surfaces surrounding that nub interact with the advancing hand to

The bluing on this P6 took a beating from holster wear, but the weapon is otherwise in fine shape.

This SIG 229 was acquired as a gently used handgun and looks and works just like Ahern's second 229, which was gotten new.

The Walther P-38 shown here is a police turn-in gun, and was designed and manufactured when full metal case ammunition was the order of the day. This one feeds hollowpoints I've tried with it, but many guns that are European police turn-ins will require getting a gunsmith to do a little work in order to achieve reliable feeding with hollowpoints.

turn the cylinder. Smith & Wesson revolvers rotate counter-clockwise, Colts the other way. If those surfaces look damaged, the cylinder may not rotate properly. Push on the ejector rod, making certain it moves freely rearward with the ejector star and returns to its forward position smoothly. Give the cylinder a couple of good spins. If the cylinder moves sluggishly or not at all, ask the seller to separate the cylinder from the crane and check for excessive fouling or debris. Cleaning that should free the cylinder. If it doesn't, don't buy the handgun. While the cylinder rotates, watch for the ejector rod to wobble. If it does – you guessed it! Don't make the purchase.

Check where the barrel emerges into the frame; this is called the forcing cone. Look for obvious signs of wear. This is especially important if the revolver in question is a .357 Magnum or .44 Magnum, both calibers which will handle their slightly shorter counterparts, the .38 Special and .44 Special. When the shorter rounds are fired – the .38 Special case is one-eighth of an inch shorter than the .357 Magnum – the bullet has a wider gap to jump as it leaves the case mouth and heads for the barrel. Jumping this gap can cause damage to the forcing cone, usually referred to as erosion.

Remember, as mentioned earlier in this chapter, to check the interior diameter of the barrel and the individual charging holes in the cylinder.

Close the cylinder carefully and hold the weapon up to a strong light. Move the revolver until you can see light between the front face of the cylinder and the forcing cone. That means you are pretty much viewing the revolver from the perfect perspective. You should see light on all four sides. These bars of light on the top, bottom and rear should be even from end to end, but not when compared to each other. At the front face of the cylinder, the light showing between the forcing cone and the charging hole in line with it will be a little narrower looking than that at the lower portion of the cylinder.

Honest holster wear – bluing is worn away in spots where the handgun rubbed against a holster, frequently on protruding edges or surfaces of cylinder or slides, or near the muzzle, or on the grip frame, especially at the back strap edges – is just that. It's honest wear and needn't bother you unless you're really hung-up on cosmetics..

There's a certain feeling of liberation in having a used gun that isn't perfect looking when you acquire it – or, at least there is for me. My first handguns were kept so perfectly it's hard for me sometimes to believe I'm the same person. I'm honest enough to admit that I only clean a gun when I feel that I have to. One of America's finest revolversmiths wiped down a revolver only when he was going to show it to somebody or it started to show signs of cylinder rotation slowing up a bit when the cylinder was spun. The advancing hand, by the way, will almost always turn even a stubborn cylinder – until you get to the point where you damage the advancing hand. Give me a dirty handgun any day of the week and some blue wear here and there. It's just character, showing the "patina of use." That's also a great way to excuse my own laziness when it comes to any sort of gun cleaning!

CHAPTER 17

DERRINGERS

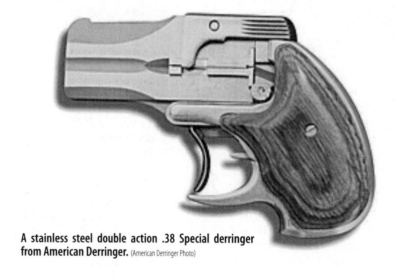

A stainless steel double action .38 Special derringer from American Derringer. (American Derringer Photo)

Sharon has come to really like handguns over the years, even carries one on a regular basis without my having to nag her to do so. But there's one handgun type Sharon just does not like. That's the derringer. As mentioned earlier in this book, the derringer as a type derives its name from Philadelphia gunmaker Henry Deringer (with one "r") and the name with the double "r" became the generic term for small, hideaway handguns, usually with only one or two shot capability before reloading. In the 19th century and, as reproductions, in the 20th century, there have been four barrel "pepperbox" pistols, which are derringers, and in the 20th century there was the COP Pistol (Compact Off-duty Police) from COP, Inc./M&N Distributors of Torrance, California. It was a four barrel weapon as well, but in .357 Magnum and .38 Special. There was also a .22 Magnum version, but that came later.

What appears to be a duplicate of or very similar to the old High Standard Derringer, this .22 Magnum derringer is from American Derringer. (American Derringer Photo)

American Derringer offers various styles of its basic derring, this one nicely engraved. (American Derringer Photo)

American Derringer offers this little .25 auto, but the principal product is the Model 1 in .45 Colt/.410. (American Derringer Photo)

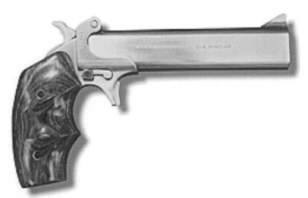

Not all of American Derringer's guns are small. This one is a long barreled .45 Colt/.410. (American derringer Photo)

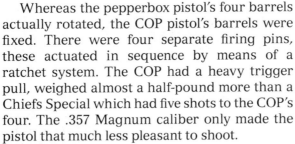

American derringer's most popular gun is the standard sized .45 Colt/.410. (American Derringer Photo)

Whereas the pepperbox pistol's four barrels actually rotated, the COP pistol's barrels were fixed. There were four separate firing pins, these actuated in sequence by means of a ratchet system. The COP had a heavy trigger pull, weighed almost a half-pound more than a Chiefs Special which had five shots to the COP's four. The .357 Magnum caliber only made the pistol that much less pleasant to shoot.

Technically, the COP is a derringer, in the broad sense of the term, and discussing this never very popular handgun is a good way to anchor a discussion on derringers. You may very well have seen a COP pistol in action – in the movies. The COP was the basis for the handgun used by Harrison Ford in the 1982 science fiction film *Blade Runner*. And, if you were a fan of *The Man From U.N.C.L.E.* and you saw the made for TV 1983 reunion movie, *The Fifteen Years Later Affair,* the rocket firing pistol Robert Vaughn's character was issued

was, in reality, a COP. With .357 Magnum loads, it just felt like you were firing a rocket.

The COP was one of several variations of hideout handguns for which my old friend and one-time co-worker, the late Bob Saunders,

Left profile shot of Bond Arms Derringer showing standard grips dismounted from the gun and oversized grips in place. Empty brass from two separate calibers is shown, .38 Special and .45 Colt.

The barrel latch swings downward and forward so the barrel can swing upward.

Note the position of the hammer and the cross bolt safety which is the large round piece near the hammer.

If you wish to remove the trigger guard so your Bond Arms Derringer has a more traditional look, this screw can be turned out and the trigger guard removed. Reverse the procedure to reinstall the trigger guard.

acquired the rights to manufacture. Bob's first acquisition was what became the American Derringer Model 1. This is a classic over/under derringer of the Remington pattern, but larger. The original guns from the original maker came out in .38 Special and the sample I examined was far from beautiful. Bob saw the potential and used the same design, but offered variations in barrel lengths and, more importantly, a list of calibers longer than your arm. You could still have .38 Special, but you could also have .45-70 or .223 or whatever. I carried one for a number of years in .45 Colt and .410, the best combination – for me – of effective caliber and manageable recoil. As another old friend who has since passed away, Dave Arnold, first alerted me to, when you have a chamber long enough to handle the .410 shotshell and fire a .45 Long Colt instead, you are taking advantage of what's called the "freebore effect," the projectile traveling a bit before entering the rifling, thereby somewhat reducing the perceived recoil.

Bob Saunders' widow, Elizabeth, still produces the American Derringer pistols and they are great looking and quite well made. Bob, however, did not stop with the American Derringer derringers, nor with the COP .357 Magnum. He also offered the COP in .22 Magnum – much more sensible for the style of handgun it was. He acquired the rights to manufacture the Phil Lichtman-designed Semmerling pistol,

a magazine fed .45 that looks like an automatic but is actually hand-cycled. You have to push the slide forward – yes, forward – to shuck the empty and draw rearward to pick up the fresh round. I've never fired one. Bob also picked up on a derringer which was very reminiscent of the High Standard Derringer, but made from stainless steel and chambered in .38 Special. It was a double action. I always thought the gun had a great deal of potential. Bob was also going to offer a single shot pistol in the shape of a writing instrument. Apparently, the Feds discouraged him from selling a pen pistol, although others have made such designs.

The High Standard Derringer mentioned above was a quite popular handgun in its day and, if someone were making it still, it's likely it would have remained popular. Two calibers were offered, .22 Long Rifle and .22 Magnum chambering. I was given one as a gift years ago. It's a .22 Magnum.

One of the most potentially versatile derringers I ever had was from the fine old firm of F.I.E., which stood for Firearms Import Export. They made a really inexpensive .38 Special Remington pattern over/under. I had the gun for a number of years and it worked just fine. The interesting thing was that I'd had two sets of insert barrels made up, one set in .25 ACP and another in .22 Long Rifle, these latter with caps that were positioned over the case

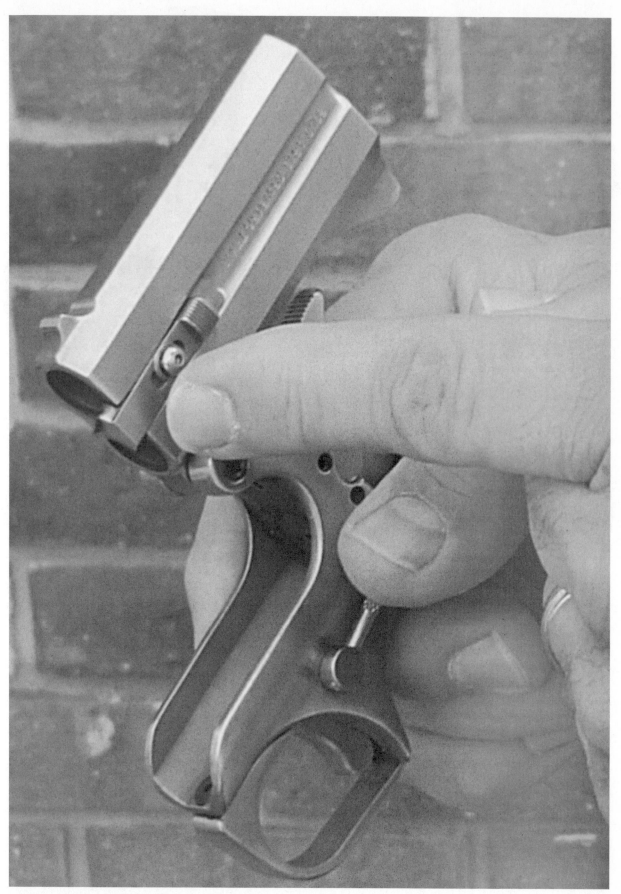

The ejector for the Bond Arms Derringer works quite well.

Swapping calibers with the Bond Arms Derringers is easy. Bond Arms Derringers have been very successful in Cowboy Action Shooting and are very well made personal defense guns.

A Cobra derringer, broken open for loading or unloading.

A stainless steel .38 Special American Derringer with scrimshawed grips, designed for women. (American Derringer Photo)

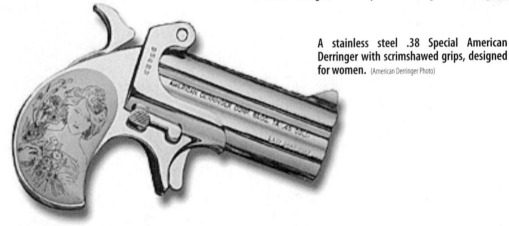

head so the centerfire firing pin would strike the cap, the other side of which had a rimfire firing pin built in.

Cobra makes some diminutive derringers that are nice little concealment guns because of their size. For some reason, the guns have a "ventilated" rib along the top, like the old Colt Pythons had. Smaller than the competition, one of these could be very handy in .32 ACP, for example.

Bond Arms offers stainless steel over/under derringers in a variety of calibers and barrel lengths, but also offers their derringers with a removable trigger guard. The idea of this is that you may wish to have the trigger guard in place for regular use. If you just wish the traditional

look or need the traditional look for cowboy action shooting competition, the trigger guard is easily removed and re-installed, as you wish. The barrel sets are interchangeable within the centerfire calibers Bond Arms offers and swapping barrel sets is very simple. I recently tested one of the Bond Arms derringers in .45/.410 and swapped to a .38 Special set with absolutely no difficulty.

Many modern derringers feature some type of safety system which must be manually "offed" or will automatically disengage when you cock the hammer. To my knowledge, no double action derringers – like the old High Standard – are currently in production, as this is written. That could change, of course.

CHAPTER 18

USE OF MULTIPLE CONCEALED WEAPONS

The H.G. Long Lapel Dagger and sheath was a concealed weapon for Allied Agents during World War II, and it's still a good concealed weapon if you wear a suit or sportcoat regularly. This is a perfect duplicate of the original.

In the old, old, old western movies, you'd sometimes see the white-hat wearing good guy draw both pearl-handled six-shooters and use them at once, but rarely firing both revolvers simultaneously, rather keeping up a steady stream of gunfire by alternating one revolver with the other. Very few people are truly ambidextrous, however, and a second handgun isn't normally carried so that both weapons can be used at once. Even in the days of the real old west, those who carried a second handgun – even a matched pair of 1851 Navy Colt revolvers, like Wild Bill Hickok carried – rarely fought with both guns blazing. Few people were good enough or took the time to learn the techniques needed. If you have a weapon in each hand, these days, you won't be able to shoot the way you shoot when you practice, namely using both hands.

Indeed, two-gun simultaneous use is all but

In order to maximize on concealed weapons options, one needs to "celebrate diversity," as they say. Clockwise from left, a SIG-Sauer P229 .40 with Crimson Trace LaserGrips, a similarly equipped NAA Guardian .380, two spare twelve-round magazines for the SIG, a Benchmade Presidio knife and, at center, a SureFire Backup tactical light.

obviated by the passion modern shooters have to grasp a handgun with both hands before shooting. You see it on television all the time, as well as in the movies. The good guy is in some dangerous situation and he holds the handgun extended at both arms' length as if his hands were glued together and his elbow joints had locked. I call this the "'Miami Vice' Water Witching Pose." Sharon and I liked *Miami Vice,* but you don't put your gun into a room at maximum extension of your arms, just inviting your adversary, who may be standing just out of view, to knock the gun out of your hands. You keep the handgun as close to your body as possible, so you can protect it long enough for it to protect you. I'm sure I'm possibly upsetting people who use this sort of isosceles stance and hold all the time and maybe even teach it. But, if I am going to use both hands on the gun, I want a Weaver position, so I can draw the gun back toward my center of mass as I do things like go through doorways, then push the gun outward when I know I'm clear.

The Blackhawk! Products Be-Warned is not a conventional looking folding knife, but it's a good one.

I've written articles from time to time dealing with the practice of two gun shooting and, of course, two gun shooting is the best way to force yourself to practice two skills vital in the real world. First, you really need to master shooting with your non-master hand. Try it two-handed, of course, for shooting around barricades that happen to be oriented improperly to your handedness. But, practice it one-handed. The reason is simple. The whole idea of being able to shoot reasonably well with your non-master hand is so you'll be able to stay in the fight, should your master hand be incapacitated.

Something doesn't have to be a weapon to be used as a weapon. The seatbelt cutting tool from Boker Plus is a perfect example.

What will hook over and cut a seatbelt only requires some imagination for use in other ways.

When you practice two gun shooting, you're achieving proficiency in three skills. First, you'll learn how to actually use two guns at the same time, should the unlikely need arise. Second, you'll be developing one-handed shooting skills. Third, you'll be improving your non-master hand shooting skills. Before you can start training, however, you must decide how your two guns will be carried. And, one of them, at least, needs to be accessible with either hand. For example, with the pistol I carry in a front pocket of my trousers, should the hand on that side of my body become useless temporarily, there's no way in which I can reach around with my other hand with any degree of speed or fluidity and conveniently get into that pocket in order to draw the gun. And, despite my age, I'm still a pretty flexible guy. If I am carrying a handgun strongside while walking around, I'll shift the holstered handgun to my left side while I'm driving. If the holster doesn't come off too easily, and the firearm is of a type which can be safely thrust into the waistband sans holster, I'll put the gun inside my trouser waistband.

The practice technique most appropriate to two gun shooting is to point both handguns downrange and raise and fire first one, then the other, repeating and repeating until the loads in each weapon are exhausted. This is for practice only. In that unlikely event of having to use both handguns in such a manner in an actual armed confrontation, you wouldn't shoot both guns empty. What are you supposed to do then? You would use what firepower you had to get yourself to a position of cover. After partially emptying one handgun, circumstances permitting, it should be reloaded. Don't teach yourself the habit of casting aside partially spent magazines. In an actual fight, you might very well wish you had those three or four rounds from the magazine that's no longer under your control. "Waste not, want not," as the old aphorism goes.

If the guns you are using are not a matched pair – and, rarely would they be – don't always shoot handgun "A" with your right hand and handgun "B" with the left hand. Switch the handguns around so that you become familiar with shooting two quite different handguns from the master hand and non-master hand.

While you are at it, practice reloading with the non-master hand. In the days when I occasionally carried two Detonics CombatMasters, I taught myself how to manipulate the standard single sided thumb safety with the trigger finger of my left hand. The slide stop can be worked that way, too, but requires more finger strength.

I have solved that problem by making certain that one handgun will be available to both hands, when possible. When this is not

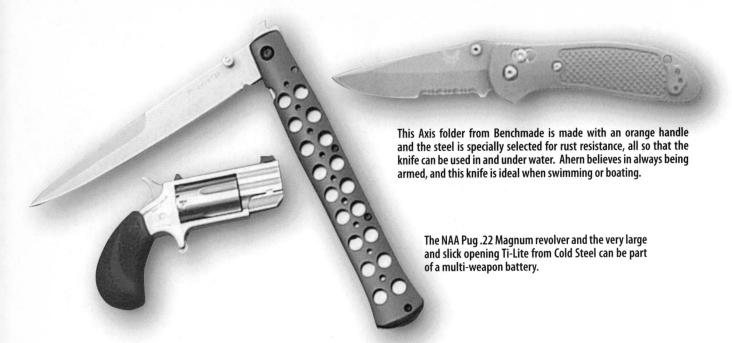

This Axis folder from Benchmade is made with an orange handle and the steel is specially selected for rust resistance, all so that the knife can be used in and under water. Ahern believes in always being armed, and this knife is ideal when swimming or boating.

The NAA Pug .22 Magnum revolver and the very large and slick opening Ti-Lite from Cold Steel can be part of a multi-weapon battery.

possible, I'm careful to have a weapon available to each hand. As Sharon and I were coming home from some errands today, my cellular phone started vibrating. I was wearing a pair of Woolrich Elite Series Tactical Lightweight Operator Pants. I like the comfort and all the pockets. My cellular phone was in the right thigh pocket, just below the actual front pocket. I'm driving along and trying to rip the hook and loop closured pocket flap open and dig into the pocket and get the phone before it stopped ringing. I made it, handing the phone to Sharon. It was an important call from our son, saving us a long and largely useless trip into Atlanta proper. But the experience made me think, once again, about how awkward it is to get to a pocket carried gun while driving and wearing a seat belt. When we next got into the car, I decided that I'd be smart and give Sharon the phone, lest we get another call. As this is written, a close relative is recovering nicely from major surgery, but we didn't want to miss a call. So, I'm digging out the telephone again. I had to take off my seatbelt for a moment just to get at it this time. Imagine what it would have been like had I been desperately trying to access a strongside carried handgun from my right side while strapped into the driver's seat! The delay while groping for that handgun would have been fatal and I don't kid myself that it wouldn't have been.

I have solved the dilemma of handgun access while seated behind the wheel of an automobile. If I am driving and anticipate the need for a weapon while driving – remember, these days, I live rural, in a pretty safe area – I carry a weapon on my left side that I can either conveniently access with my right hand or get at easily with my left hand. So, let's say I'm armed with my trusty old Seecamp .32 in my well worn Pocket Natural front pocket holster, in my right pocket, and one of my full-size or compact semiautomatic pistols or even a revolver, this carried elsewhere. That other handgun is going to be carried crossdraw, just forward or just aft of my left hip bone, butt forward, of course. That way, I can reach the larger handgun with either hand, as the situation requires, and I'm clear of the seatbelt. When a handgun is worn in a classic strongside position, for a right-handed person driving an American car with the steering wheel on the left side of the vehicle, reaching around behind one's body and getting past the seatbelt in order to grab the handgun is very close to impossible, if one expects any degree of speed on a reliable basis.

While developing the ability to use your guns with both hands, remember that the off-hand is not as accustomed to drawing and re-holstering safely as is the master hand. Be extra conscious about safety with all aspects of developing this skillset.

CHAPTER 19

MEDICAL MALADIES ASSOCIATED WITH CONCEALED WEAPONS

The reason we acquire, train with and carry concealed weapons in the first place is to ward off death or injury at the hands of an attacker. But sometimes the "injury" part can come about because we habitually carry concealed weapons. Does this mean you should stop? Hardly, but it does suggest that you may want to vary where and how you carry.

Let's start with a very simple and basic malady about which you've likely never heard – unless you wear a shoulder holster with a crossover strap that passes under the gunhand side armpit and you have a bit of bad luck. A furuncle is a bacterial infection of a hair follicle. A cluster of these is known as a carbuncle. To fight off this infection, the body walls it off, much like a coffer dam. The dammed area is

an abscess. A reddish lump is formed that is severely painful to the touch. Although carbuncles can be precipitated by other factors, all that would be needed to get one going in the context of carrying a concealed weapon is for the crossover piece of your shoulder holster to rub the seam of your shirt against the area where some particle from the shirt or some other foreign object transfers bacteria to one or more follicles of underarm hair. Although warm compresses can help, you'll usually need to see a doctor in order to have the resultant abscess lanced and drained. Antibiotics may or may not need to be administered.

The sheer weight of the handgun itself is often the problem.

We hear the term "ergonomic" used to

describe the design for a handgun's grip or something similar, but ergonomics is a complex study that investigates and, of course, tries to prevent activity related muscle strain and pain. Over the summer of 2009 while I was doing some stretching exercises with my legs, I zigged when I should have zagged apparently and pulled a ligament in the back of my left leg. The result was that I actually had to go to my doctor and get a prescription for anti-inflammatory medication. The condition went away. As this is written, it may be coming back. Muscle strain or cramping can be associated with any part of the body and it is the result of muscle fatigue or abuse of the muscle. If you suffer muscle strain and have no idea why, it is probably because of some normal activity that you perform in slightly the wrong way. Damage your muscle sufficiently and you can experience more than discomfort. There can be bruising and even internal bleeding. If you are about to embark upon a serious shooting regimen or will begin to carry a firearm that is much more than a pound and a quarter or a pound and a half on a regular basis, you should realize that, like any other physically demanding activity, the better your overall muscle tone, the better you will be at the activity and the better you will feel during and afterward.

Tai-Chi exercises are excellent for limbering up and warming up before engaging in a physical activity or simply for overall good health. The more physically strong you are and the better toned your muscles – man or woman – the better your body will be able to take perceived recoil comfortably and the more steady your aim is likely to be. But, in the same spirit of the fickle finger of fate with the carbuncle, there are some things you can do to yourself for which no amount of physical training will help or guard against.

When wearing a shoulder holster, it is imperative that the harness not be positioned in such a manner that the weight of the gun, spare ammunition and the holster unit sits on your neck. When one wears a balanced shoulder rig, wherein the gun is on one side and two spare magazines and maybe a cuff case are located on the other side and the two sides of the harness are joined by a coupler of some sort, as one finds in shoulder rigs from Galco, DeSantis and others, the rig should be comfortable. The weight should be suspended from your shoulders. If the coupler is sitting right where your neck joins your torso, the weight is on the neck instead. This, at the least, will be uncomfortable and may well bring on headaches because the muscles at this location will tense up and blood flow may be restricted. The solution, of course, is to wear the holster rig properly, adjusting it so that the coupler is at least three fingers below the bottom edge of your shirt collar.

If you regularly carry a substantial handgun of any kind in an ankle holster, you are placing undue strain on ligaments, muscle and cartilage in the subject leg. You may also risk some spinal complications because of the weight factor – one side is regularly a pound and a half or two pounds heavier than the other. This is why, normally, although I have in the past and probably will in the future carry something as heavy as a Detonics CombatMaster in an ankle holster, I normally recommend nothing heavier than a J-Frame Smith & Wesson. One of my very best friends carried an alloy framed SIG 230 .380 in an ankle holster for years and years and finally had to stop because of leg problems.

Moving right along, carrying a heavy object on one side of your body, day in and day out, other than on your leg, is a terrific way in which to do spinal damage, the most frequently presented symptom being an aching back.

The worst possible place, from a standpoint of doing damage to your body, for you to carry a handgun of any substantial size is over the spine. The damage you can do can prove severe. Consider several factors, from the mundane to the opposite extreme. You are seated at least for part of the day, or may have an occupation which requires you to be seated much of the day, like a truck driver or cab driver. As you lean back, that gun is going to be pressed against your spine. It's not comfortable at all. Press against the spine log enough and hard enough and discomfort can turn to damage.

Similarly, if you have a handgun of any size over the small of your back and you should take a fall, whether by accident or during a fight, your gun will be impacting your spinal column. Even if you have a gun with a polymer frame, the polymer frame is rigid and the slide is still steel and the handgun will still possibly hurt you. If the gun is worn to the right or left of the spine, again depending on just where the gun is positioned, you might bruise a kidney.

When you aren't wearing the handgun, but you're holding it in your hand or hands while firing, depending on the handgun's weight and the caliber and the frequency with which you shoot, you run the risk of damaging some of the smaller bones in your hand or damaging your wrist or even your elbow. I have fired intensely recoiling small handguns in the course of earning the portion of my living derived from firearms related writing. I do what I have to do in order to fairly and accurately report test results and the like. I do not go out of my way to try to see how hairy chested I am. I fire .45 autos large and small. .357 Magnums and .357 SIGs are fine, too. I used to shoot a goodly amount of .44 Magnum and I may do so again. I fire hot .45 Long Colt loads out of my Cimarron Arms single action. And so on. All of my handguns are steel framed, except for a couple of semi-autos which are polymer framed. That's just me. I am not terribly recoil sensitive in my hands, which doesn't mean I'll go out of my way to fire the biggest and baddest recoiling handguns there are, nor will I avoid them should shooting them be necessary. Years ago, I knew a young man who was a bullseye champion shooter. He was about 25, and he could probably have outshot a Ransom Rest. He could cloverleaf an unmodified production DA .45 all day long with such consistency that it was almost boring. The pistol never moved when he triggered off a hardball round or a high speed hollow point. He confided to me that his doctor had warned him that he should stop shooting because he had already mutilated several of the bones in his right hand. He was in his mid-twenties. How great were his hands going to feel or function by the time he was in his forties or fifties? So, you don't fight the recoil quite as much; maybe your group size expands a quarter inch or so and you can still use your hands when you're older.

Am I saying you shouldn't wear your gun this way or shoot that kind of handgun? Not at all. If weight of the revolver you carry, for example, is all that important, if the budget allows, get one with a steel or aluminum alloy frame and the essentially identical handgun with the super light weight frame. Shoot the super light handgun enough to know that it functions reliably and will work for you should you need it in order to save your life or the life of an innocent. Then, practice with the steel or alloy

framed gun so you can get really good with it. In the middle of an adrenalin rush, the practice has a good chance of carrying over to the very similar, lighter weight handgun. Anyway, that's what I would do if I wanted a super light revolver for carry, which I don't.

What about small of the back carry or similar? Well, when you think about it, although lots of fine holsters are made for that application and it is convenient, small of the back carry really doesn't conceal that well at all. When you reach for something above you, a short jacket will pull up and display the handgun. When you bend over or stand up, your jacket or other covering garment will likely pull pretty tightly over the gun butt, so you'll be advertising that you are carrying. Under some circumstances, however, that carry may be just the thing.

There's a great deal to consider when it comes to muscle memory, as the phrase goes. There is a serious school of thought that holds that, during a crisis, if you carry your weaponry in different locations you may not remember where you have the gun and you'll reach uselessly for a gun on your right hip when, today, it happens to be holstered in a diagonal shoulder rig under your left arm. I'm not going to say that is good or bad advice, although there's probably a great deal of good sense to that way of thinking. However, bone damage and the like cannot conveniently be undone, if at all.

My lifestyle does not allow me to carry a handgun in exactly the same spot all the time. Different kinds of handguns carry differently, anyway. Someday, God forbid, I may rue the decision to sometimes carry crossdraw, sometimes strongside, using different holsters and the like. I hope I don't. But I never wanted to rue the day that I decided to give myself chronic back trouble because I just have to carry in that one certain way no matter what the consequences, especially considering that, in this age of the automobile, what might be the best carry while walking around is downright unmanageable while one is seated because the handgun cannot be accessed with any degree of speed or reliability. Hopefully my muscle memory will prove it can "think on my feet!"

CHAPTER 20

"GUNS ARE LOADED, KNIVES ARE SHARP; DON'T TOUCH"

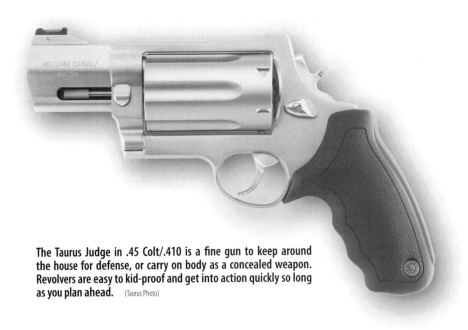

The Taurus Judge in .45 Colt/.410 is a fine gun to keep around the house for defense, or carry on body as a concealed weapon. Revolvers are easy to kid-proof and get into action quickly so long as you plan ahead. (Taurus Photo)

Sharon and I have two adult children, a son and a daughter. When they were little, we always had guns and knives around because working with guns and knives, whether in association with our novels or my articles and columns, was just what we did. Our children knew better than to touch a gun or a knife without adult supervision, but you can't rely on other people's children.

If you go armed on a regular basis, and you want that security in your home, the only way to do it if you have children or untrained adults in the environment is to carry the gun and not

The Taurus 709Slim is an outstanding little 9mm, this one with a slide in natural stainless finish. To kid-proof one idea might be to place the pistol empty in a spot where only an adult can reach it, lock up all the ammo except one or two magazines which you keep on your person, loaded and ready to go. Either that, or wear the gun loaded and ready to go or get a biometric security container for quick access. (Taurus Photo)

set it "somewhere safe." Children and cats have in common both curiosity and the uncanny ability to climb onto or get into things you would have thought impossible.

Whenever our son or daughter had friends come over, after greeting them, I issued that warning: "Guns are loaded, knives are sharp; don't touch! If you want to see something, ask." That was the same philosophy we used with our children. On those rare occasions when one of ours or a visiting child actually wanted to see a rifle or handgun or knife, Sharon and/or I would stop what we were doing and supervise the safe investigation of the weapon in question. Just like you are supposed to do, we stored guns and ammunition separately and locked away, except for a few weapons secreted around the house for immediate emergency use. These were artfully hidden and entirely impossible for anyone to get at.

We started our son shooting centerfire handguns at age five, our daughter – smaller – at age seven. They knew what guns would

do. As our children got older (and so did we!), if we'd go out for ten minutes, to rent a videotape movie or pick up a bottle of wine or a jug of milk, we'd leave a handgun that both children knew how to use out and available, telling our son, "If somebody breaks in, you shoot him."

Am I recommending you do this? Not at all. It worked well with our son and daughter because they were always exceptionally mature, looked at weapons as being as natural a thing to have around as a sofa or a coffee table and we were with them seven days a week, because Sharon and I were blessed to be able to work from home. We both saw both of our children take their first steps.

If you carry a concealed weapon and you take it off but want to leave it loaded, depending on the age and height and temperament of your child or children, the top of the refrigerator is a pretty good place for short term use while you're in the same room. Otherwise, it's on body or empty.

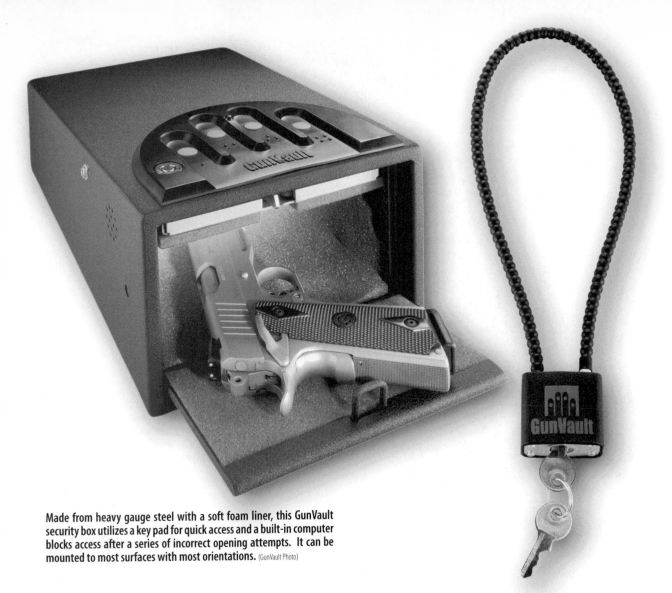

Made from heavy gauge steel with a soft foam liner, this GunVault security box utilizes a key pad for quick access and a built-in computer blocks access after a series of incorrect opening attempts. It can be mounted to most surfaces with most orientations. (GunVault Photo)

This "gunlock" is from GunVault and is typical of the look of these bicycle style locks which, when properly applied, can help to kid-proof a gun. Emphasis on properly applied. (GunVault Photo)

When you are storing concealed carry handguns that you want sort of ready but must keep safely away from kids, here are some things you can do. Buy yourself a pair of handcuffs. The potential for recreational use aside, handcuffs – get the good Smith & Wesson kind, like those sold in police equipment stores – are a terrific way to secure a handgun. When you take off your gun, you can empty the weapon and lock one shackle to the handgun and the other shackle to something extremely sturdy. Use your imagination.

The best handguns for this application are revolvers. When you open the cylinder of a revolver, you have the frame cut out as a natural spot for one of the shackles. Close the shackle around the frame top strap. Then, carry a speed loader or Bianchi Speed Strip in a pocket along with a key ring with a cuff key on it. I read the account of a man who stashed four-inch K-Frame Smith & Wesson police turn-in revolvers in various spots around his house. They were all .38s or .357s, so a speedloader or Speed Strip loaded with .38s would work just great in any of the handguns. If the man had children about, he could cuff each of the revolvers, but would only need one key. Unlike the handcuff key silliness shown so often in movies, unless you are using maximum security handcuffs or some off- or foreign-made brand, the keys are identical and one key will open any standard, American handcuff. Obviously, check that your key will open each set of cuffs reliably, if you use this method, before locking the cuffs onto a handgun and having to say, "Oops!" in the event of a home invasion.

This full size safe from GunVault offers secure storage, fire-resistance and a quick to use keypad entry with audio feedback. (GunVault Photo)

long. If you utilize such locks, make sure these keys work as well and familiarize yourself with working them in a hurry.

Today, there are wall safe units that are hidden behind paintings. There are biometric safes which will only open for you. There are small safes and larger ones that can open almost instantly via key pad combinations. Hollowed out books work great for hiding snubby revolvers and medium frame semi-automatics and small frame autos, as well. Years ago, I encountered a firm that offered hollowed out encyclopedia sets for hiding rifles and shotguns. You'll give the impression of being extremely well-read while hiding your guns at the same time!

And, of course, there are always the locks which come with most handguns, unless the handguns have built-in locks like those found in Taurus and Smith & Wesson products. If you have an older firearm and it didn't come with a lock and you really want one, for a medium size handgun, you'll want a bicycle lock that will have a plastic covered shackle about eighteen inches

If children or less than responsible adults are definitely not in the picture, you have considerably more latitude in hiding your guns. When I'm working during the day, aside from the handgun in my pocket and the handgun a few paces down the hall in either direction, there's a loaded handgun on one of our desks. When the grandchildren come over, everything

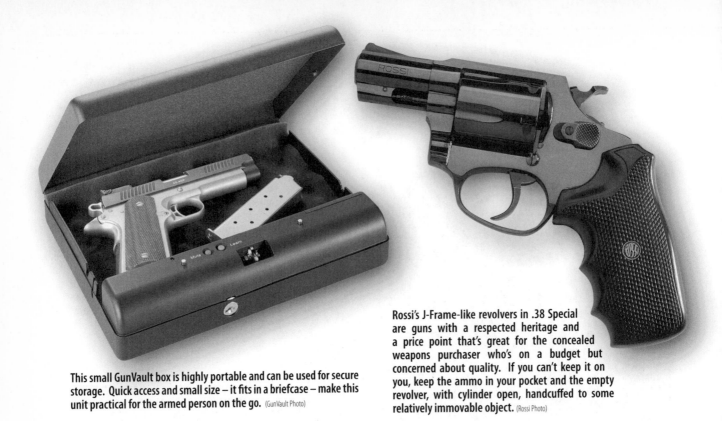

This small GunVault box is highly portable and can be used for secure storage. Quick access and small size – it fits in a briefcase – make this unit practical for the armed person on the go. (GunVault Photo)

Rossi's J-Frame-like revolvers in .38 Special are guns with a respected heritage and a price point that's great for the concealed weapons purchaser who's on a budget but concerned about quality. If you can't keep it on you, keep the ammo in your pocket and the empty revolver, with cylinder open, handcuffed to some relatively immovable object. (Rossi Photo)

goes away securely, except for the handgun I'm wearing and a handgun located out of reach of all of the kids, except the thirteen-year-old, who isn't a problem. Not only do Sharon and I have to see to the firearms, but the swords, too. As some readers may know, in addition to my columns in gun publications, I write a column in the bimonthly magazine *Knives Illustrated,* which means I've always got modern reproductions of older swords and daggers around, all of these blades as sharp as if we were readying ourselves against an attack by angry Vikings who'd sworn a blood oath against us.

On body or locked is the general rule when children or other unauthorized persons are around. When such persons are not around, if you are particularly security aware (read as "paranoid"), as are we, have a few strategically placed weapons and leave the rest safely away. In the event those Vikings really do come, there's a limit to how many weapons you can successfully handle at once or in rapid succession.

CHAPTER 21

CLOTHING CONSIDERATIONS

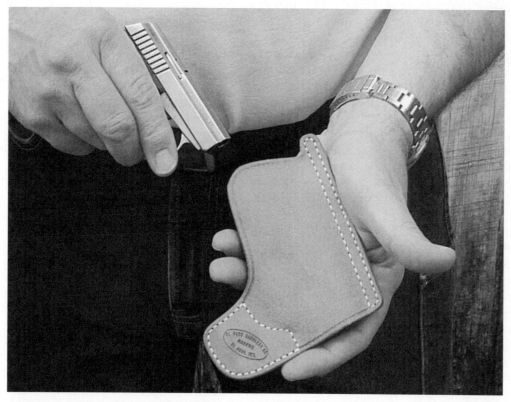

A Seecamp in a well-designed pocket holster like this one from El Paso Saddlery will conceal in anything from shorts to blue jeans to a tuxedo – Ahern has tried all three.

Ever since Gene DeSantis invented the fanny pack style of concealed weapons holster, if you observe someone wearing a fanny pack, these days, no matter who the person is, the thought has to at least cross your mind that the wearer – even if the fanny pack is pink and the wearer is some sweet little old lady who looks like "Granny" from the Warner Brothers cartoons – is armed. This carry system was designed to obviate conventional concealment requirements. There are, however, other things you can do. And, I'm not talking about changing your style of clothing or dressing inappropriately to the temperature or social conditions.

Rather than changing your style of clothing in order to mask your armed condition, adapt the armed condition to how you would normally dress. Sounds like an aphorism, doesn't it? In an earlier period of my life, I wore a suit and tie six days a week at least. With sport clothes, I often wore a bush jacket, when bush jackets were quite commonly seen. Such clothing lends itself well to hiding a gun, of course. But living in the oft-times steamy South and answering to no one's dress code save my own for the last thirty plus years, I rarely wear a suit and tie. If it's cool enough or even cold in the morning, almost invariably it warms up enough in the afternoon that, much of the time, even in the winter, it may even be too warm for one of my Woolrich Elite Series Tactical Algerian Field Jackets. For seven or eight months a year, I almost never wear any kind of jacket at all, unless it's raining. As I write this, however, in all fairness, I must mention that the blower on our heating system went out and we're waiting for the repairman's arrival with a replacement unit. So I'm freezing my you-know-what off, I'm "field testing" my Woolrich Elite Polyester Fleece Jacket as my hands fly over the keyboard. It's a good, warm jacket with zip closure side pockets which have elastic bands inside to secure magazines or even small handguns. It can be worn by itself or layered under the Woolrich Elite Series Tactical Waterproof Parka I used throughout the winter of 09/10, an exceptionally cold and wet winter for Georgia – global warming theories notwithstanding.

To carry a fighting handgun when wearing just a shirt and slacks or shorts, you must determine on body position very carefully, keeping in mind the type of carry (holstered or holsterless) and always mindful of safety considerations. It should be noted before proceeding that concealed carry permits may carry with them a caveat for how the weapon is to be lawfully carried, i.e., a holster must be employed, ankle holsters are prohibited, etc. When we first moved to Georgia, I was quite impressed that my old favorite Barami Hip-Grips were written into Georgia concealed carry law.

There are holsters available from several makers which allow inside waistband carry beneath a shirt tucked into the trousers. The system was a long time coming, but is deceptively simple. A standard inside holster of rigid leather is built with no attachment system at or near the holster lip. Rather, a shank rises from the toe of the holster, its upper end attaching to the trouser belt. The shirt is tucked between the holster and the shank, the shirt tail drawn up in order to access the gun. The Galco SkyOps, mentioned earlier, is of this general type.

An alternative method, but only if carrying crossdraw, is to open the shirt enough so that the gunhand can be slipped inside to accomplish the draw. Unless wearing a snap front cowboy shirt, this latter technique can be time consuming. It has been recommended by others that shirts be specially equipped with hook and loop closures (i.e., velcro), the button(s) in question sewn into the button hole(s) to match the appearance of being closed. The hook and loop material actually keeps the shirt together. There is nothing wrong with this practice; but, unless one only rotates through a half-dozen-or-so shirts, there is an awful lot of sewing involved.

This technique with the rip-away shirt front – the entire shirt front – has also been recommended for use with a shoulder rig. The idea is to carry a diagonal shoulder holster underneath a loose fitting shirt and merely rip the shirt open to get at the gun. In my opinion, this is hardly concealable. An upside-down shoulder rig, like those offered by Ken Null for snubby revolvers, can work well under a loose shirt or sweatshirt, but anything larger quite probably will not. Unless the diagonal shoulder rig is adjusted to a nearly upside-down position – as one can do with the Galco original Jackass shoulder rig – the muzzle of the gun is quite likely to protrude from behind the arm. And, honestly, using this carry method would also mandate wearing a T-shirt underneath the shirt – something I never did even during Chicago winters years ago – and the shirt itself would have to be of heavy fabric, too heavy for Georgia summers. As my writings likely reveal, I like to be comfortable and am not a great fan of hot days.

The inside waistband carry, crossdraw or strongside, when utilizing one of the inside waistband holsters designed to be worn with the shirt tucked in, can be quite effective indeed, especially if the belt which supports the holster is of the same color and texture of leather as the tab which secures certain of these holsters to the belt.

The attachment tab itself is the only potential giveaway with this style of holster, if the rig is worn correctly. The experienced eye is quite likely to spot this tab. One way around this, of course, is to go holsterless. There are cautions to consider. First, it may or may not be legal under the conditions of your permit to carry. Second, carrying holsterless is not as safe as carrying with a holster, or at least some other means of support for the gun, other than mere friction.

The best holsterless carry in the world is the Barami Hip-Grip, the praises of which I

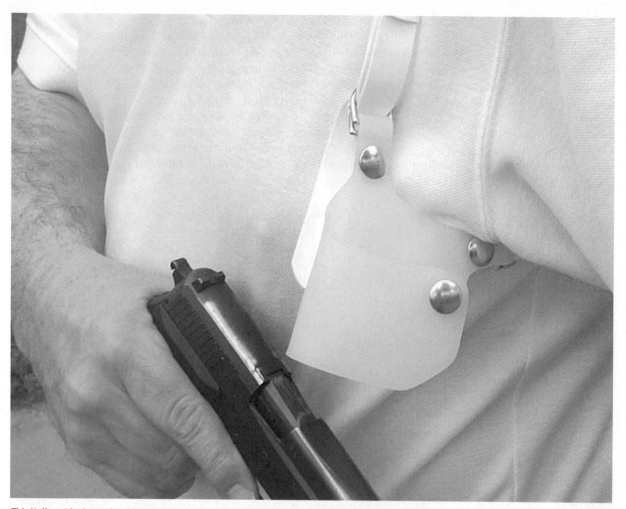

This Null upside down shoulder rig works with a SIG P6 (225) when worn under loose or baggy clothing.

sing relentlessly. It is still available for J-Frame (round or square butt) and K-Frame (round or square butt) Smith & Wessons, Charters, certain Taurus and Rossi revolvers and Colt Detective Specials and Cobras (but not in the color black for these latter; only off-white). A shelf-like hook extends from the right plate of these replacement grips. Wear the gun strongside or crossdraw merely by slipping it inside your waistband, the hook portion of the right grip going over the waistband, with or without a belt. It is possible to wear a Hip-Grip fitted revolver underneath one's tucked in shirt, merely by letting the portion of the Hip-Grip which hooks over the belt hook over a little bit of the shirt, too. My old friend, author, antiques expert and holster manufacturer (Lawman Leather), Jerry Ardolino, had told me that when he used to be a Chicago cop, he would sometimes use a Hip-Gripped revolver without masking over the Hip-Grip. Depending on the fabric of one's shirt, it might not be noticed at all.

If you can live with a two- or three-inch barrel revolver, it's hard to beat the Hip-Grip for convenience and comfort with terrific concealment.

I make considerable mention of crossdraw carry, despite the fact that many of my firearms writing colleagues decry crossdraw's use because of the possibility of gun snatching. I'm not letting someone get so close to me that he or she can access my crossdraw-carried handgun. If someone is so seriously in my space, my hand will be on my gun at the very least and I'll be stepping back to get more distance between myself and the potential gun grabber. If I can't step back, however regrettably, I'll draw. This harkens back to your condition of readiness. If you're in Condition White and you're not asleep, you've got bigger problems than avoiding a crossdraw carry can solve.

Crossdraw is the way to carry when seated, of course. When just walking around out and about, crossdraw is terrific because, with practice, one can easily access the gun with either hand, a virtual impossibility with a strongside carry. And, when one goes to sit down or reach above one's head, etc, there is no gunbutt to poke against the covering garment and profile, thus revealing that the wearer is armed. The gunbutt is pointing forward, so it cannot point rearward.

Wearing clothing that is uncomfortably warm or doesn't fit the season or the social occasion, simply because it is perceived as some sort of super secret way to conceal weapons when it really isn't that at all is poor judgement.

Certain clothing has been designed for men and women which facilitates concealed carry and supports concealed carry. By "supports concealed carry," I mean such items may well be specially designed to keep spare magazines or other equipment secure. By "facilitates concealed carry," I mean the clothing is specially designed to hide concealed weapons. In recent times, for example, I've found myself quite

Ahern's taking a Kel-Tec .32 from a hidden zipper closure under-pocket in this Woolrich Elite Series Tactical lightweight shirt.

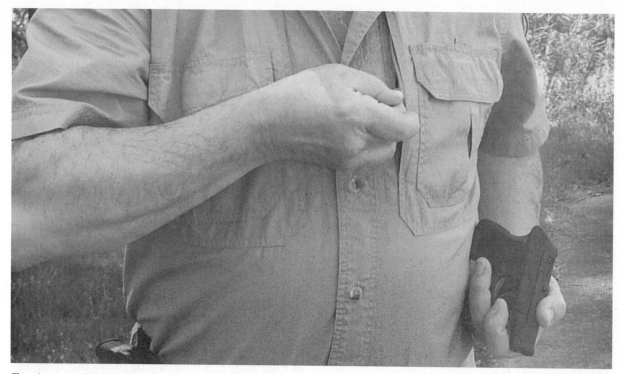

There is a concealed pocket on either side in this Woolrich Elite Series shirt, designed for hiding documents or cash or, in this case, capable of handling a small, light, thin pistol.

often wearing trousers, jackets, often times shirts and, in the summer, even shorts from the Woolrich Elite Series Tactical collection.

One of my favorite items is the Algerian Field Jacket. Constructed from nine-ounce 100% cotton herringbone and garment washed for comfort, this jacket became an instant favorite for me. It has thirteen pockets, four of which are nicely tailored bellows style, two on each side and two on the chest. The chest pockets have zipper closure security pockets behind the bellows pockets. Woolrich recommends that spare magazines or a small automatic or revolver can be carried in these zippered pockets. I think the first handgun I tried in one of these pockets was my Century International Arms Walther PP .32. It fit just fine.

Not long after that, I was taking my Detonics CombatMaster .45 from the glove compartment – I never leave a handgun in the car overnight – to go back into the house and decided to try the CombatMaster in one of these zip closure hidden pockets. It fit like a glove and the weight, somehow because of the comfortable design of the Algerian Field Jacket, wasn't at all uncomfortable. I often use this carry for short periods rather than merely stuffing the pistol into the waistband of my trousers. And, as a father and grandfather, I appreciate anything that facilitates having some fun

with my children and grandchildren. With no gun in the pockets, my oldest granddaughter enjoyed counting those thirteen pockets the first time she saw the Algerian Field Jacket and my grandsons and my son, their father, all like kidding me about hidden zippered pockets in the Elite Series shirts I'll sometimes wear.

In association with another project, I tried a pair of Blackie Collins "Toters," extremely high quality all USA made blue jeans which aren't so much designed to conceal weapons as to carry weapons securely and comfortably. But you can conceal smaller handguns and spare ammo and folding knives in these pants quite well.

Although not specifically designed to carry weapons or conceal weapons, it's hard to beat a well made leather bomber jacket for covering a handgun in a shoulder holster. Years ago, I quested after the ultimate, perfect bomber jacket that was built to last and looked good. I didn't want something pre-aged, figuring that time and normal wear would handle that for me. I selected an A-2 bomber jacket. They're available from Cockpit USA (formerly Avirex Ltd.) and are the official jackets for the United States Air Force. You have to dig around to find these jackets on the website, but they are there. Mine is the original style with just two flap closure patch pockets, but Cockpit also offers the current Air Force model, with side hand warmer pockets under the patch pockets and interior pockets as well. These jackets are made from goatskin and really wear long and well. I've had mine for twenty years or so and I've concealed weapons in shoulder rigs under it with perfect confidence. The side patch pockets will carry a small automatic with ease.

Leather is a great cover for weapons because leather doesn't break over bulges like fabric will, having less give. That being the case, leather is a natural. One will find leather vests that are specifically made for concealing handguns, designed with built-in pockets. But, there are other fabrics that make their own unique contributions to concealed weapons carry. How about mesh and stretchable fabrics?

I have concealable body armor from Protective Products. It wears well and is a great fit. But to really get the most out of armor, one needs a base layer. Blackhawk! Products offers long and short sleeved, round and V-necked base layers and, if you order a size smaller than you might normally wear, the stretchy base layer will provide what is called a "compression fit." When a garment has a compression fit, it molds to the body like a second layer of skin, supporting muscles and guarding against what are called "hot spots," equipment rubbing where there's a wrinkle or less than perfect clothing fit.

Men's and women's undergarments are also available utilizing this compression fit concept, undergarments which incorporate built-in handgun holsters, molding handgun and holster as closely to the body as possible and completely obviating any method of belt attachment at all for the holster. This is an ingenious solution to the inside waistband carry concept. It's available through Masters of Concealment. Elasticized tops for men and women are also available, incorporating built-in holsters which position the handgun much like a vertical shoulder holster would do.

Kramer Leather began marketing specially designed undershirts some years ago, these mesh-like garments incorporating built-in shoulder holsters.

A lot of the time, men don't really need special concealment oriented clothing, although it can surely help so long as it's not obvious. Women, on the other hand, if they are to carry on body, have more complicated issues. For example, when a guy wears a shoulder holster, he doesn't usually have to worry about the butt of the handgun or the thumb break rubbing or even hitting uncomfortably against a breast. Women's clothing is usually from lighter fabrics that will do just the opposite of leather – instead of covering a bulge by not breaking over the gun and holster, the fabrics will accentuate the bulge. Women's clothing is designed to be more form fitting, of course, and form fitting clothing and concealed weapons make for an awkward combination, if not an impossible one. The approach a woman must often take with on-body concealed weapons carry is to deceive the eye. This can be done with patterns in the material, but specially tailored garments are available for women which will mask the presence of handguns. As with men's clothing specially crafted for concealed carry, one must merely be careful that the clothes themselves don't draw attention because of some odd look.

PART 2

TESTFIRES

CHAPTER 22

TESTING SELECTED HANDGUNS

As this book was written, a great many handgun models were still in short supply because of high demand. A list was compiled of test and evaluation guns and the borrowed guns included in these pages are what we were able to obtain from that list. In order to round out the representative sampling of brands and types, guns owned by Sharon and I and guns owned by friends were also included, both for testing and photography.

I established testing procedures that would not necessarily pit gun against gun, shooter against shooter. Nor did I wish for every handgun tested to be limited by my perennially mediocre marksmanship. I enlisted the aid of two fine shots, Danny Akers and Bradley Fielding. Throughout, Birchwood-Casey Shoot-N-C targets were used, in several different sizes. A variety of different ammunition brands were utilized as well, these mentioned as the individual guns are discussed.

Since this is a book dealing with concealed carry handguns and not target handguns, virtually all testing was done at no greater distance than ten yards. Over a period of some months, those guns not borrowed specifically for this endeavor were fired at ranges as distant as fifty feet and as close as five feet. Depending on initial performance and firearm type, certain of the guns borrowed from manufacturers for this work were also shot at extremely close range, i.e., derringer pistols and, to a lesser degree, mini-revolvers. There are certain persons who shoot derringers a great deal in Single Action Shooters Society side matches, and these persons get to be really good hands with these little over/unders. I am not one of these persons. Nice and close was the order of the day.

For a handgun's accuracy to be remarkable in these shooting sessions, it had to be remarkably bad. Almost any handgun will shoot more accurately than a human being can handle it. With that understood, and since I was using multiple shooters, I expected at least one of the groups fired by one of the shooters – there were at least two shooters and usually three on each weapon – to be six inches or under when the handgun was fired two hand standing unsupported rapid fire. Results were generally better than anticipated. Remember, these guns need to be able to cluster rapidly fired shots into the center of mass of an attacker who is close. Most of these handguns would have acquitted themselves well at fifty feet or even greater distances, in the right hands. But, if someone is attacking at a protracted distance, the prudent person will opt for using cover as he or she beats a retreat, especially if all one has as armament is a handgun. That's an advantage of being a civilian, rather than a law enforcement professional. Police don't usually have that option.

None of the handguns reported on here was "remarkable" in the context of doing badly. One handgun, which shall remain nameless, would not function properly because of what appeared to be an improperly fitted firing pin. I did what any consumer would do and contacted the manufacturer, informed the manufacturer of the difficulty and returned the gun. Rather than waiting for repairs to be effected, since this was a borrowed handgun to begin with, another handgun was sent in its place. This worked perfectly.

Stiffness of the controls, fingers pinched between the bottom of the trigger and the inside of the trigger guard, excessive recoil, tendencies toward shots touching one to the other, exceptionally smooth or exceptionally heavy trigger pulls and the like – all of these, for good or bad, are duly noted, as they occurred.

With many of the handguns featured in these pages, I felt it would enhance the reader's perspective to know the background of a particular weapon or weapon family or manufacturer. There are, as well, occasional references to certain individuals whose involvement with a particular firearm or firearm type has actually shaped that handgun's role or even caused a particular firearm to come to be. Being involved at one time or another in virtually every aspect of the firearms business since 1973, I've been privileged to know quite a few people and quite a few stories.

The following chapters detail some of my experiences.

CHAPTER 23

SIG-SAUER P6 (P225), SIG-SAUER P229 & SIG-SAUER P238

In the mid-1970s, while I was working as Associate Editor of *GUNS Magazine,* we got a catalog in the mail, unlike any catalog I've seen before or since. Sadly, I misplaced it years ago. On the catalog's pages were pictures and schematics, one after the other, of some of the most modern looking and functional appearing handguns I'd ever seen. There was a .45 automatic, there was a 9X19mm, there was a .380 ACP. They were all double action for the first shot, looked to be quite sensible dimensionally and, as they appeared in the catalog, seemed to be examples of handguns concerning which the designers had thought of just about everything.

And the name! I mean, everybody had heard of the great gun making firms which had come together and put their names on these pistols. One was J.P. Sauer und Sohn of (then West) Germany and the other was Schweizerische Industrie Gesellshaft of Switzerland. Sauer and SIG! The idea, we immediately figured, was to produce these new SIG pistols in Germany, where they could be made perfectly well but

The SIG 238 was a great little shooter. A single action .380, it's small, light, but pleasant.

Right profile shot of the SIG 238.

less expensively than in Switzerland. Swiss-produced SIG P210 pistols were fabulously expensive, comparatively, even then. The .45, which was to become known as the SIG P220, originally was imported by Browning Arms and marketed as the BDA (Browning Double Action) .45. The .380 eventually became known as the SIG P230, the earlier version of the current SIG P232. The 9mm never did

particularly well here, a single column pistol that came along just as everyone was starting to go wild over large capacity double column magazine "wondernines." Yet, even though the SIG P225 didn't really catch on in the USA, as the P6 in Europe, the P225 became a widely disseminated and very much respected police service pistol.

A gentleman we know here in Georgia, one of our first new friends when we moved South in 1978, had a pair of these pistols put away in a pistol case which proved to be the next best thing to a sponge as it sucked humidity out of the air, into the foam padding and subsequently deposited said moisture on his SIG P225s. One side of each pistol was covered in heavy rust. What a shame!

In 2009, I learned that Century International Arms was importing the P6, these P225s police turn-ins, handguns displaying some holster wear but very little shot. Each pistol came with a spare magazine, a good thing since the P225s were never exactly wildly abundant in the United States and there are, consequently, precious

Right profile shot of the SIG P6, known in the USA as the P225.

few extra magazines to be had in this country. If you own a P6, whether marked as that or a P225, and you see a good quality magazine, you may want to grab it, because factory original magazines aren't about to get more plentiful, the P6 no longer in production, to the best of my knowledge.

The SIG P6 is an 8+1 pistol, length overall is just a tenth of an inch over seven inches, while the barrel is one tenth under four inches. Weight without a magazine is a tenth of an ounce under 26 ounces. An empty magazine weighs two point seven ounces. Height is five and two tenths inches, while the width is only one and three tenths inches.

The SIG P6, if you can live with a 9X19mm pistol that can only pack nine rounds with the chamber loaded, is an excellent handgun for concealment. And, unlike some of the first SIG-Sauer pistols which started showing up in the USA in the mid-1970s, the P6 has an American style push button magazine release.

There is a peculiar hole in the spur of the hammer. I've heard various reasons for this, but the one which sounds most plausible (because it seems the silliest) is that a tiny wire was threaded through the trigger guard at the very upper rear portion all the way behind the trigger and this wire was run through the slit or hole on the hammer spur. In this manner, the police department which issued the weapon could tell instantly whether a weapon had been discharged, even if the officer scrupulously cleaned the firearm and never reported "shots fired."

Whatever the reason for that peculiarity concerning the hammer spur, the P6 is an outstanding little firearm. If you need a good, reliable pistol from one of the top handgun manufacturers in the world at a low price, look for an unsold P6 at your local gunshop. This police turn-in pistol is one of the very best handgun deals around.

The success of the SIG P220 .45 from among

those first SIG-Sauer pistols led to this full-size double action police/military pistol being re-designed as a double column magazine 9X19mm which competed head-to-head with the Beretta 92 in the final of three separate pistol trials during the 1980s, which led to the adoption of the Beretta as the new U.S. service pistol, the M9. The SIG 226 reportedly matched the Beretta in every way, except price. The Beretta is a large pistol. When the Air Force went looking for a weapon with which to arm pilots, a reasonably new compact version of the SIG 226, known as the SIG 228, was selected. The 228 was and is a superb compact pistol. It became the M11. SIG introduced the 229, essentially a slightly beefed up version of the 228 with a stainless steel slide, available in 9mm, but also in .40 Smith & Wesson.

SIG announced the introduction of the .357 SIG cartridge in 1994. The 229 can be had in that caliber, as well, or, if one has a .40 Smith & Wesson SIG 229, one need only secure a .357 SIG barrel and some ammunition to be able to have dual caliber versatility. Production of the SIG P228 ceased in light of its near total duplication with the 229. A version of the 229 has been adopted by the United States Coast Guard and the Federal Air Marshals very wisely chose the the SIG-Sauer P229 chambered in .357 SIG.

I own two SIG 229s, one acquired as a gently used handgun and the second purchased new. Both pistols are superb shooters. I acquired a .357 SIG barrel, which I have used with the first 229 and I have since been field testing one of the SIG-Sauer .22 Long Rifle conversion kits for the 229. Both 229s are fitted with Crimson Trace LaserGrips. These are earlier pistols, without Picatinny Rails. I purchased both pistols during the period when the Assault Weapons Ban silliness was in force, and therefore have a reasonable number of ten-round magazines. Once that craziness was past, I acquired a number of twelve-round magazines.

The P229 is the Ahern Family's designated main battle pistol, I suppose.

The P229s I use are the standard double action kind, not double action only. With a twelve-round magazine in .40 S&W or .357 SIG – the magazine works with both calibers – the 229 is a nice compromise between cartridge effectiveness and capacity/ time between reloadings. To give the pistol more versatility for practice and other purposes, I can switch to the .22 conversion kit merely by removing the 229's magazine, clearing the chamber and dismounting the slide, barrel and recoil assembly all as one unit. Just like field stripping. Then, I place the .22 Long Rifle slide, barrel and recoil spring unit on the pistol's frame. Insert the provided ten-round .22 LR magazine and away you go. For those so inclined, the .22 kits can be had with barrels that are pre-threaded to accept a suppressor.

When the 229 isn't being used as a concealed weapon, with its cartridge versatility, the pistol would be ideal to take hiking or camping, the heavier caliber providing ample power against smaller predators, including humans, while the .22 conversion kit would be great for shooting small game.

The original 229, which I purchased used, is one of the more accurate handguns I own, but both pistols are fine shooters. Any pistol chosen from among the SIG Classics will prove to be a fine and reliable weapon and the SIG-Sauer P229 is definitely one of the most versatile in the line.

SIG's P238 is not part of the original SIG-Sauer offerings, but it should look somewhat recognizable, especially to persons familiar with the no-longer-available Colt Mustang. Both single action .380 ACP pocket pistols, the cosmetic similarities are striking. However, the P238 is a SIG, through and through, and even in a single action semi-automatic, SIG-Sauer innovation can be counted on to deliver.

Despite the number of witness holes in the magazine, the SIG P238 handles 6+1, not 7+1. The pistol's sights are large enough for easy pickup, coarse enough for speed. Although Black Hills and Remington jacketed hollow points were used, the ammo this particular P238 seemed to shoot the best with was the remnants of an old box of aluminum case Blazer hollow points. Trigger pull with the little pistol was smooth with virtually no overtravel and everything about the shooting experience with the P238 was pleasant.

My sample pistol has an aluminum alloy frame, although pistols with stainless steel frames are available. Slides are all stainless steel, by the way. The alloy framed P238 weighs 15.2 ounces with an empty magazine. For reference, a Walther PPK weighs about twenty-one ounces, as does an original two-inch J-Frame Smith & Wesson. Perceived recoil with the P238 was barely noticeable. As one would expect with any product bearing the name SIG-Sauer, the pistol worked perfectly. It even looks good.

There is no grip safety on this quite miniaturized 1911-ish pistol, but there is a

A police turn-in gun sold on the used market, this P6 is an outstanding value, if you can still find one. Century International Arms imported these SIGs.

thumb safety which works hammer up or hammer down. When the hammer is down, the slide cannot be retracted if the safety is engaged. When the hammer is up, the slide will work with the safety engaged. The owner's manual for the P238 suggests that one should not attempt to lower the hammer over a live round and that, once a round is chambered, the pistol should be kept cocked and locked. This does not thrill me with a pistol of this size, but I could live with it because the P238 is not so "1911-ish" as to be absent an internal safety which blocks the firing pin from striking the primer of a chambered round unless the trigger is pulled. That said, however, users of the P238 are admonished to avoid a muzzle drop.

The Colt Mustang, which the P238 so closely resembles in size and overall appearance, was a terrifically popular little .380 and the P238 will doubtlessly prove to be the same, especially with the upgraded cosmetics of the current guns (i.e., nicer looking grips). Looking like a perfect miniature of a 1911, for those whose firearms experience is most closely aligned with a 1911, carried cocked and locked, this pistol's similar manual of arms will prove quite comfortable.

If a pistol carries the SIG-Sauer name, I've found, that means it is well-built, has a good trigger, is capable of serious accuracy and is reliable. When you come to think about that list of qualities, it's what a handgun is all about.

All three of the SIG pistols included here easily met the accuracy/shooting standards I had set, the 238 fired by three different shooters, I being one of them.

CHAPTER 24

DETONICS USA (PENDERGRASS) 9-11-01 AND DETONICS (PENDERGRASS) COMBATMASTER

When we think about big bore handguns, although there are certainly more powerful cartridges to be had, our thoughts naturally turn to the Government Model .45 auto. Years ago, I owned a Colt Series 70 and it was a good gun, but not anything truly special. When I was tasked with running the Detonics USA operation in Pendergrass, Georgia, a few years back, one of the things I truly wanted to do was have the firm produce a full size combat pistol. The original Seattle company produced a full size pistol, of course, known as the "ScoreMaster," a target sighted pistol which was perfectly serviceable as a combat gun except for those target sights. So, while Detonics USA got the little CombatMaster .45s into production again, at my request, our master gunsmith worked out the details and the Model 9-11-01 was born. He did an excellent job with that project. I picked the name "9-11-01"

These are not Detonics USA (Pendergrass) pistols, but examples of the guns, as this is written, to be coming from the Illinois operation, known simply as "Detonics." Unique front sight placement and barrel configuration are only some of the new features. (Detonics Photo)

A Detonics USA (Pendergrass) CombatMaster .45, in right profile. With the exception of the sights, the aluminum trigger and the wooden grips, everything is stainless steel, including the springs.

because, in some very small way, I wanted to do whatever I could to help keep the events of that historic day in people's minds – sort of a "Remember the Alamo!" type thing. And what better way to remember than with a supremely reliable combat pistol with which our good guys might kill some of the terrorist bad guys?

I had spoken with a knowledgeable military gentleman, an owner of an original CombatMaster, and he had told me about some of the difficulties the armed services were having with finding a handgun through which you could get thirty thousand rounds. That seemed kind of pathetic, really, and I was certain any number of fine handguns could do that. With the co-operation of Black Hills, preparations were made to conduct a thirty-one thousand round test. We arranged for a group of law enforcement personnel, one of them a woman, all of them members of the Georgia Tactical Officers Association, to do the actual shooting. The tests would be conducted over the course of five to six days. Before the test took place, two of the nation's leading cannoneers were engaged to drive to Georgia and haul their Union Army mortar with them. The Model 9-11-01 that was to be used was fired out of that mortar, travelling a distance of a few hundred yards. There was no damage to the pistol.

The test took exactly five days, and at the beginning of the test an accuracy group was shot. Sometimes, as many as five hundred rounds would be fired in a matter of minutes, several of us reloading magazines. The gun

Detonics pistols are bushingless and feature triple recoil springs surrounding a guide rod.

grew too hot to touch at times. Ninety percent of the ammunition was Black Hills reloads 230-grain full metal case (hardball), the remainder Black Hills 185-grain jacketed hollowpoints. Around twenty-five thousand rounds, the heat generated by the constant firing caused one of the dual recoil springs to break. We never knew until we examined the gun at the end of that string, because the Model 9-11-01 kept working flawlessly. The master gunsmith replaced the spring. At between thirty and thirty-one thousand rounds, the firing pin spring broke and the other of the two recoil springs broke. We never knew that until the pistol was examined at the conclusion of the testing, because the gun kept going. Keep in mind that the recoil springs and the firing pin spring in a 9-11-01 are stainless steel and cannot take such high heat.

The action was slow at times, the gun fouled like crazy. The master gunsmith wiped it off, but never cleaned the weapon. At the conclusion of this test – there was never a failure to feed or fire throughout all five days of the test – the master gunsmith fired a one-hole group with the weapon. After the test, he discovered the two broken springs and replaced them. For publicity purposes, the weapon was never cleaned. A year later, when my old friend Michael Bane of The Outdoor Channel came by to do an episode on Detonics USA on *Shooting Gallery*, we hauled out the test gun. Another fifty or so rounds went through the never cleaned pistol and there was never a failure to feed or fire.

Government Model style pistols – the 9-11-01 was that, certainly, but with Detonics touches

– are known for their amazing durability and strength. I read an article some years ago in which a well-respected firearms writer told of discovering some 1911 magazines which had been loaded since World War I. He put a couple of them into a full-size 1911 and – amazed as he was – the magazines functioned and the cartridges all went bang.

Silly stories about full-size .45s with their punishing recoil and terrible accuracy problems notwithstanding, the pistol like the one heroic Sergeant Alvin C. York used in his Medal of Honor winning capture of four Imperial German officers, one hundred twenty-eight enlisted personnel and a number of weapons, on October 8, 1918, was a .45. Sergeant York, armed only with his 1911 and a bolt action rifle, led the survivors of his unit against the German position, York personally killing twenty-eight of the enemy and becoming the most decorated American combatant of World War I.

If you have a full size, five-inch-barrel 1911/1911A1-pattern .45 automatic and it works faultlessly, despite the fact that I carry lots of other handguns, I'll admit it's kind of hard to see any logic behind carrying something else. I have neither knowledge of nor connection to the Detonics company of Illinois, other than to wish them well. I talk about Detonics USA pistols because they worked. I look at my Detonics USA (Pendergrass) Model 9-11-01 as a magazine-fed, eight-shot version of the Sword Excalibur.

But Excalibur could be a little large to carry around on a daily basis, hence the development of the original Detonics CombatMaster during the 1970s. A man by the name of Pat Yates wanted a small-sized 1911 for himself and couldn't get it to work as it should. Sid Woodcock, an explosives expert, martial arts expert and firearms expert, liked the concept and, sometimes file stroke at a time, designed a fully functional pistol made largely from 1911 parts (except for the three and one-half inch barrel, recoil spring guide rod, springs, etc.) that was a true 1911 and – dare I say it – was actually an improvement on Browning's design. The finished product was about the size of a Walther PP or a Chiefs Special revolver. It was a production gun, although there was a great deal of hand work involved with it. The company had its ups and downs and that is not a concern in these pages. What is a concern is that the little CombatMaster – the first major caliber semi-automatic made from stainless steel which required no exotic lubrication – was and is an outstanding personal defense weapon with every detail covered.

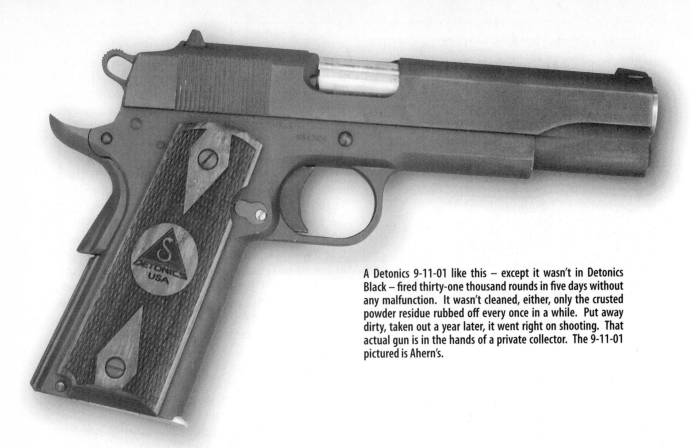

A Detonics 9-11-01 like this – except it wasn't in Detonics Black – fired thirty-one thousand rounds in five days without any malfunction. It wasn't cleaned, either, only the crusted powder residue rubbed off every once in a while. Put away dirty, taken out a year later, it went right on shooting. That actual gun is in the hands of a private collector. The 9-11-01 pictured is Ahern's.

This example should illustrate the excellence of the little CombatMaster's design. Sid Woodcock had seen men cleaning 1911s in the field, only to launch a recoil spring off into the brush, never to be seen again. The 1911 less recoil spring was largely useless as a fighting handgun. When Sid designed the CombatMaster, because of its size and not in spite of its size, he was able to make the entire recoil system captive so the barrel and slide and recoil assembly could be dismounted without any risk of losing parts. In fact, if you know how, the entire firearm can be detail stripped using only the gun parts themselves and no tools. I'm a fan of the gun and count Sid Woodcock as one of my best friends. A Detonics USA (Pendergrass) CombatMaster .45 is on me every day.

As far as I am able to ascertain, the Model 9-11-01 has been discontinued by the current owners of the Detonics company, and the CombatMaster has been re-designed. These Detonics pistols about which I have just written are the last of their breed, traditional and basic handguns. By the time this book sees print, the entirely new generation of Detonics pistols may well be available. The guns are coming; and, I for one wish the Detonics firm well with these new projects.

CHAPTER 25

GLOCK 22, GLOCK 27 AND GLOCK 17 GEN 4

Right profile shot of the Glock 27.

The Glock 17, first seeing service with the Austrian military in 1982, was a pistol unlike anything ever seen before when it first appeared in the United States in 1992, during the days of the shooting public's wondernine crush. Contrary to the logical assumption that the Glock 17 was named the way it was because of the magazine capacity – seventeen rounds, an eighteenth in the chamber – the Glock 17 was actually the company's seventeenth product (an American-made version of the Steyr GB; the GB was developed as an earlier Austrian military sidearm and was marketed for a short period in the USA as the Rogak P-18, because it really did have an eighteen-round magazine). Glock soon followed up with a wide range of variations on the same basic Glock 17 design, some longer, some smaller, some even in different colors than black. And, there were different calibers, of course.

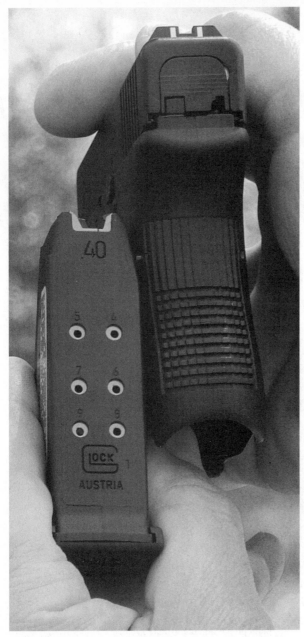

At nine plus one rounds, you can also use the larger capacity Glock 22 magazines as spares.

chamber is loaded, as it should be, of course, neither the Glock 22 nor any other Glock should be carried holsterless. If you should have, for example, the Glock 27, the smallest of the .40 caliber Glock pistols, you cannot drop it in your coat pocket without a holster if a round is chambered. Glock refers to its system of operation as "Safe Action"; and, indeed, it is a safe pistol, so long as nothing depresses the safety lever built into the trigger and takes the trigger rearward at the same time. For this reason, lest this might happen, any holster for a Glock must cover the trigger guard so both that trigger and the lever within the trigger are protected. Now, in fairness, a wise person will want similar trigger guard coverage for any semi-automatic pistol, regardless of make. Years ago, you would see police uniform duty holsters and off-duty belt holsters for revolvers which left the entire trigger guard exposed. This was in the heyday of the Hollywood holsters for the Colt Single Action Army, as worn on such classic television westerns as *Cheyenne* and *Have Gun – Will Travel*. When it came to fully exposed trigger guards on police duty and off-duty revolver holsters for double action Colts and Smiths, to my way of thinking, too much was exposed.

The Glock buyer must be careful when he or she acquires a holster that the holster designer, in his zeal to protect the trigger, has not constructed a holster where the holster lip essentially abuts the root of the trigger guard (where the trigger guard emerges from the grip front strap). If the design brings the lip and root in such close proximity, it will be impossible to get a full combat grip as you draw the weapon.

What is meant by obtaining a "full combat grip," of course, is being able to grasp the pistol in such a fashion that the middle finger can be placed in contact with the underside of the root of the trigger guard without having to adjust the shooting hand on the pistol after the weapon has been started out of the holster. In other words, initial contact between your hand and the pistol butt places your hand in the ideal position for the weapon to be fired, once the muzzle is on target.

Much of the time, my Glock 22 wears a Surefire 300 WeaponLight, affixed to the pistol's Picatinny rail. For most but not all holsters, however, the light precludes use. Regardless of the holster, and whether the light is on or not, my Glock 22 is fitted with the Crimson Trace LaserGrips unit. The Glock 22 is one of my few concessions to modern tastes in pistols.

The Glock 22 is a Glock 17 that happens to be chambered for .40 Smith & Wesson, its capacity only fifteen rounds, plus one in the chamber. The length of the Glock 22 is 7.32 inches, while the height is 5.43 inches. Weight of the empty pistol is 23 ounces. Barrel length is 4.5 inches. Width is 1.18 inches.

The Glock 22 is a full-size battle/law enforcement duty pistol, yet is easily enough concealed for most concealment scenarios. There are certain special considerations which need to be observed when one carries a Glock of any sort, however. First and foremost, if the

The Glock has a polymer frame and a light. I'm one of these older pistoleers who doesn't mind shooting one handed if the target is close enough and always believed that the source of tactical illumination – what we used to call a "flashlight" – may be better off held in the off hand and well away from the body, rather than positioned under the pistol. So, I'm working with the Glock 22 and another Picatinny rail-equipped pistol from Taurus in order to make myself feel more comfortable with this newer technique. I will say that the Surefire 300 WeaponLight is a superb "flashlight." As this is written, I've acquired a SureFire X400 WeaponLight, which also incorporates a laser. I'm looking forward to trying it.

Ahern took quite a liking to this .40 S&W Glock 27. Its natural pointing qualities make it a good candidate for body index shooting.

Right profile of the Glock 17 GEN 4.

My Glock 22 is a factory re-conditioned pistol. I have no worries that its service life may be diminished. Glock claims it has gotten three hundred thousand rounds through a pistol kept at their Smyrna, Georgia, facility. The FBI, it is reported, put fifty thousand rounds through a .40 S&W Glock. If I live as long as Methuselah, I might have a problem with my Glock 22. Otherwise, I think I'm safe.

I have always been someone who appreciates durability and that goes for looks in a pistol as well as the mechanical side of performance. Glock slides and barrels utilize a Tenifer finish, which is not an actual finish, per se, but a metal hardening process which imparts a Rockwell hardness of 64 to these parts, as Glock notes, nearly as hard as diamonds. And, the process, of course, guards against rust. I believe it was the noted firearms authority Chuck Taylor who recounted a test in which a Glock pistol was left immersed in sea water for a protracted period. When the pistol was retrieved, one barely

noticeable rust spot was on the slide and that was it. That's tough to beat. The Tenifer process is not performed in the United States, as this is written, and it would, frankly, be really good to see this treatment more widely in service.

The Glock 22 is a superb piece of equipment and a great shooter. Pair it with the comparatively diminutive Glock 27 as your backup gun and you can even use the Glock 22's magazines as spares for the smaller pistol. I know a good thing when I see it – usually – and my Glock 22 is certainly that.

When it came time to test fire the Glock 27 we had borrowed from Glock for the purposes of this book, I'll confess that I was rather looking forward to it. If there's a downside to writing firearms books and columns and articles – discounting, for a moment, schlepping guns and ammunition cans in and out of safes and cars and cabinets – it's having to deal with a wide range of trigger pulls. By way of example, when I'd wind up test firing thirty or thirty-five

A SureFire X300 WeaponLight or similar accessory can be mounted on the accessory rail of this Glock 22.

Detonics USA pistols while I was running the Pendergrass, Georgia, operation, my usually mediocre handgun marksmanship was at its Zenith. All our trigger pulls were pretty close, one pistol to the other, and I'd pick up a gun, load it and shoot it and move on to the next one. When you go from brand to brand, that doesn't happen. Even if all the trigger pulls are really good, they will never be essentially the same.

The borrowed Glock 27 – about the size of Chiefs Special two-inch snubby – had the crisp and even trigger pull to which I have become accustomed with my Glock 22 and an original Glock 17 which I owned years ago, a firearm which I gave to a friend who was going off to Operation Desert Storm. Danny and Bradley, both using Black Hills hollow points (red box/new manufacture), got their usual excellent groups, bullet holes touching. Even I, using 200-grain truncated cone full metal case reloads in Winchester cases, ammunition that I was taking out of a plastic sandwich bag it

had sat in for five years or so, got a nominal three-inch group.

All three of us thought the Glock 27 was a pleasure to shoot. I've heard people talk about shooting ultra small pistols in .40 Smith & Wesson, specifically referring to unpleasant recoil. None of us found that to be the case with the Glock 27. I liked it so much, I just may buy the sample.

The last of the three Glocks to be shot was the Glock 17 Gen 4. My Glock 22, for example, is a Gen 3 gun. The Gen 4, which shot well for Danny and myself and printed a series of hole to hole touches for Bradley, has a heavily textured grip frame, the Gen 4 guns coming with two additional back strap pieces for the grip frame, allowing owner modification of grip size and shape. The magazine release catch is larger than on previous models and reversible according to hand preference. Probably the principal feature of note is the addition of a second recoil spring unit which has necessitated a slight enlargement

Even in broad daylight, a powerful light can still be seen, this SureFire unit mounted on a Glock 22. If you look really closely, you may just be able to see the red laser beam as well.

of the frame. All other features of the Glock 17 Gen 4 are classic Glock.

These pistols are actually growing on me. There is something certainly to be said for a semi-automatic pistol that can be that fast into action and right out of the holster and has a trigger that requires so short a stroke that strings of shots or follow up shots are more easily accomplished. Any of these three Glocks would make a fine concealed carry gun, obviously the little Glock 27 being the easiest to use in close concealment.

CHAPTER 26

SMITH & WESSON MODEL 686, MODEL 637, MODEL 642, MODEL 640 (OLD STYLE), MODEL 60 (OLD STYLE), MODEL SW9VE, AND M&P 9C

Full-size, medium and small-size revolvers still have their place, of course, even in this age of so many wonderfully reliable service automatics. I remember years back when I was Associate Editor of *GUNS Magazine* and we had recently hired on Bill Jordan for a monthly column. Bill Jordan, of course, was a wonderful gentleman, who happened also to be a lightning quick and deadly gunman with a heroic record in both the United States Border Patrol and

the United States Marine Corps in the Pacific, during World War II, and in Korea. He retired from the USMC as a Colonel. During his career as a lawman, he made famous his phenomenal abilities with Smith & Wesson double action revolvers and was responsible for the .38 Special K-frame revolvers being made available in .357 Magnum, what was to become one of Smith & Wesson's most important police sidearms of the era, the Model 19.

Right profile shot of the M&P Compact, an outstanding little pistol.

Jordan always gave primacy to the revolver. When he went jogging in the mornings, he'd have a two-inch J-Frame snubby .38 in the muff pocket of his sweats, as I understand it. When Smith & Wesson came out with the first Model 59 automatics – large capacity magazines, double action first shot capability 9mms – the company gave Jordan one. I remember him remarking in one of his columns or an article that he really liked the little Model 59. It made a great backup gun if you were in a gunfight and hunkered down behind cover. For Bill Jordan – and several generations of American lawmen – a fine double action revolver was the ultimate sidearm.

American cops and their department administrators became more and more concerned about bumping into heavily armed criminals with superior firepower at their command and, soon, department after department began phasing out the wheelgun and switching to the semi-automatic. But, as my old pal Ron Mahovsky of Mahovsky's Metalife used to say about revolvers as opposed to semi-autos, "Six for sure."

Even though double action revolvers are more complicated mechanisms than semi-automatics, typically, and double action revolvers are less able to handle dirt and other environmental concerns, revolvers are simpler to operate and much less ammunition sensitive. Considerably slower to reload, even with speedloaders, in all-but the most experienced hands, their capacity between reloadings is considerably less, even in more modern revolvers with seven or more rounds.

My revolvers would almost qualify as antiques, I'm sure, and my Model 686 is only a six-shooter. The Model 686 is, indeed, what might be called the spiritual descendant of that revolver Bill Jordan so much influenced, the Model 19. Here's the chronology. The Model 19 Combat Magnum in blue and nickel finishes was a .357 Magnum version of the Smith & Wesson Model 15 Combat Masterpiece, both revolvers K-Frames with adjustable sights. The fashion in

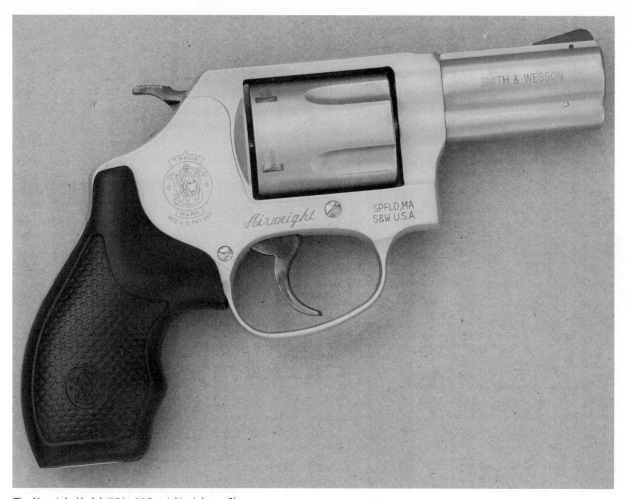

The Airweight Model 637 in .38 Special in right profile.

those days for Smith & Wesson was to take a popular revolver and make a version in stainless steel. This Smith & Wesson did with the Model 66, this revolver available in six-inch, four-inch and 2 ½-inch versions, the latter a round butt.

The trouble was, whether the Model 19 or the Model 66, this was still a K-Frame revolver firing the .357 cartridge. There were complaints about perceived recoil and worries about the revolvers holding up over prolonged use. At the time, Colt had a slightly larger medium frame revolver which was somewhat between Smith & Wesson's K-Frame and much larger N-Frame in frame size. Smith & Wesson decided to develop a similar sized frame, called the L-Frame. The first guns in this configuration were the blued Model 586 and the stainless Model 686, both four-inch .357 Magnums. Fixed sight versions, the 581 and 681, also four-inch revolvers, appeared for a time and soon disappeared. The 586 left the scene, too, but the 686 became the basis for the continuation of the enlarged medium frame revolvers currently in the Smith

& Wesson line. K-Frames themselves, as the smaller of the two medium frames, are hanging on in various models, including .38 Specials like the original fixed sight Model 10, .22 Long Rifle ten-shooters and even .357 Magnum seven-shot adjustable sight modernized versions of the K-Frame Model 66, the 619 and 620.

My Model 686 was converted to a round butt grip frame when Ron Mahovsky did all the other work on it – slab siding the barrel, polishing the stainless steel, adding a crane lock for greater strength and doing an action job. The rear sight's corners have been rounded to guard against snagging. Today, that 686 wears Crimson Trace LaserGrips and is a dependable family heirloom, my name on the barrel in gold letters. When we were writing *The Survivalist* series of novels, we used this revolver as the basis for the brace of revolvers given to one of the principal female characters, "Natalia," by the President of the United States. Hers had American Eagles on them. In another series we wrote, titled *Track,* the main character had a

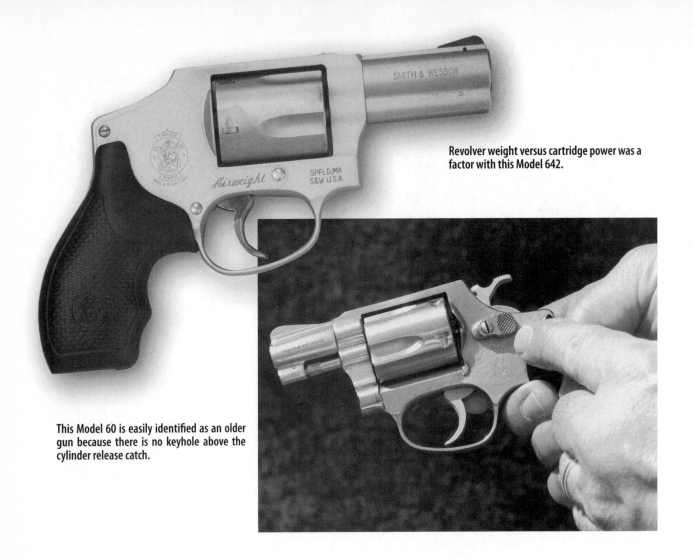

Revolver weight versus cartridge power was a factor with this Model 642.

This Model 60 is easily identified as an older gun because there is no keyhole above the cylinder release catch.

revolver just like mine, minus the name on the barrel. I keep a few Safariland Speedloaders for the Smith & Wesson 686, just in case. If I do wear the revolver, I have to choose between some very good shoulder holsters and belt holsters. A fine revolver makes for some of the best handgun shooting to be had and the Smith & Wesson 686 is among the finest, with the added strength over the K-Frame, without much added size at all.

Where revolvers are still going hot and heavy in sales is in the small frame models, of course. Those who predicted the demise of the double action revolver because of the popularity of the semi-automatics were – fortunately – mistaken. The small-frame revolver has, instead, morphed into a series of specialized carry guns. Charter Arms offers its small frame .38 in both right- and (mirror image) left-hand models. Taurus fields a full range of small revolvers as well. Smith & Wesson took many of its J-Frame revolvers and experimented with different metals, slightly longer barrels and added safety features.

I am a great fan of Smith & Wesson revolvers,

but I am not a fan of ultra-lightweight revolvers that are so extremely painful to shoot that they discourage practice. For Danny and Bradley and me, the Model 637 (exposed hammer) was just that: painful. Smith & Wesson shows the gun weighing 16 ounces. Our postage scale shows 17 ounces. The 642 (fully enclosed "Centennial" hammer), which was not as punishing, is also shown by Smith & Wesson at 16 ounces. Our scale registered 18 ounces. Apparently, an ounce made an appreciable difference. The old Smith & Wesson Airweight models (aluminum frame) were 19 ounces, if memory serves. Snubby Airweights can now be had at a weight of 15 ounces. All three of us utilized 158-grain lead semi-wadcutter hollowpoint +Ps, what used to be called the FBI load, Danny and Bradley firing ammunition made by Winchester. I fired the same load, but from Federal.

As this is written, I have been carrying and shooting Smith & Wesson J-Frame .38 Specials for almost forty-three years, getting started with the little revolvers about a decade before either Danny or Bradley was even born. All three of

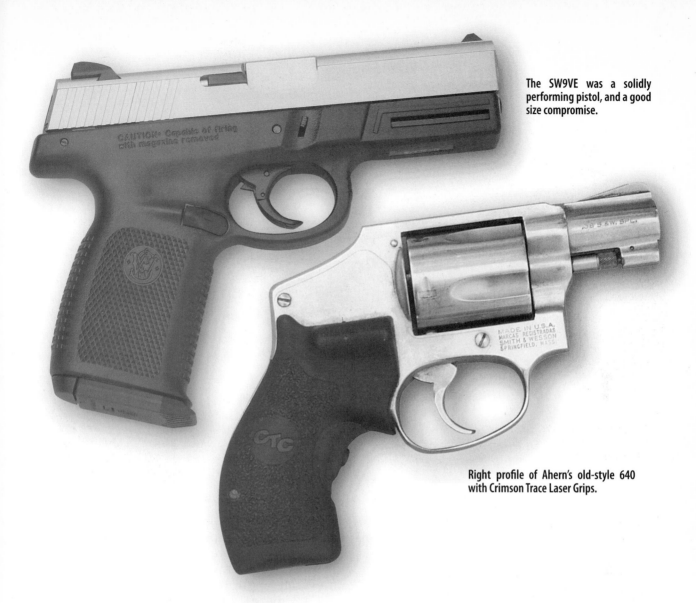

The SW9VE was a solidly performing pistol, and a good size compromise.

Right profile of Ahern's old-style 640 with Crimson Trace Laser Grips.

us had terrible results. I handle handgun recoil extremely well. Why, then, did all three of us do really badly? Certainly, it's not the gun, per se, but the weight. Smith & Wesson builds revolvers of undisputed quality. After the first shot with the 637, using a solid two-hand hold, my dominant hand was in pain, so much so that I suppose I was flinching. Danny and Bradley had the same problem, although Bradley shot the best.

My conclusion regarding the 637 and, to a lesser degree, the 642, is that there is a weight boundary – at least for the three of us – that shouldn't be gone below in a .38 Special revolver chambered for +Ps. Let alone .357 Magnums!

One of my favorite concealable handguns is the old style .38 Special all-steel Model 640, as manufactured by Smith & Wesson from 1990 to 1995. Wearing Crimson Trace LaserGrips, it weighs in empty at what I consider an ideal weight for a handgun of this type – 21 ounces. My old style .38 Special Model 60 – again, all

steel – is fitted with a Barami Hip-Grip "pistol handle holster" and weighs in a little closer to 20 than 21. With factory wooden grips – they really used to put skinny checkered walnut grips on the little guys – it would weigh the full 21 ounces.

The .38 Special Model 60 is the first stainless steel handgun, introduced in October of 1965, a stainless steel version of the Chiefs Special Model 36. It was an enormous hit and started the stainless steel handgun craze which endures to this day, although lighter weight has surpassed the demand for stainless construction. The result can best be typified by a handgun like the SW9VE Sigma 9X19mm semi-automatic. Its slide and barrel are stainless steel, its frame polymer. A true bargain financially, this striker fired handgun has a lot going for it.

The SW9VE Sigma's specs include an array of desirable features. Overall length of this four-inch barrel pistol is 7-1/4 inches, while weight empty is 24.7 ounces. Capacity is ten plus one.

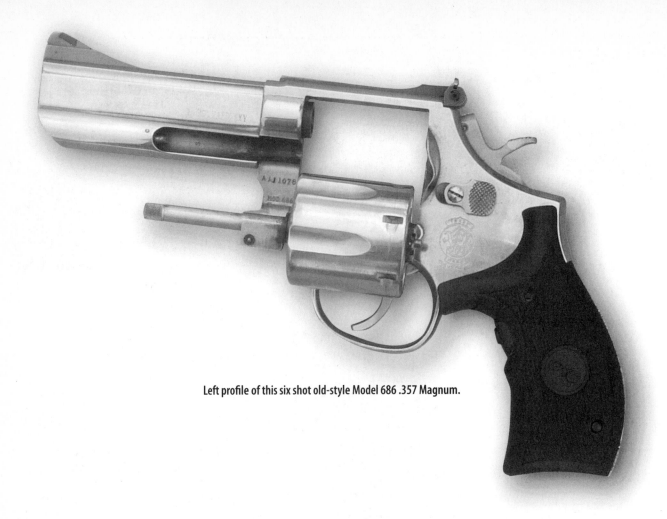

Left profile of this six shot old-style Model 686 .357 Magnum.

Sights are the three-dot type. Smith & Wesson engineers carefully determined what they felt to be the most natural grip angle – eighteen degrees – so that the gun points naturally when grasped, thus facilitating accuracy and speed of target acquisition.

Danny, Bradley and I all had good results, the groups tight, bullet holes touching and nothing unpleasant. This was an accurate handgun and, in our testing, perfectly reliable. Bradley and I both used Black Hills 124-grain jacketed hollow points, while Danny used Federal 124-grain JHPs and 147-grain JHPs.

Another Smith & Wesson semi-auto, part of a family of semi-autos, actually takes its name from one of the most popular revolvers ever made – the Smith & Wesson Model 10 M&P, standing for "Military & Police." The Model 10 was THE police service revolver for droves of uniformed police, those who did not carry a Colt Official Police or Police Positive Special, at least. The particular member of the M&P family examined here was well-suited indeed to carry as a concealed carry personal defense handgun. A 9X19mm, with twelve plus one capacity, it is the M&P Compact, with 3-1/2-inch barrel and an overall length of just 6.7 inches. Height is only 4.3 inches. Empty weight is just shy of 22 ounces. The barrel, slide and other parts are made of stainless steel, while the frame is polymer. A very convenient pistol to operate, Danny fired it with Federal 147-grain JHPs, while I used a more than three decades old box of Remington 115-grain JHPs I purchased in Waukegan, Illinois, for use when I was testing a Walther P-38K. Neither of us found anything remarkably good or bad accuracy-wise with the M&P Compact 9mm. It was a serviceable, concealable, reliable handgun and wore the M&P name well.

In all but handgun hunting and concealed carry/personal defense, the double action revolver is favored considerably less than the semi-automatic pistol. But where the revolver is still highly valued, it shows little if any sign of being supplanted.

CHAPTER 27

SEECAMP .32 AND SEECAMP .380

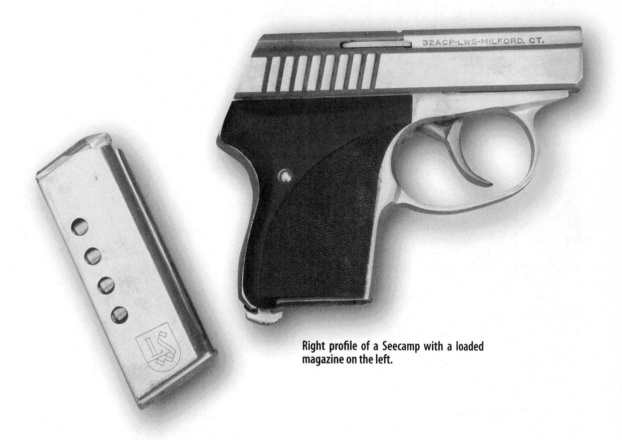

Right profile of a Seecamp with a loaded magazine on the left.

Larry Seecamp and his late father are firearms geniuses of the first ranking. Anyone who has even seen a Seecamp, let along tried or owned one, knows that for the fact that it is.

Let's talk about the Seecamp pistols and how they came about. Larry Seecamp's father, trained in pre-War Germany as a gunsmith, became greatly enamored of the 1911 pistol, yet liked the instant responsiveness and convenience of

the double action Walther P-38. He once used a P-38 to save his life. After retiring from his position as gun designer for O.F. Mossberg, he began making the well-respected Seecamp Double Action Conversions for the 1911, thus combining the P-38's first shot capability with the 1911. The first of the two Seecamp conversions I have seen was on a nickel-plated Series 70 Colt that belonged to a Chicago cop. I happened to be visiting the esteemed old gunshop down

With no sights, the Seecamp is a point and shoot proposition and one of the most sought after pistols ever made.

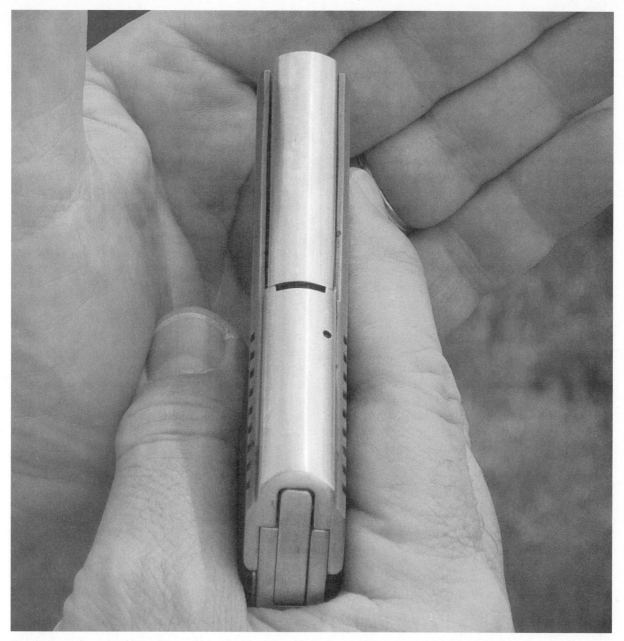

Viewing the Seecamp from above, if you catch it at just the right angle you can see if the weapon is chamber loaded.

the street from Chicago P.D. Headquarters at Eleventh and State when the young cop came in, delighted to see his gleaming nickel plated Colt converted for DA first shot capability. The second example was on a Detonics pistol which belonged to a very nice gentleman who kindly came to visit the Pendergrass manufacturing facility one day.

The advent of factory produced double action .45s – namely the SIG-Sauer P-220, in those days sold as the BDA .45 – largely obviated the need for such conversions.

Ludwig (Louis) W. Seecamp and his son, Larry, set about to produce a double action

only .25 automatic in stainless steel, a project at which they were quite successful. In 1981, the gun debuted and was perceived as a marvel, a hammer cocking (DA) stainless steel pocket pistol with no sights. In 1985, the .25 automatic, about the size of most .25s, was discontinued in favor of a pistol that literally revolutionized personal defensive handgun design. Also in stainless steel – in fact, identical to the .25, except in caliber – the LWS .32 was born, chambering the .32 ACP (7.65mm Browning). All that most Americans knew about .32 ACP was that James Bond's Walther PPK was chambered for the round. Today, .32 ACP hollow points and even solids are respected rounds from the smallest of concealed carry semi-autos. Seecamp had the smallest .32 ACP in the world, the most powerful hand gun of its size in the world. The guns worked and worked well, designed to use the Winchester Silvertip .32 ACP cartridges, which the Marshal and Sanow tests revealed to have a 60% one-shot stop rating. The Seecamp .32s became the most sought after handgun of the type in the world. In those days, it was not uncommon for these pistols to be acquired then re-sold for insanely high prices. Larry Seecamp never made a dime extra out of such scalper prices.

Meanwhile, while numerous companies were trying to create their own super small .32s, Larry was working on his next re-chambering, making the same pistol that started out as a .25 as a .380, this released to the public in 2003. The guns are so identical dimensionally that they cannot be told apart unless you check out the bore size. They fit into the same precisely molded holsters and, at least for me, felt pretty much the same when it comes to recoil. Having a Seecamp in your pocket, regardless of caliber, is rather like having a Rolex on your wrist. There are other ultra-fine watches and extraordinary handguns, but a Rolex is a Rolex and a Seecamp is a Seecamp.

Whatever the caliber, Seecamps have no sights, but they point very well.

If you look in the chamber with a bore light of some sort, you'll be shocked. For the guns to work as supremely well as they do, the chambers have to be made that way – cratered. Seecamps use a heel-of-the-butt magazine release, which is actually ideal for a small handgun which will be pocket carried and rarely reloaded under combat conditions. All stainless steel, Seecamps take abuse – dirt, lint and neglect – extremely well. I should know. I've carried one in my pocket for one side or the other of twenty years. The springs in their six-round magazines are sensational. A few months back, I had the occasion to fire my pet Seecamp. I hadn't shot it for well over a year, and very possibly over two years. Pocket dust and, despite the pocket holster, sweat and no cleaning for a couple of years, etc. – well, the pistol worked perfectly when I used the body indexing technique at close range on an Usama Bin Ladin target. I nailed that vile person's image with all six plus one .32 Silvertip rounds, placing them in the lungs, the sternum and the pump.

The .380 Seecamp comes with an extra set of recoil springs. Larry suggests that you do your practice shooting with one set of springs in the pistol and change to the other set for carry, this based on the idea that the springs for the .380 will weaken because of the tremendous pressure they endure. Larry had, initially, estimated the number of rounds before fatigue to be quite a bit lower than it has turned out to be. Take Larry's advice, to be sure, but I wouldn't be too worried over the springs for a Seecamp .380, unless you do an awful lot of shooting.

Larry Seecamp has new projects he's working on, of course, but you won't see those new guns until he's able to make them work perfectly, because that's the way Larry is – and people who depend on a Seecamp for personal defense or as backup really appreciate that, myself included. Seecamp pistols are outstanding and Larry stands behind every one that he makes.

CHAPTER 28

BERSA THUNDER CONCEALED CARRY .380, BERSA THUNDER .380, BERSA THUNDER PLUS .380 AND BERSA THUNDER .45

I'll confess that I had never fired a Bersa before preparing this book. I'd heard good things about the pistols for years, even had a friend who owned one he raved about. But a bargain-priced .380 from Argentina just really didn't excite me that much. When Sharon and I were going through GUN DIGEST to check on new items we might not have heard of or a brand we might have ignored, however, we bumped into that Bersa name and decided it was high time

to try their guns. I contacted the Bersa people, confessed my lack of personal experience with the line and asked for their suggestions. Three of the four handguns Bersa loaned for testing and evaluation were .380s (the fourth one was a really terrific little .45).

I was impressed with trigger pull, accuracy, reliability and ease of use of the controls. These were great guns!

The Bersa Thunder Concealed Carry is nickel

The Bersa Thunder .45 proved to be another fine value.

The Thunder .380 Concealed Carry is nickel plated.

The Thunder Plus is a larger capacity version of the basic pistol.

I tried the pistol with Black Hills 90-grain JHPs. My first round failed to feed, but after that everything fed smoothly. The Black Hills jackets are segmented and, in more than one handgun, the first time one of these rounds was to be chambered, there was a hang-up. After that, feeding was perfectly fine. I was aiming for my last bullet hole as I continued shooting and had some good two- and three-shot mini-groups.

Bradley Fielding, initially a friend of Danny's and now a friend of mine as well, is a really good pistol shot. He used some old aluminum case Blazer hollow points I must have had for twenty years to print a very tight group.

Inspired by Bradley's performance with the Blazer ammo, I tried the Bersa Thunder 380 (the Bersa plain blued .380). At twenty-one feet, I got several clusters where bullet holes were touching. In my hands, that's good shooting. My technique of sighting on the last hole worked great again and showed the sights were better regulated than my aim. Bradley turned in a nice tight group with the Black Hills – no feeding problem – and Danny, using the Remington

plated. It works pretty much like a Walther PP series pistol, the thumb safety in the up position allowing the shooter to fire, the thumb safety in the lowered position rendering the pistol safe and dropping the hammer. The Concealed Carry was the only one of the three .380s about which we found anything to complain. At about twenty-one feet, my son-in-law, Danny Akers, a good pistol shot, found the the sights easy to see, but the accuracy less than ideal. All shots on the Birchwood Casey Shoot-N-C target were clustered within a few inches, but there was no truly good group. The 88-grain Remington JHPs didn't seem to be a favored diet for this pistol.

The magazine of the increased capacity Thunder Plus.

ammunition, got a group well within our parameters, but it was low and to the left. After seven years of being my son-in-law, as this is written, I hoped my standard aiming problem wasn't catching.

The Thunder .380 Plus, a blued, wide body magazine version of the basic Thunder .380, revealed that my chronic shooting complaint – low and to the left – was not catching. Danny fired Black Hills hollow points into a quite tight group, as did Brad with the old Blazer ammo and even I with Remington fodder. I very much liked the smooth, even double action pull and the single action pull was nice and clean. All of us were impressed with the good feel of the rubber-like grips of the Thunder Plus. This was a nice shooter, indeed.

The Bersa .380s proved what all of us should know. Although price can be indicative of quality, that is not always the case. The Argentinian-made Bersa .380s evidenced

careful attention to quality with good looks, good accuracy and great performance. I'm glad I tried them! When Danny and I tried the Bersa Thunder .45, we were happier still, both of us preferring slightly more meaningful calibers. I brought along one of my favorite personal defense loads, the Federal 230-grain Hydra-Shok JHPs, a load I use quite often. Pinpoint accuracy and great groups in Danny's hands and mine proved elusive, both of us shooting to the left. Danny's trigger finger got pinched between the bottom of the trigger and the guard. The gun worked flawlessly, however, and keeping all hits consistently into something the size of a man's chest cavity center-of-mass was ridiculously easy. Controls and trigger pull were extremely good with this traditional double action. The Bersa Thunder .45 might well be looked at as a larger version of the .380s – and not all that much larger. This .45 is a serious compact.

CHAPTER 29

WALTHER PP, WALTHER P-38 AND WALTHER PPS

The Walther PPS was a truly fine performer and Ahern thinks this is destined to become another Walther Classic.

When Hitler and his Nazi Party rose to power in Germany in the early 1930s, Germany began to prepare for war – surprisingly early on, actually. Part of this preparation was the development of a new service pistol which could be produced more simply and easily and cheaply than the quite complicated P'08 Luger, with which officers and other personnel requiring a sidearm had been armed during World War I. This was an important military contract to be awarded and the people who had developed the first commercially successful double action pistol – the PP and the subsequent PPK – competed for the prize with the Heeres Pistole which, when awarded the contract and accepted into service, became the Walther P-38.

The P-38, at that point in history, was arguably the most technologically advanced military pistol on the face of the earth. Certainly, the Browning P-35 (Hi-Power), with its thirteen round magazine, was innovative, but nothing quite matched the double action first round capability of the Walther P-38. Although the pistol was not as ruggedly built as the 1911, the principal complaint I've heard concerning P-38s was that the dust cover on the upper rear of the slide, when removed too often for detailed stripping, could fly off the pistol when a shot was fired.

If you get a used P-38 in your hands and the dust cover seems loose, you may want to hunt around for another gun. If it doesn't seem loose, you're probably fine. I've owned several P-38 pistols over the years and never had a problem

The trigger guard on the PPS is hinged and works as an ambidextrous magazine release.

Right profile shot of Walther P-38.

of that sort or any other. Typically, you may find that this pistol will need some slicking of the feed ramp in order to reliably handle hollow points, the gun having been designed in the age of solids alone, as well as being a military weapon. The Walther P-38s hang well in the hand, are simple to operate and simple to field strip and they shoot well. During the War, they were made with steel frames. After the War, as the West German P1 service pistol, they were made with alloy frames. My current P-38 is a German police turn-in gun, but marked as a P-38. It was imported as surplus by Century International Arms. As this is written, no more seem to be currently available, but that might change by the time you read this.

The whole thing started in 1929 with the Walther PP. In Europe, the PP was considered a police holster pistol. In America, it's a pocket pistol in the truest sense. Although double action systems had been tried before, commercial success was not to be. Walther, on the other hand, got everything right with the PP. Double action first round capability, hammer dropping safety, loaded chamber indicator, decent sights,

good reliability and rugged construction, ready to fire at an instant's notice and a caliber that was and is again quite popular. Who could ask for more than the PP? Mine has Crimson Trace LaserGrips. Considering it's a design that is pushing toward the century mark, it's still quite modern, although mechanically more complicated than many of today's designs.

The PP led to the ever-so-slightly-smaller PPK (the gun with which "James Bond" routinely saved the world and Adolph Hitler spared the world the anguish of the war crimes trial to end all war crimes trials) and, after the silliness of the USA's Gun Control Act of 1968, the PPK/S, a PP-length frame with a PPK length barrel and slide.

The P-38, albeit a design that was the hot new thing back in 1938, is still quite modern, as well. Like most double action pistols, it is double action for the first shot only, single action after that. Some decry this switch from one trigger pull to another. I don't, since much of the time, with a double action auto, I'll thumb cock the hammer and fire the first shot single action anyway. The advantage of the double action system is that one can usually lower the hammer with impunity and carry the pistol hammer down in more or less perfect safety. I know – I'm peculiar.

The thumb safety also drops the hammer on these older classic Walther pistols. Rather than leave the trigger in a rearward position, Ahern always works the safety off, then back on when the gun is to just be carried.

The P-38 has an eight round magazine and a five-inch barrel and easy to see sights. Albeit alloy framed, firing the 9X19mm, perceived recoil is precious little. The magazine release catch is another thing many shooters will gripe about. It's heel-of-the-butt style. For a true pocket pistol or a military pistol to be taken onto a battlefield, such a magazine release can be a better arrangement, since lightning quick magazine changes won't be required and the magazine is locked more firmly into place than any push-button style magazine release could hold.

The PP series pistols have an "American" style push button magazine release. Capacity in .32 ACP is eight rounds plus one, in the PP itself.

The P-38 is not too large for concealed carry, about the size of a 1911. I've carried P-38s in shoulder holsters, over the years, and inside the waistband. The PP works fine in a holster, a purse, a large pocket or tucked holsterless into the waistband, if you deem that a safe practice.

A feature of the P-38 which cannot be ignored is that it has style. With the exposed barrel, like the barrel of a revolver, and the black finish and, as a used gun, some bright spots from holster wear, the Walther P-38 exudes character. It's one of my favorite handguns.

But the new Walther PPS 9mm is superb in its own right. One of the first of the guns we tested in association with this book, it jaded me, at least, with its fine accuracy, wonderful trigger pull and faultless operation. The PPS is a 9X19mm that is extremely pleasant to shoot, accurate even for me and compact enough for perfect ease of concealment. If anyone thought that Walther might rest only on its laurels or fade away, etc., no way! I would venture to say that, if there were a real "James Bond," he'd be getting "Q-Branch" to stock up on the PPS ASAP!

Using both 115-grain JHP Federals and 124-grain Black Hills hollow points, this "Large Magazine Floorplate" version of the PPS carried eight plus one. With the medium size, capacity is reduced by one round, and with the

This used Walther PP in .32 has been modernized with Crimson Trace LaserGrips.

small size two. I did some of my best shooting with this pistol using the Federal ammo, one of my favorite 9mm loads, the 115-grain JHP 9BP. The PPS's trigger pull was nice and light, but the lower edge of the trigger did pinch my finger against the trigger guard. Protracted shooting would have been less than pleasant. Neither Danny nor Bradley had that problem. Both of them used the Black Hills ammunition. Danny didn't like the feel of the grip, finding it too skinny. Bradley found no problem with grip size and turned in the kind of tight group that seemed to be pretty much the norm for him.

As is becoming more and more common these days, the PPS features "swappable" grip back straps. There is a rail, of course.

The Walther is polymer framed and all black. The sights are of the three dot arrangement. The slide stop is not ambidextrous, but the magazine release is. Merely depress the bottom of the trigger guard from either side. It is hinged at the root of the trigger guard and this is the magazine release catch. Although marked "Smith & Wesson" on the right side of the slide, the left side of the frame indicates the pistol was made in Germany.

From a standpoint of accuracy and ergonomics – except for the tip of the trigger – the Walther PPS was an outstanding shooter and is truly fit to bear the Walther banner.

CHAPTER 30

TAURUS MODEL 809B AND TAURUS 709 SLIM

Left profile shot of the Taurus 809B which proved to be an outstanding performer and incorporates virtually every desirable feature one might look for in a modern semi-automatic.

Taurus is a manufacturing giant, making everything from helmets (the motorcycle kind) to handguns, albeit we in the United States merely think of Taurus in the latter context as one of the largest firearms manufacturers in the world. The first Taurus handguns I ever saw – decades ago – were copies of Smith & Wesson revolvers. Taurus's revolver plant was, at one time, owned by the same people who, at that time, owned Smith & Wesson. The people at the Brazilian revolver plant and the Massachusetts plant exchanged information. Eventually, Bangor-Punta divested itself of the Brazilian operation and sold Smith & Wesson. Taurus started importing handguns into the United States.

As luck would have it, Beretta had a plant in Brazil for a time and, when Beretta decided to close it, Taurus bought up everything and started

The 809B features fully ambidextrous controls and Novak sights and a Tenifer finish.

making its own versions of the Beretta 92. Not long after that, Taurus, continually upgrading performance, looks and overall quality, not only began to broaden the line of model variations, but introduced totally original models. One of Taurus's newest handguns is the Taurus 809B. The 809B really has essentially any feature anyone could ask for in a compact full-size semi-automatic pistol.

The 809B is a 9X19mm pistol with a seventeen plus one capacity. Mine actually takes eighteen plus one, but I load the eighteenth round into the chamber off the top of the magazine. The 809B is a conventional double action, when used as a double action. By that, I mean that the 809B can be carried cocked and locked and used as a conventional single action. All controls – thumb safety and slide stop and dual disassembly actuators – are ambidextrous. The trigger system incorporates an automatic double action reset, should you hit a bad

primer. If the primer doesn't go off on the second strike, the hammer returns to full stand and you clear the action by use of the slide, as you would with any pistol. Don't like the grip back strap? There are two other shapes from which to choose. The grip is nicely textured for a positive hold.

There's a spare magazine included in the case. The push-button magazine release catch is ambidextrous as well. The magazine base has a built-in finger rest, sometimes a dubious feature at best. This is a good one.

If you need to mount a light or any accessory under the frame, there's a Picatinny rail. Front and rear sights are adjustable and quite easily picked up. They are Novaks. It's a three dot system. The slide has deeply angled serrations for good contact and there are forward slide serrations as well, these to facilitate a press check as needed.

Clearly, this is a pistol into which went a great

This Titanium version of the 709 Slim would be an interesting pistol to shoot. Ahern tested quite extensively the 709 Slim, but with stainless slide. This was an excellent little gun. (Taurus USA Photo)

deal of thought. It incorporates every desirable detail. The 809B shoots great, as well. Accuracy and feeding with several 9X19mm cartridge types was without a hitch.

The frame is polymer and the slide is Tenifer. Tenifer is considered a finish, but it isn't, really. Tenifer is, rather, a metal surface hardening technique which makes the surface almost as hard as a diamond. The Tenifer surface resists rust and corrosion because the surface is so hard that rust and corrosion can't get started. It's a fascinating process.

Eight and one-half inches long, with a four inch barrel, the 809B weighs a little over 30 ounces. I speak very highly of the Taurus 809B because I view it as a world class pistol anyone would be lucky to own. I own one. Size and handling qualities are outstanding.

Yet, if a smaller handgun in 9X19mm is better suited to your concealment needs, the 709 Slim is just about as good as you can get. That's a compliment I don't toss out lightly. Polymer framed with a stainless slide, my sample is about the size of a Walther PPK, only a little slimmer, maybe, and has every feature you could want

in a hideout handgun. 9X19mm may not be the best man stopper, but it's no B-Complex shot for your adversary, either. The 709 Slim is a little wonder. Length overall is six inches, just one tenth on an inch shorter than a Walther PPK in .32 or .380, and the 709 Slim – it really is, slim – is a 9X19mm, don't forget. Capacity is seven plus one. Weight is 19 ounces, and the pistol is extremely comfortable to shoot in two-hand aimed fire or when body indexing from the hip with one hand. The frame is polymer. The barrel is three inches long, and the slide can be had in black, stainless or, lighter weight still, titanium. I have never fired the titanium version but found the stainless slide version an ideal shooter.

I tested the 709 Slim in a rather lengthy shooting session a short while ago, at The Firing Line in Bogart, Georgia. I used a variety of 9X19mm cartridges, and accuracy was consistently good at a variety of distances. My favorite Federal 9BP load, of course, worked just great. This was a terrific, naturally pointing little gun to shoot from the hip, by the way.

This 709 Slim is a superb personal defense handgun I recommend unhesitatingly.

CHAPTER 31

CZ USA CZ83 .380 & 2075 RAMI 9MM

Both CZ pistols seemed to have strong springs and stiff controls, but quality of workmanship was quite evident. This is the Rami 9mm.

I f you happen to be a firearms manufacturer and one of the world's most highly regarded special forces organizations uses one of your products, it's a real plus.

Then, if one of the world's most well-respected firearms experts says that product is one of the best of its type to be had, that helps.

And if a brand new gun that gets lots of publicity is designed using that other gun as the basis, those circumstances certainly generate even more notoriety.

And then, if another fine firearms maker starts copying the weapon, that just creates even greater interest.

Add in the fact that, in certain parts of the world, the gun is almost impossible to obtain and you get quite a lot of "buzz."

The special forces organization was the Soviet-era Spetznas. Although the Commies were the "evil empire," no one disputed the taste these men had in firearms. The firearms authority was the late Jeff Cooper, one of the men most trusted for his

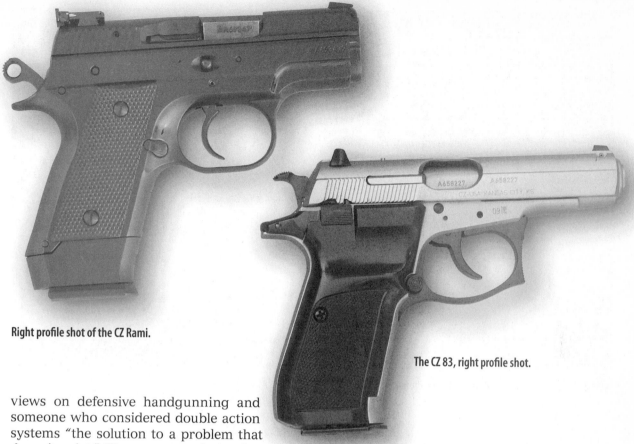

Right profile shot of the CZ Rami.

The CZ 83, right profile shot.

views on defensive handgunning and someone who considered double action systems "the solution to a problem that doesn't exist." The new gun design based on the weapon was the ill-fated Bren Ten. It will be recalled that the character of "Sonny Crockett" on *Miami Vice* had enough Bren Ten magazines to drop them to the ground, even as he practiced his shooting. The majority of Bren Ten owners didn't even have one magazine to put into the Bren Ten, rendering the guns a single-shot proposition. The well-respected Italian firearms maker Tanfoglio produced and produces excellent near identical seeming duplicates of the gun; other firms did and still do. Because the gun was made in what was then Czechoslovakia, inside the Soviet Bloc, precious few reached the United States, those that did coming by way of Canada. What's that they say about forbidden fruit tasting the sweetest?

After all, the pistol was/is only a blued 9mm!

The gun was the CZ-75 9X19mm. Internal rails machined into the frame, ala the crème de la crème of 9mms, the SIG P-210, and a Browning style short recoil design combined to make the pistol developed by the Coucky brothers for Ceska Zbrojovka an all-time classic.

Ceska Zbrojovka was founded in 1936, production actually underway in early 1937. Stalin's Russia used the aftermath of World War II as the means by which to absorb various smaller nations and turn them into "satellite" countries to the Soviet Union. In 1918, after World War I, Bohemia changed its name to Czechoslovakia, in honor of the Czech and Slovak ethnicities. Czechoslovakia was a casualty of appeasement diplomacy when, in 1938, it was sold out and ordered to turn over the Sudetenland to Hitler's Germany, this to help assure Neville Chamberlain's concept of "peace in our time." The rest of the country was occupied by the Nazis in March of 1939 when that "peace in our time" thing didn't quite work out, Czechoslovakia being "liberated" by the USSR upon the collapse of the German war machine. The present-day Czech Republic was established in 1993, after the fall of Soviet Communism and the breakup of the Soviet Union. What this meant for the CZ-75 was that more of these guns could be sold to police and others in the United States and elsewhere in the West and that CZ could grow into the world class arms house it is today.

While sticking to that same basic design of the Coucky brothers, while adapting alloy frames in some models, adding new safety features, making compact versions, incorporating light rails, caliber selection has even broadened. The 2075 RAMI is a

The CZ 83 was very much a quintessential medium frame automatic.

compact 9X19mm pistol which worked well for Danny, Bradley and me. Much of the shooting was done with Sellier & Bellot 124-grain full metal case ammunition, also from the Czech Republic, but we combined these sure-to-work solids with Winchester Supreme 9mm JHPs in the same fourteen-round magazine. The shorter ten-round magazine would allow the pistol to conceal more easily. Clear, easy to use sights – the rear sight rather large – and a comfortable feel to the gun in the hand lent to accurate shooting from all three of us and a pleasant experience.

The one criticism with both CZ pistols shot in association with this project was the strength needed for operation. Springs were obviously strong and working slide stops was not easy.

With the CZ 83, for example, loading Remington 88-grain .380 JHPs into the twelve-round magazine was quite a chore. While the hand-filling grips were comfortable and the pistol was inherently accurate – even in my hands – the stiffness of the controls was disconcerting. Trigger pull, conversely, was quite nice. When I used Black Hills .380s in the CZ 83, the hollow point design mentioned elsewhere here gave me a slow feed on the third round I fired. As one might do with a 1911, when not in a gunfight, of course, a little bit of a nudge of the slide did the trick and everything continued smoothly with the CZ 83.

The CZ 83 has a distinctly European look, tapering gracefully along the slide. The trigger guard is squared and slightly hooked. Fit and finish were excellent.

CHAPTER 32

NORTH AMERICAN ARMS GUARDIAN .380, GUARDIAN .32 NAA, GUARDIAN .32, PUG .22 MAGNUM, LONG RIFLE MINI-REVOLVER

The people at North American Arms are some of the nicest people I know, whether it's Sandy Chisholm, who owns the company, or Ken Friel, who's the General Manager and runs the day-to-day operation, or any of the other members of the staff. For a number of years, North American Arms wanted to have its own automatic pistol to add to its already well-respected line of NAA Mini-Revolvers. The first of these semi-autos was the Guardian .32. If the

Guardian .32 my wife, Sharon, carries is typical – and, I strongly suspect that it is – Guardian 32s have a quite heavy trigger pull. For a handgun that will be banged around in pocket or purse, that may not be such a bad idea.

The Guardian .32 is the smaller of the two Guardian models, this larger frame gun the Guardian .380. I quite often carry a Guardian .380 that is equipped with Crimson Trace LaserGrips. Sharon's little .32 and my slightly

For a reasonably powerful handgun, the Guardian .32 NAA is still quite small. Fortunately, as Ahern sees it, NAA wisely made the little gun all steel.

The Guardian .32 NAA had stout recoil, but was manageable and not painful.

larger .380 both hit what they're aimed at and function with perfect reliability. Otherwise, we wouldn't carry them.

Readers will recall that the search for the ultimate handgun, whatever that is, often focuses on cartridge power. J.B. Wood got involved in that quest when he worked to develop the bottle-neck .25/.32 round. J.B.

Wood is a gun writer, of course, but only in the same sense that, say, Frank Sinatra was just a singer. NAA was already working with cartridge effectiveness authority Ed Sanow and Peter Pi, the president of Cor-Bon. It was during this period that J.B. Wood contacted NAA. While Sanow's and Pi's work went on apace, work on the .25/.32 JBW cartridge hit a snag relating to feeding. J.B. Wood's cartridge worked great, but feeding precipitated nosedives, the bullet sinking and the cartridge failing to chamber. Sanow's and Pi's work with the .32 NAA succeeded and Sanow and Pi went to work on the .25/.32 JBW, lengthening the case and deleting the rim. The .25/.32 JBW is not the same cartridge as the .25 NAA, but served as the inspiration for the cartridge.

The result of NAA's collaboration with Cor-Bon on the .32 NAA, all based on Ed Sanow's research and experimentation, was a necked down .380 with a .32 ACP bullet. At over 1200 FPS velocity and nearly two hundred foot pounds of energy, it is a serious cartridge, to say the least. Both Danny and I fired the .32 NAA version of the Guardian – it's chambered in the .380-sized pistol, of course – and came to similar conclusions. Combine heavy trigger pull with long length of pull and vestigial fixed sights and quite noticeable recoil – I found it much more "noticeable" than firing the ordinary .380 ACP Guardian – and you have a gun that needs

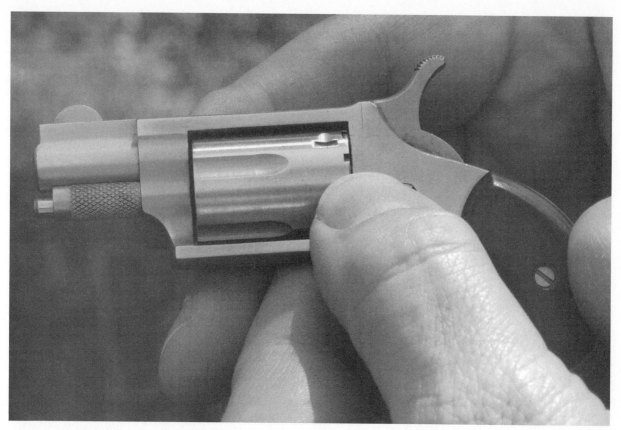

The NAA Long Rifle Mini-Revolver with 1 1/8-inch barrel is a reliable weapon at what amounts to contact distance or nearly that.

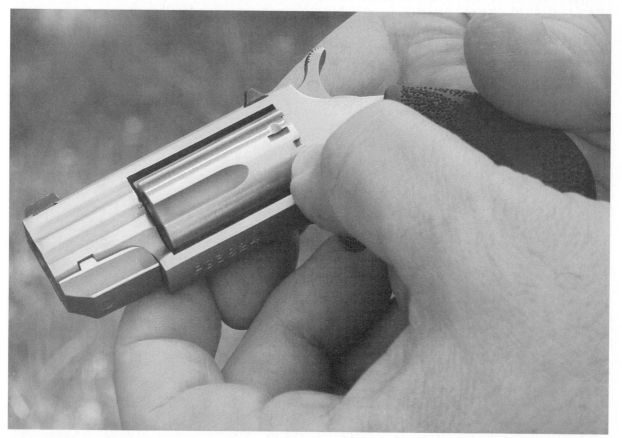

Because it offers more to hold onto, the .22 Magnum NAA Pug could be a best choice among Mini-Revolvers for an ultimately tiny backup.

to be fired quickly and at close range. When Sharon first tried her Guardian .32, the trigger pull weight and length issue for conventional deliberate shooting was unmanageable. So, I asked Sharon to try pointing the gun at her target, look across the sights and then pull the trigger as fast as she could, before that length and weight of pull caused wobbling. She shoots the Guardian .32 just fine now, at the close range for which the gun is intended.

Danny got a pretty decent group, despite grousing over trigger pull weight, length and subsequent recoil. I groused just as well, but shot a large group that would have done its work on a human center of mass but was nothing one would want to photograph or even discuss. Additionally, both Danny and I experienced the trigger finger being pinched slightly against the inside of the lower portion of the trigger guard.

If you are close to your target and sure that you must shoot, shoot fast and these guns will serve you well.

Much the same can be said for NAA's Mini-Revolvers. They are not for long range shooting. There are numerous variations. NAA's .22 Magnum Pug is among the newest and is well suited to close range defensive shooting. Yes, the gun can be had – like mine – with night sights; but, in darkness, this would just be to find the gun if it had been set down or dropped or to orient the muzzle toward the target. The bulbous rubber grips make the Pug easier to hold onto than more conventional Mini-Revolvers and do nothing to detract from concealment. At ranges between one to three yards, with practice I can keep my shots in the chest area of a silhouette. That's acceptable to me with a Mini-Revolver, keeping in mind the gun must be rotated in the hand after each shot is fired in order to cock the hammer – at least the way I hold a Mini.

The Pug is a sensational tiny backup or backup to your backup. The same can be said for the less powerful one and one-eighth-inch .22 Long Rifle Mini-Revolver. Shorter barreled Mini-Revolvers like this can be hidden in rather unconventional places on body. The same general accuracy can be obtained when I'm shooting one of these. In most real life situations, a Mini-Revolver that is used for personal defense will only be used in the most desperate circumstances and, quite likely, at contact distance. Lots of cops use these little guns. A friend of a friend saved his life with one in a law enforcement situation. Possessing at least one North American Arms Mini-Revolver is an essential requirement for the true concealed weapons aficionado.

North American Arms handguns – whether revolvers or automatics – are made from stainless steel. Even more stainless, however, is the reputation North American Arms has earned over the years for customer service and standing behind their products, whether the watch-like Mini-Revolvers or the ever-evolving autoloaders with their wide array of custom options.

CHAPTER 33

RUGER LCP, RUGER KSR 9C & RUGER LCR

The LCP .380's magazine can be fitted with a finger rest extension, if desired.

R uger has an enviable reputation for fine handguns, of course, but is somewhat new to the field of smaller, personal defense handguns, their LCP .380 creating quite a stir with its arrival on the scene. Then, of course, following the 2008 Presidential Election, the ammunition buying frenzy kicked in and endured through 2009 and even beyond with many loads. Everybody wanted the hot new Ruger .380 auto and the ammunition to shoot through it.

Ruger kindly loaned me a sample LCP for this work. It is a fine looking all-black pistol with an amply dimensioned trigger guard for almost any hand. I did pinch my trigger finger between the bottom of the trigger and the interior surface of the trigger guard. Although all three of us – Danny, Bradley and myself – own Ruger firearms and both Danny and Bradley are great fans of Ruger semi-autos, not one of us was taken with the LCP.

Shooting results were not good. There were

The LCP is a tiny, light weight .380 hideout pistol.

no malfunctions, but I shot just miserably with the LCP using the Black Hills hollow points. I found perceived recoil to be stronger than I experience with my NAA Guardian .380 or what I experienced with the diminutive Seecamp .380. Danny used the Remington hollow points and fired the LCP very poorly as well. Danny put into words something I also had experienced. The gun wanted to jump out of his hand in recoil. Neither Danny nor I could be accused of having a weak grip, and this problem surfacing for both of us was unnerving. Bradley Fielding shot the best target, getting the only results acceptable by the standards I had set, using the very old aluminum case Blazer hollow points.

Compounding the recoil problem with the little gun was the issue of the sights. These were virtually non-existent. Now, I like small sights or no sights at all on small handguns, but the sights were just enough to make all of us think that we should use the sights.

This is clearly – at least in my hands and those of Danny and Bradley – a gun best suited for extremely close range, especially if follow up shots might be called for. If one of the issues could be taken out of the mix, conventional marksmanship results would be more readily achievable. For example, weight of the LCP is just 9.4 ounces. The discontinued Beretta 950 BS Jetfire single action .25 ACP weighed 10 ounces. The steel-framed NAA Guardian .380 weighs in at 18.72 ounces, almost twice as much as the LCP. The frame of the LCP is glass-filled nylon. I cannot help but feel the LCP would have handled better weighing more.

If the LCP were offered in .32 ACP, I, for one, would find it a much more viable proposition. The weapon displays the obvious quality of materials and manufacture one expects from Ruger, of course. Taking all safety considerations into account, to be sure, if you find yourself armed with this firearm, you may well want to practice at extremely close range and limit practice session duration.

Totally the opposite of the LCP, for us at least, was the KSR9C 9X19mm compact. All three of us shot the weapon well, Danny getting a group falling well within our parameters with some of my old Remington 115-grain JHPs, these cartridges well over thirty years old. I shot not as well, but stayed within the parameters. I found the pistol's trigger pull to be excellent, the trigger itself incorporating a safety lever within it; when not depressed, the trigger is inoperative.

There's also an ambidextrous manual safety.

At a hair under seven inches in length, sight radius is good and the sights themselves are large but no overly so. Bradley did the best shooting of the day, stringing shots, one hole touching the other. A compact full-size 9mm, it features a seventeen plus one capacity and weighs a quite acceptable 23.4 ounces.

As with so many handguns these days, there's a light rail on the underside of the frame.

Around the time of the 2010 NRA Convention and Show, Ruger announced the LCR revolver was being offered in .357 Magnum. At thirteen point five ounces, it won't be something for a casual day's plinking. This model is in .38 Special.

The pistol comes in all black finish – the alloy slide matching the glass-filled nylon frame – or, as was our sample, with brushed stainless steel slide. Either finish option, you should have a good looking, good shooting, accurate 9mm in the SR9C.

The third new Ruger we tried was the radically designed LCR Double-Action Revolver. Had I realized that this revolver weighed in at only 13.5 ounces – almost half a pound less than a steel-framed J-Frame Smith & Wesson, I would have brought along some standard velocity .38 Specials. Yet, despite the lack of weight, the revolver's recoil was not unpleasant, which I find remarkable and can only attribute to Ruger's design personnel and the choice of materials. The sample had the Hogue Tamer grips, rather than Crimson Trace LaserGrips, which are optionally available.

Crimson trace LaserGrips would make a great addition to this remarkably innovative revolver, since the consensus arrived at by all three of us was that the revolver's fixed sights are not conducive to terrific accuracy.

All three of us, although we complained about the sights, shot decently enough. Bradley got the tightest of the group, using Winchester

Controls for this modularly constructed revolver from Ruger are refreshingly straightforward.

The Ruger SR9C is a conveniently sized pistol, pleasant and easy to operate.

Ruger semi-autos, like this SR9C, are justifiably well-respected for good value.

Super X 158-grain lead semi-wadcutter hollow point +Ps. Bradley was able to get a cluster of five shots hole touching hole near the center of the target. Using the same load from Federal, Danny got a proportionately larger group. My eyes are twice as old as either of theirs and the black front sight and diminutive black rear sight blended in to one another hopelessly. My shots were all over the place with Federal 129-grain jacketed Hydra-Shok hollow points. Had the target been a man's torso, I would have hit it every time, but my accuracy was dismal.

My advice would be that, in order to take advantage of this modularly constructed, lightweight but manageable Ruger revolver, go for the Crimson Trace LaserGrips.

CHAPTER 34

KEL-TEC P-32 AND KEL-TEC PF9

About the size of a medium frame autoloader in .32 or .380, the PF 9 is a 9X19mm.

el-Tec CNC Industries came on the scene some years ago with a 9mm pistol that was about the size of a slightly larger Walther PP. The gun instantly became quite popular because of its size and caliber. Kel-Tec was an experienced entity and seemed to take considerable pride and care in product manufacturing.

But what really caused Kel-Tec to take off big time was a small, small gun. While everyone was trying to get their hands on the Seecamp .32 and other .32s were being designed and heading toward the market, Kel-Tec produced a polymer framed .32 ACP that has developed an admirable following. One of the most knowledgeable gun

guys I know oftentimes carries a Kel-Tec .32 in his shirt pocket. The barrel for the Kel-Tec is made from 4140 ordnance steel, as is the slide. The grip frame is made from DuPont ST-8018, a high impact polymer. Although longer magazines can be had, which would be self defeating for concealment, the standard magazine holds seven rounds. Firing from a locked breech, this double action only pistol claims to be and is the "lightest .32 auto pistol ever made."

The Kel-Tec .32 is a pistol that feels comfortable in the hand. Double action only with no manual safety, it is very much a diminutive version of a larger handgun. It is, in fact, identical in every

The little Kel-Tec .32 has become a very well-respected personal firearm and Ahern has never heard of any complaints with the gun.

Right profile shot of the Kel-Tec PF 9.

The Kel-Tec PF 9 is compact and reliable. Diminutive 9mms were Kel-Tecs first firearms products.

way except size to the PF-9 pistol. The parts diagrams for both pistols, if you compare them, are essentially identical except for size. The PF-9 has a seven round magazine and Kel Tec claims the gun "…is the lightest and flattest 9mm Luger caliber ever made." Both Danny and I found the P .32 quite pleasant to shoot with Winchester Silvertips. Neither of us really liked the sights and Danny found that the pistol shot low for him. With my older eyes, I was shooting around my point of aim but both of us wound up with groups that were well within our established parameters for rapid shooting. The overall impression of the gun was the same I had some years ago when I first fired one. The Kel-Tec .32

is smooth functioning and easy to use. Once you get past the idea that the sights will do little good for you, the gun is actually easier to work with. It's obvious why this Kel-Tec .32 is so popular.

The Kel-Tec is also available, of course, in .380 ACP.

When it came to the PF-9, we had mixed reviews. Using Sellier & Bellot 124 grain solids, Danny found the gun shooting well to the left for him. I used Winchester Supreme 124 grain JHPs and found the recoil to be quite unpleasant, but the 124-grain JHP is a +P. I failed to get a group that would fall within our parameters. The PF-9 weighs in at around fifteen ounces, which is very light for a full power cartridge. Despite that, using the same Winchester ammo, Brad, who found the gun shooting a little to the right for him, got not only the best group but one with most holes touching.

This is the classic situation of do you want a firearm that is extraordinarily light and therefore easier to carry or can you handle a little more weight with a gun that is more pleasant to shoot. If weight when you're carrying it is the ultimate critical factor for you, the PF 9 could be just what you're looking for. But, I would go to standard velocity 9X19mm ammunition and avoid the +Ps. Both Kel-Tec pistols functioned flawlessly and Kel-Tec products are a good value.

CHAPTER 35

ROHRBAUGH .380 AND R9

Right profile of the Rohrbaugh R9.

The Rohrbaugh .380 was created for persons thinking that the R9 would be too tough with recoil. The R9 is not that tough to shoot. And, the Rohrbaugh .380 is a fine little pistol in its own right.

The Rohrbaugh R-9 is to 9 mms what the Seecamp was to .32s. It does something that has never been done before. The R-9 and the .380 version deserve a little bit of explanation here. When Rohrbaugh invented the gun, he was teaching pistol and found that many of his students were as taken with the Seecamp .32 as was he. Inspired by what Seecamp had done in terms of miniaturization and alert to the fact that there was a considerable wait to get a Seecamp, Karl Rohrbaugh tried his hand at designing a smaller-than-ever before 9mm.

The reason that there is a .380 ACP version of the Rohrbaugh is because many people were reluctant to shoot a 9X19mm that weighed only 12.8 ounces. I don't blame them. When Rohrbaugh and I spoke concerning borrowing a couple of his guns for this book, I asked him quite bluntly about the 9mm. I recounted that, even though I'm a great fan of the Detonics CombatMasters, I had found the old Detonics Pocket 9, which was a straight blowback, to be the most unpleasant to fire pistol I have ever handled. Shooting that gun, which had

The Rohrbaugh R9 was surprisingly pleasant considering it is an ultra-small 9X19mm.

Either Rohrbaugh easily carries in a pocket. This is the .380.

to weigh well more than the Rohrbaugh, is an experience that I will never forget. Karl Rohrbaugh assured me that I could rest easy, this pistol of his design firing from a locked breech. The shooting experience with the Rohrbaugh was an odd one when it came to the 9mm. Even though this pistol weighs less than 13 ounces, neither Danny nor Bradley nor I found it punishing to shoot. Danny used the Sellier & Bellot 124-grain solids and had the only ammunition problem of our tests when he had a hit from the firing pin but the round did not discharge. After examining the round, it was disposed of safely. Other than that, Danny's shooting experience with the Rohrbaugh was not remarkable and, unsolicitedly, he volunteered that there was not a lot of recoil. I used Federal 124-grain Hydra Shok JHPs and shot a group within our established parameters. And, I was, frankly, amazed that the noticeable recoil was not punishing. Part of this has to be grip design. That is the only explanation I can think of. Brad used the Sellier & Bellot full metal jacketed ammo and got his usual good group. All three of us were impressed with the Rohrbaugh and it's easy to see why this small pistol is so terribly popular.

The .380 version was produced simply for those persons who could not be persuaded that the 9mm wouldn't rip their hands off. I used the Remington 88-grain JHPs that I normally use these days when I'm shooting a .380. The sights on the Rohrbaugh were small, of course; but, since they were not black on black, they were sufficiently visible and I got my usual mediocre group. Trigger pull, as with the 9mm version, was smooth and pleasant. Both Danny and Bradley used Black Hills 90-grain hollowpoints and both shot well with them. Curiously, Danny complained that the grips on the .380 felt too slick to him. The grips are identical on the 9mm and the .380 , so this would indicate to me that, in anticipation of super strong recoil, Danny had a death grip on the 9mm and, expecting far more moderate recoil with the .380, he held the pistol more loosely. Bradley had no complaints with the .380.

The Rohrbaugh .380 is a perfectly satisfactory .380 that is considerably smaller than the classic medium frame auto. But, where the Rohrbaugh design really shines is in the original R-9. Here is a 9mm, although one not designed for +Ps, that can easily be hidden in a trouser pocket and doesn't produce recoil so severe that you will never practice with it. This did indeed do for the 9mm what Larry Seecamp and his father did for the .32 ACP. They dropped a full frame size. Both Rohrbaugh calibers were good performers; but, clearly, the 9mm option would be what I would go for. In size it is unmatched.

Overall length of either gun is 5.2 inches with a barrel that is 2.9 inches. Height of the pistol is 3.7 inches. The six round magazine is secured with a heel of the butt release. The slide and barrel are machined from stainless steel and the frame is from aluminum. Double action only, of course, the pistol is ready to go when you need it. I was impressed.

CHAPTER 36

COBRA SHADOW REVOLVER AND COBRA DERRINGER

The Cobra Shadow revolver is a close copy of the S&W Model 640, and very lightweight. It's a bargain alternative truly worth considering and will even work with Crimson Trace LaserGrips made for the S&W J-Frames.

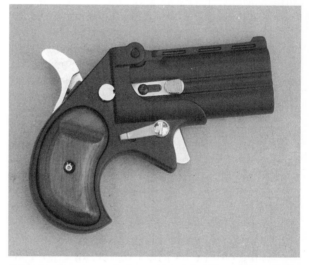

Cobra Derringers are close to the original Remington pattern handguns.

The people at Cobra produce an eclectic mix of firearms. Based in Utah, the company is very aggressively pro-gun and this is extremely commendable. One of the guns that they make is so close in size and other features to the Smith & Wesson current production Model 640 that the guns will even take the same Crimson Trace LaserGrips. The Cobra Shadow, as that revolver is called, has a great deal in common with that famous Smith & Wesson. The Shadow weighs just under 16 ounces on our postage scale and it got mixed reviews as relates to recoil. Danny found the Shadow reasonably pleasant to shoot, despite the weight, while Bradley complained about a lot of recoil. The weight question really depends on who is holding the gun and how that person experiences the recoil and what that person considers to be severe.

The Shadow's double action pull is very

Handling qualities with the Cobra Shadow are quite satisfactory and quite familiar.

smooth and light. I used Federal 158 grain lead semi-wadcutter +Ps as did Danny. This is the load that I use in my own J-Frames and that both Sharon and Samantha use in theirs. The same bullet design in Winchester is what Brad used. All three of us were able to obtain groups that met our testing parameters for shooting rapid fire. That said, all of us would have shot better if the rear sight channel were more defined. In this one aspect, the Shadow diverges from the typical Smith & Wesson J-Frame. As someone used to the J-Frame sights, I found the Shadow's a little hard to pick up. On the plus side, with the barrel being bright metal and the frame being black on our particular sample, the contrast was helpful. The frame is made from aluminum and, aside from the black anodized version, the frame can be had in a variety of colors, to include pink or gold. The cylinder and barrel are made from stainless steel. Barrel length is the classic 1-7/8 inches. Cobra makes a point of the fact that these 100% American made revolvers are attractively priced and they are attractively priced indeed. Add to that the gun comes with a lifetime warranty and the Cobra Shadow is definitely something to consider. It does not feature an integral safety lock, a fact which does not break my heart.

The Cobra Derringer in .38 Special was the size of the old FIE Derringer from many years ago. There's a very modest ventilated sighting plane running between a low front blade and a notch. As triggers go in derringers, the Cobra Derringer has a pretty good one. The one thing I will say is that neither Danny nor Bradley nor I would ever be a force to be reckoned with in a derringer side match if we engaged in Cowboy Action Shooting. I had not shot a derringer in well over a year and a half and I was woefully out of practice. What I normally do when I'm firing a derringer is a technique I actually picked up from television westerns! As you are going to fire the derringer, you essentially punch it forward and pull the trigger. The technique actually works at extreme close range and allows you to hit near the center of something the size of an adult male torso, but neither one of the three of us could get a group with something which had to be manually cocked and turned in the hand to do that. We used both Federal and the Winchester +Ps and all of us came away feeling that, as derringers go in the shootability department, the Cobra Derringer was perfectly acceptable. It's a nice looking and well made derringer that is also sold by Cimarron Arms as a private label item.

The Cobra Derringers are also available in a more diminutive version, offered in .22 LR and in .22 Magnum. Whereas barrel length of the .38 Special is 2-3/4 inches, and overall length is 4-2/3 inches, the rimfire version, which weighs only a little over a half-pound, has a barrel length of 2 inches and an overall length of only 4 inches. The .22 version is about a half-inch shorter in height, too.

Whether or not a derringer is right as a defensive option for you is a question I cannot answer. Years ago, I carried a beautifully made American Derringer chambered in .45 Colt and .410 and found it to be a reliable personal defense weapon. I have also tested and reported on the Bond Arms derringers, these derringers too being extremely well made. The key to whether a derringer is right for you rests partially in caliber selection. .38 Special or smaller caliber is perfectly pleasant to shoot. When you go above .38 Special, you want to have the freebore effect found with the .45 Colt/.410 combination. The difference without this freebore effect is profound when it comes to recoil.

The Cobra Shadow and the Cobra Derringer seemed to all of us to be a good value.

CHAPTER 37

SPRINGFIELD XD-40 AND SPRINGFIELD XDM

The XDM 9mm in right profile.

The XD40 came packaged with its own holster and double magazine pouch as well as a magazine loading tool.

Springfield first got its handgun business going with a series of fine 1911 pistols that have developed a very solid following. All assembly and other work is accomplished in their Illinois plant but certain of their parts are made in Brazil, a country well respected for firearms manufacturing quality. As the polymer frame passion swept the firearms industry as a result of the success of the Glock pistols, various firms endeavored to have their own unique firearms capitalizing on some of these exciting new features. The initials "XD" stand for "extreme duty" and the XD pistol series from Springfield has captured a great deal of the American market. We worked with two XD pistols, one the XD 40 in – you guessed it – .40 S&W and the other the XDM in 9mm. Curiously, all three of us did better with the Springfield XD .40 than the XDM.

Let's cover some features first. The XD series incorporates a grip safety, a loaded chamber indicator, a striker status indicator and is engineered with good ergonomics. The Springfield XD .40 is a sensational little

The 9mm Springfield XDM is a good shooting handgun.

The Springfield XD40 is a good-handling concealment pistol. Yet, the little gun has an accessory rail on the frame.

subcompact, wide bodied .40 S& W which has a nine plus one capacity. Made in Croatia, exclusively for Springfield, the little gun features a light rail, slide serrations which allow a positive grip, an ambidextrous magazine release that works conveniently, the afore mentioned grip safety and trigger safety and a frame that extends just slightly rearward of the mating spot between the slide and the frame, this to protect the web of the hand. Three dot sights and a comfortable heft in the hand make this little .40 a good shooter.

Using 200 grain .40 S&W cartridges of unknown ancestry, Danny got an extremely tight group, well better than our basic parameters. Bradley did the same. I shot like I usually do, but found the gun rewarding. We also used Winchester Supreme Elite 180-grain JHPs, some Black Hills 180-grain and Cor-Bon 140 grain DPX as well. The gun was a genuine pleasure to shoot. As to how the gun was packaged, it comes with a standard magazine and an extended magazine that handles twelve rounds. Danny liked the extended magazine better than the standard length. As concealment guy, I, of course, liked the shorter magazine. Our sample came packaged in a nice looking case which not only included the spare magazine, but also a magazine loading tool, a holster and a double magazine pouch. Basically, you've got a kit and you are ready to go.

The XD-9 comes with a similar kit. This is a very sound marketing idea. The XD-9 has an eighteen round magazine, what many of us in the trade refer to as a bicycle lock and two additional backstrap inserts which allow customizing the grip to your own specifications. Danny used some of my old Remington 115 grain 9mms, as did I. Then he also shot three different types of ammo out of the same magazine, Remington 115 grain, Federal 115 grain and Sellier & Bellot 124 grain solids. I used Remington 115 grain from the old box and Bradley used Federal 115 grain, the 9BP. None of the three of us did as well with the 9mm as we did with the .40. Bradley remarked that, although the pistol felt good in his hand, he thought it shot rather high. The best group of the day with this gun was Danny's, with a magazine of mixed ammunition.

The same safety and convenience features on the little .40 are also on this larger 9mm, but I do have some very minor reservations about the length versus height issue. Overall length of this pistol is just 6-1/2 inches. Overall height of the pistol, because of the eighteen round magazine, is 5-1/2 inches. Had I been designing this pistol and I had an eighteen round length grip, I would have extended the overall length of the gun another inch. This is just personal preference, but it would make this gun no less concealable and probably a little bit more effective.

Springfield, which first became well known because of their fine rifles, continues their pursuit of excellence.

CHAPTER 38

KIMBER ULTRA CARRY II

Kimber can always be counted on for good looks and good performance. The Ultra Carry II is no exception.

The Ultra Carry II from Kimber is accomplished with Kimber's usual attention to detail. Weight of the pistol is 25 ounces, according to Kimber's own stats, putting it at over three quarters of a pound less weight than a full size 1911. The weight factor is important, because in many ways we're talking about a more compact version of a Commander size pistol. The Commander, when it was originally introduced by Colt, had an aluminum alloy frame. There was much chest beating about aluminum alloy frames holding up, but aluminum alloy frames have proven to be quite acceptable for hard duty with a heavy caliber pistol.

Barrel length is where this pistol is quite radical. The barrel is only three inches long, making it 1-3/4 inches shorter than a Commander and a half-inch shorter than the Detonics CombatMaster. Magazine capacity with the

There's a certain "comfort factor" to be found in shooting a reliable .45. Shooting the Kimber Ultra Carry II was a pleasant experience.

The Kimber Ultra Carry II .45 is made for concealed carry needs, yet shooting qualities are not compromised.

pistol is a full seven rounds, as in traditional 1911 pistols. Overall length of this pistol is 6.8 inches. The slide is stainless steel and the trigger is match grade aluminum. The added length in the grip in order to accommodate seven rounds allows getting the entire last three fingers on the grip frame.

Danny and I both shot the Kimber Ultra Carry II using Federal 230 grain Hydra Shok ammunition. I did my best shooting of the session with the Kimber and this did not surprise me. In my hands, it shot slightly to the left, which is a chronic problem with my shooting. My group

was nice and tight. It should be remembered that I would sometimes test fire more than thirty 1911-style automatics in a session, so that even with my lackluster marksmanship, I tend to do better with a .45. Danny is also a good hand with a .45 and got a better group than mine, both of us well within the parameters set for the test. The pistol was quite pleasant to shoot and perception of recoil was not a factor.

Kimber recommends that, with the Ultra Carry models, the recoil spring should be changed every 1800 rounds. I had asked one of my contacts at Kimber about swapping recoil springs as often as recommended in their manuals. It was made clear to me, as I had assumed, that once you hit the magic number of rounds you shouldn't expect catastrophic spring failure. Instead, Kimber views this as a way to ensure there will not be spring failure. That certainly makes sense.

Sights on the Ultra Carry II are fixed and extremely rugged. They are left black and, if this pistol were mine, I would add white markings on the sights to assist my older eyes. The thumb safety is single sided, but extended, and the grip safety features a beaver tail. The beaver tail amply protects the web of the hand. The Kimber Ultra Carry II is a classy looking pistol and performed quite well.

CHAPTER 39

HKP2000 SK

The HK P2000 Sub-Compact .40 was a unique gun with unique features.

Heckler & Koch manufactures purpose driven firearms. At least, it has always seemed that way to me. Heckler & Koch is a firm that has always been associated with some of the finest military weapons on the planet and the Heckler & Koch name on a battle rifle is a symbol of obvious quality and durability. Heckler & Koch is also known for "odd" handguns. I mean "odd" in a good sense. For example, the HK P7 M8 squeeze cocker was extraordinarily unconventional, yet quite, quite good.

These days, the number of HK pistols has grown substantially and HK has a serious position in the law enforcement and military market. The P Series P2000 SK is a 27 ounce polymer frame, nine-plus-one-shot .40 S&W that is also available in 9x19mm and .357 SIG. Overall length is 6.42 inches and barrel length is 3.27 inches. The controls on the gun are

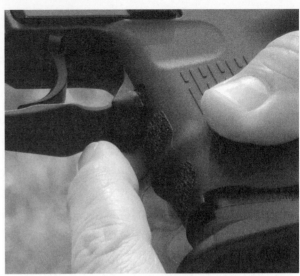

Shooting the HK P2000 was a pleasant experience.

One of the unique features of the HK P2000 was this ambidextrous magazine release, a lever rather than a button.

interesting. Everything is ambidextrous and, when it comes to the magazine release catch, that ambidextrous control would take a great deal of getting used to – if you had just picked up the gun. You have to press slightly downward on the release, which is located below and is part of the root of the trigger guard. The root of the trigger guard, of course, is where the trigger guard meets the grip frame. The gun comes with a flat grip backstrap installed and a curved back strap which can be switched into the pistol. Sights on the HK, although black against a black gun, are quite visible with their three white dots.

Since we were getting toward the end of our shooting session and we had ammunition left over, it only seemed appropriate to shoot up more of it in the HK. Using the .40 S&W solids with Winchester cases, all three of us – yes, even including me – shot perfectly well and stayed well within our parameters. We moved then to Winchester Supreme Elite 180 grain JHPs and Black Hills 165 grain hollowpoints. Danny used both of these rounds and got some really tight groups, holes touching. I did some more shooting with Federal 185 grain Hydra Shok and, once again, I got a perfectly satisfactory group. Bradley used Black Hills 180 grain blue box and got his usual fine group. Danny was clearly the best performer with the HK.

Bradley remarked about the HK's light trigger pull and, indeed, although there is a great deal of take up, the single action pull is quite good, if peculiar. Once the pistol is cocked, you'll notice that the hammer does not stay at full stand, but returns to the position it would have if you had the weapon chamber empty. As you draw the trigger rearward, you're drawing the hammer upward with absolutely no pressure at all until you approach the break point. Because of this, if you started to draw the trigger back and realized you did not want to shoot, as you ease pressure on the trigger, the hammer would settle into rest. Suffice it to say, with the HK you have a weapon that is unique in its operating characteristics and, in order to fully take advantage of this truly fine little pistol's features, you have to take the time to learn the gun.

Overall length is 6.42 inches, while barrel length is 3.27 inches. Height with the magazine inserted is 4.61 inches according to the manual and weight, with an empty magazine, is 25.8 ounces. The little gun feels good in the hand and a person with smaller hands would be able to comfortably rest the little finger on the floor plate extension. I wound up curling my little finger under the magazine.

This gun is worth learning.

CHAPTER 40

PARA USA CARRY 9MM

Right profile shot of the Carry 9. It was a pleasant handgun to work with.

The Para USA Carry 9mm is a very nicely performing 1911 style pistol that happens to have a double action mechanism which is really light and smooth and allows one to get some seriously good shooting done. Three dot sights aided in this as well. The sights seemed to be a little off for Danny and he found himself getting a nice group with holes touching but not exactly where he was pointing. Both Danny and Bradley used Winchester Supreme 124 grain 9mm +Ps and I used 147 grain Federal. All three of us obtained results that were well within the test parameters and all three of us were impressed with the pistol's functioning.

It is a little odd to be holding what looks and feels and in many ways functions like a 1911, but has no hammer spur. The Para Carry 9 LDA features a discrete grip safety that does not have much of a tang and might allow persons with fleshy hands to be bitten by

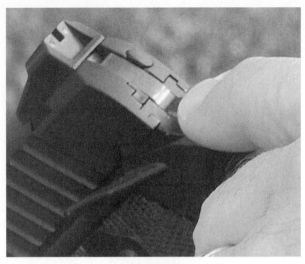

There's a flat mainspring housing, a grip safety and magazine release is familiar, too.

The Para USA Carry 9 has a spurless hammer.

Note the extended thumb safety of the Carry 9.

the slide as it leaves battery or returns. Alloy framed, the Carry 9 is not only a 9mm but is a nine shot pistol with its eight plus one capacity. The barrel is three inches and overall length of the pistol is six inches. Height is just a hair over five inches from the rear sight to the base of the magazine floor plate and three fingers easily get on the pistol for a very solid hold. Whether with the Winchester Supreme or the 147 grain Federal, it was quite pleasant to shoot this gun. Weight of the Carry 9 seems to be bang on twenty-four ounces, which is just a few ounces more than an all steel J-Frame S&W revolver. Although this is a compact gun, the Carry 9 would probably conceal better if the grip frame were a round or two shorter. That is my only criticism of the gun and I would have to say, with the grip frame as long as it is, the gun might be better offered with a longer barrel as well. Just nit-picking!

I was very impressed with the feel of the gun and how it functions and would heartily recommend it. That Light Double Action felt really good!

CHAPTER 41

BERETTA PX4 STORM 9MM, BERETTA 3032 TOMCAT .32 ACP AND BERETTA 21A .25

The Beretta Storm has stylish looks and worked well. (Beretta USA Photo)

The looks of the Beretta Px4 Storm are intriguing. Even without a laser or light mounted on the frame, the appearance of the gun makes it look like something from the future. This thirteen plus one 9X19mm, for all its science fiction looks, functions with comforting familiarity. The pistol is a conventional double action, meaning, of course, that the first round can be fired by a long pull of the trigger or the hammer can be manually cocked to full stand and the weapon fired single action. After the first shot, unless you lower the safety for the de-cocking function to kick in, the hammer will remain at full stand. Only the safety is ambidextrous, the slide stop and magazine release catch being set for right hand use. Dismounting of the weapon for cleaning is particularly simple.

Once again, all three of us took turns with the gun. Danny and Bradley and I all found the

Beretta Storm to have a staged double action – almost like one can learn to stage with a well-timed revolver – that was easy to pull through and a very crisp single action that broke cleanly with little over travel.

Perceived recoil with Federal 124 grain JHPs and Winchester 9mm +P Bonded Personal Protection ammunition was not any sort of bother. Although you can only get two fingers on the Storm's Polymer grip, there was a very good, solid feel to the gun, which also enhanced perception of recoil. For anyone who finds the grip not quite to his or her liking, there is another housing that can be swapped onto the gun. All three of us obtained groups well within the test parameters and no one had anything even slightly negative to say about the gun. I would recommend the Beretta Storm

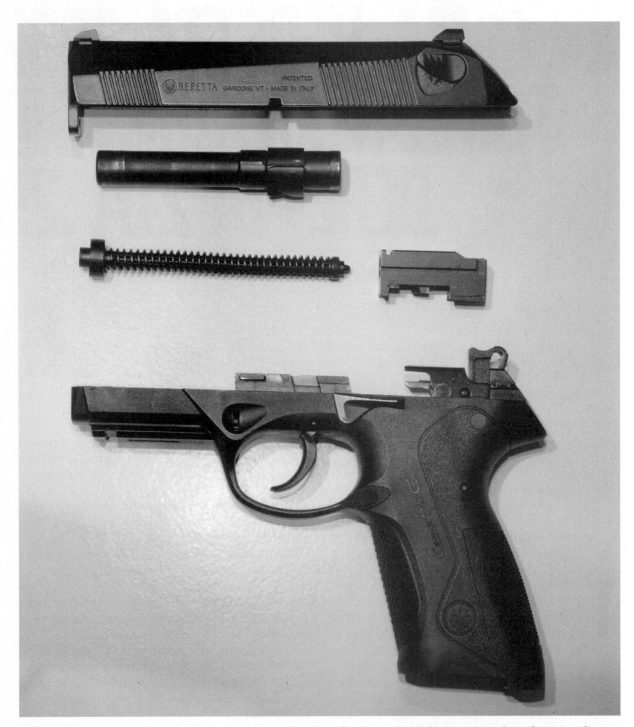

Field stripping of modern pistols like this Beretta Storm is often times far simpler than field stripping handguns from an earlier era.

(Photo courtesy Praiyachat)

The 21A is Beretta's double action version of the familiar Jetfire 950 BS .25.

Px4 as an excellent choice in a compact, highly concealable 9mm that is a good shooter — and it looks really cool.

The Beretta 3032 Tomcat .32 ACP came out as .32s from other makers hit the scene; the popularity of the .32 ACP was driven, of course, by Larry Seecamp's universally acclaimed pistol. What Beretta did with the .32 Tomcat was to take the Model 21A and enlarge it. Initially, the 3032 Tomcats were not offered in stainless steel and there were some dimensional changes with the gun. The 3032 Tomcat Inox, is in fact, quite interesting. The slide and the barrel are machined from stainless steel. The alloy frame is anodized to give it a stainless steel appearance. Other parts are black, including the rear sight.

Weight of the gun is 14-1/2 ounces and, depending upon how you will use the gun, you may want to take advantage of a luminous Tritium front sight that is an option. The rear sight is drift adjustable. You can get two fingers on the gun with ease. The tip-up barrel makes chamber loading quite easy. In a defensive situation, if one were going to draw and immediately fire, the first round double action capability can be taken advantage of; but, for deliberate aimed fire against a target at the range, the double action pull is long and heavy, despite the fact that Beretta advertising uses the words "smooth" and "crisp." Single action pull is where it is with this gun for aimed fire and the single action pull stacks only as you near the break. And, there is virtually no overtravel.

Magazine capacity is seven rounds, giving the Tomcat a one round edge over much but not all of the competition. I volunteered to try the Tomcat first because I always liked small Beretta pistols. That double action trigger pull made my first shot a total throwaway, but subsequent 60 grain Silvertips fired single action kept me well

Beretta's tip-up barrel .32 is a mixture of stainless steel and alloy. The tip-up barrel feature is convenient for safe loading and unloading.

Considering the size of Beretta's smaller pistols, the magazine release catch is ideally located.

within the testing parameters. As usual, both Danny and Bradley fired better groups.

The Tomcat 3032 is not the smallest .32 to be had in this new breed of sub-medium frames; but, it does have a substantial feel. Weight of the gun on our postage scale is just about 17 ounces and the experience of perceived recoil was essentially nonexistent.

One of my first handguns was my Beretta 950 Jetfire, back in the days when J. L. Galef was the importer and the guns could still be brought in from Italy because GCA 68 hadn't happened yet. We've had one of the little Jetfires in our immediate family for literal decades and it is only in the last couple of years that I talked myself out of owning a .25. The 21 A is a double action version of the 950 or Jetfire, and features the same tip-up barrel as found in the original gun and as found in the 3032 Tomcat. The tip-up barrel feature, regardless of gun or caliber, is a good one for persons with insufficient finger strength to allow for manually functioning a

semi automatic slide. Eight round capacity in .25 ACP and the ability to rapidly interchange magazines because of a push button release are positive assets. The caliber is nothing to scream about, but lots of bad guys have been shot with .25s and that's something that's not going to change too radically in the future.

Any pistol that you get from Beretta is going to be of highest quality because Beretta is the oldest company of its kind in existence.

I never asked Bradley if he owned a .25, but I know Danny does – a Beretta, actually -- and as already stated, I used to. I took the 21A and loaded up with Federal 50 grain full metal case ammunition. I opened fire on one of the Shoot-N-C targets. The holes are so small! Danny and Bradley used the same ammunition, as well. The 21 A functioned just as it should, grouped decently for all three of us and was very much a typical high end .25 automatic. If you must have a .25, Beretta's is one of the first product lines you should examine.

CHAPTER 42

FINAL RECOMMENDATIONS

A Beretta .25, this the 21A, is an outstanding gun for its type, the only complaint most people have with a .25 being that it is a .25. These are guns to use in a pinch, and they have saved lots of lives.

There are certain fundamental principles to take away from this book.

Don't be a price snob. Just because a handgun may be less expensive than others of the type doesn't mean you should ignore it. I own two wristwatches – a thirty-year-old Rolex Sea-Dweller, for which I've been offered well over $6,000, and a Timex Expedition I bought at Wal-Mart. Both watches are terrific, rugged and keep great time.

If it isn't a certain brand, that doesn't mean the handgun is not worth investigating. Many readers will know that in our science fiction adventure series *The Survivalist,* our character of John Thomas Rourke carried "... twin stainless Detonics .45s." Had I been one of these guys who said, "If it's not a Colt, it's not a .45 automatic," I would have missed out on a handgun with which I have been intimately involved for more than three decades and which I carry virtually every day.

The gun is a Smith & Wesson M&P and – yes – that's a bayonet on the Picatinny Rail. In a life or death brawl with multiple adversaries, a bayonet might be just the thing, but it's not a normal concealed carry accessory. But, use your imagination! (Laserlyte Photo)

That's a Laserlyte NAA-1 laser on this 1 1/8-inch barrel North American Arms .22 Long Rifle Mini-Revolver. It would actually be a useful combination, giving the little gun a bit more reach. (Laserlyte Photo)

Albeit this gun is one of the superb single actions from Cimarron Arms, don't forget Colonel Colt's sage advice!

Some few of the guns mentioned here were acquired as used guns – the Walther P-38 9mm, the Walther PP .32, the SIG P-6 (225), one of my SIG 229s, two of our family's J-Frame Smith & Wessons, etc. A used gun can be a superb gun. You just have to look at it a little harder when you buy it. If you can save a few bucks or find a handgun no longer available new, but one that is great for meeting your needs, that's wonderful.

The important thing is that, whatever handguns you select, learn their limitations and their strengths and teach yourself or otherwise get taught how to use those guns to maximum effect. Be a responsible concealed weapons carrier. Vote for persons who will support your Right to Keep and Bear Arms and be a credit to the firearms owning/using/carrying community.

Finally, instill in your children, and whichever other young people on whom you might have influence, the paramount importance of having the capability to be responsible for one's own safety and well-being and the ability to defend yourself.

Remember the old saying engraved on the oldtimer's Colt? It's still true today.

"Have no fear of any man, no matter what his size. When in danger, call on me – and I will equalize."

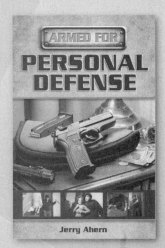

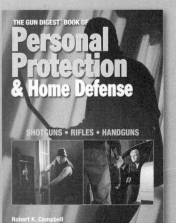
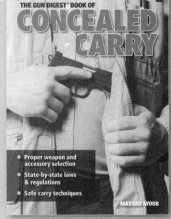